Born in 1951, on the Indonesian Island of Java, in the village of Surabaya, Joyce Di Lorenzo repatriated with her family to The Netherlands in 1952. At the age of 10 years old, she and her family immigrated to America in search of a better life. She grew up in the San Francisco Bay Area, where she met her husband. Being of Italian descent, one day, her husband suggested buying a vacation home in Italy. Now, the couple divide their time between living in Idaho and Morcella, a lovely medieval village in Umbria.

For Vince; mio marito
"Thank you for my life."

Joyce Di Lorenzo

LANDING ON A STAR IN UMBRIA

AUSTIN MACAULEY PUBLISHERS

LONDON • CAMBRIDGE • NEW YORK • SHARJAH

Ordering Information
Quantity sales: Special discounts are available on quantity purchases by corporations, associations, and others. For details, contact the publisher at the address below.

Publisher's Cataloging-in-Publication data
Di Lorenzo, Joyce
Landing on a Star in Umbria

ISBN 9781685624811 (Paperback)
ISBN 9781685624828 (ePub e-book)

Library of Congress Control Number: 2022918039

www.austinmacauley.com/us

First Published 2023
Austin Macauley Publishers LLC
40 Wall Street, 33rd Floor, Suite 3302
New York, NY 10005
USA

mail-usa@austinmacauley.com
+1 (646) 5125767

Table of Contents

Preface
"You Need a Project"

August 2007: I was sitting at the computer on a sunny afternoon, aimlessly surfing the internet, not looking for anything in particular, unmotivated and certainly not feeling creative enough to start a project. I was just hoping that something would catch my eye or capture my interest and point me in a direction.

Without warning, my mother suffered a stroke on Mother's Day and passed away in the hospital a week later. After her death, in my grief, it helped me to stay focused on preparing her house, my childhood home, for sale. Mom was a collector and I had a mountain of her worldly possessions to sort through. I made a million decisions about what to keep, donate, sell, or toss and now, at long last, the house was sold and her estate liquidated. The emotionally draining task was behind me and here I was, feeling sad, lost, disoriented.

Vince, my husband of nearly nineteen years, entered the room, kissed me on my neck and seeing me spinning my wheels at the computer, asked how I was doing. I shrugged my shoulders and gave him a half, almost non-receptive answer. He looked at me and said, "You need a project. You need something to do, something to focus on. Why don't you find us a house in Italy?"

"What, to buy?" I replied. I couldn't believe it! He couldn't be serious. "Are you kidding me? Vince, you want to buy a house in Italy? Do you mean as a second home, a vacation home? Oh my God, really? I would love that!"

That was the incentive I needed. That was my gift from God, my distraction from the sadness. I immediately went to the computer, typed in 'properties for sale in Italy' and was pleasantly surprised to see a few that we could afford! Vince pulled up a chair and sat beside me. We clicked on some of the listings that looked interesting and we talked about what kind of property would be suitable for us. Something with an outdoor space and a garage, a farm house, or an apartment, and where? In which region of Italy? We agreed immediately that we wanted a building made of stone, brimming with historic character and architectural details. We certainly did not want a project dwelling in need of repair or restoration.

I barely slept that night or on countless subsequent nights. Instead of dozing and drifting off to sleep, visions of us living in Italy danced through my head. In the middle of the night, I would sit at the computer and search for more listings. I printed my favorite ones and showed them to Vince in the morning. Suddenly we had a new and exciting goal to talk about, dream about. Throughout the years, we had been to Italy several times. We always loved the time we spent there. Italy is full of those welcoming and engaging Italians who know how to make you feel right at home and with Vince's Italian heritage, Italy was a natural place for us to buy a holiday home.

1. Discovering Italy
My First Trip

I made my first trip to Italy at the age of eighteen, in the summer of 1969. My mother, grandmother, younger sister Ellen and I left the day following my high school graduation. For Ellen and I, it was also our first return trip to the Netherlands since immigrating to the United States in 1961. We were staying with family in Schiedam for two weeks, before traveling by tour bus to destinations in France, Switzerland and to Lago Maggiore in northern Italy. We were very excited about our family vacation!

I still have wonderful memories of that trip. It was my introduction to traveling abroad and becoming curious about how people lived in other countries. I was fascinated with international culture, music, art and food! *Especially* the food! I tasted everything and quickly identified my favorite local dishes. In France I couldn't eat enough of the fresh seafood served on oversized platters of crushed ice. I loved eating chunks of dark chocolate, cheese and fruit for dessert and in Paris I never passed by a pastry shop without going in to buy one of those out-of-this world French baguettes to munch on, while strolling along the tree-lined Champs-Elysees. In Switzerland, among my favorite treats, were the exquisite chocolate truffles that had to be consumed within a few days because they were made with fresh dairy cream and butter. A potato dish called *rosti* became my addiction. I was crazy about cheese fondue and the apple and onion quiche which every restaurant served.

My absolute best-loved country, though, was Italy! It was easy to understand why everyone calls living there *La Dolce Vita;* the Sweet Life. The pace is slower, people are warm and friendly and the food is divine. A fellow tourist described authentic Italian cooking as *forgetting about celebrity chefs and fancy restaurants, Italian cooking is all about combining a few fresh ingredients to complement and enhance the best flavor of each.* I would recall this accurate description every time I returned to this ancient, delightful country. Italy touched my soul right from the beginning.

My Trip with Ellen and Eileen

My second trip to Italy was in 1983 when Ellen, my best friend Eileen and I decided to take a three-week European vacation without an itinerary or schedule. Our only plan was to begin and end our trip in Holland.

We arrived in Italy on a ferry from Greece, at the Port of Brindisi on the Adriatic Coast. Ecstatic to be in Italy, we couldn't wait to disembark, gather our mummy-sized luggage bags and board our train to Rome. Completing the luggage screening and the passport control process was hectic. It was the first time I saw the use of drug-sniffing dogs to identify suspicious passengers who were pulled out of line and interrogated.

As a port of entry, the town of Brindisi was overcrowded with people. The scene was completely chaotic and everyone seemed to be going in a different direction. By the time we finally made it to the street, our luggage had become heavy, cumbersome and difficult to manage. People shoved and elbowed their way to the curb to compete for a taxi. As a Pan American flight attendant, Ellen had been to Italy several times before and warned us not to get into an unmarked cab without a meter on the dashboard. In the midst of the chaos, a man, speaking little English, suddenly offered to take us and our massive bags to the train station. We jumped at the chance. Relieved to be rid of our luggage, we completely forgot Ellen's warning and didn't notice, at first, that our bags were not being loaded into a cab. Instead they were thrown onto a hand cart which our "driver" pushed through the streets. *Oh, my God! What have we done?* We were dumbfounded when we realized our predicament and ran after our luggage all the way to the train station, laughing, taking pictures in case the bags took a quick turn into an alley and disappeared from our view. What a priceless first experience in Italy! Later, when we were safely on the train to Rome with our luggage shaped into comfy headrests for our night journey, we talked and giggled about the comical incident. It was truly a firsthand lesson never to carry more luggage than you can personally manage!

After a long train ride, we finally arrived in Rome. Ellen was eager to take us to her favorite Italian delicatessen near the train station. She showed us how to order a fresh Bufala Mozzarella cheese sandwich with tomato and basil. We ate our lunch sitting on the steps of the Vittoriano Monument; Tomb of the Unknown Soldiers. Absorbed in our surroundings, I fell in love with Italy right then-and-there. I was completely captivated by the energy and vibrancy of Rome, the cafes, restaurants and shops. We went to the Vatican and visited the Sistine Chapel, saw the Coliseum and the Forum, climbed the Spanish Steps and threw coins in the Trevi Fountain. Rome is a city of contrast with ancient and new, Baroque and Roman and I found it a spellbinding place to be with my sister and my best friend! Italy was completely fabulous!

Throughout my thirties, I made several subsequent visits to Italy with friends, exploring Florence, Pisa, Verona and Venice.

Vince's First Trip

Dad's Hometown; San Pietro Avellana

Mamie; Vince's mother, is of Sicilian descent. Her family is from Palermo, in the Northwest part of the island of Sicily. Oriente (Orry); Vince's father, was born in the small village of San Pietro Avellana in Italy's south-central region of Molise. Until 1963, Molise formed part of the region of Abruzzi. The split did not become effective until 1970, making Molise Italy's newest region.

When Vince was eleven years old, Orry brought him to Italy to meet his grandmother. With friends, they flew from San Francisco to Rome. As an impressionable, wide-eyed, young boy, Vince was taken by the dazzling uniforms and plumed helmets worn by the sword carrying *carabinieri;* the national military police of Italy. They were the best uniforms he had ever seen.

After spending several days in Rome, Vince and his dad traveled by bus to Orry's hometown, where Vince met his grandmother, aunt and cousin. They stayed in the house where Orry was born and lived until he moved to the United States at the age of seventeen. In spite of the language barrier, Vince played with the local kids on the street.

There were no restaurants in town, every meal was prepared at home and served at the kitchen table. Neighbors who were eager to see Orry and his son, often stopped by for a visit bearing gifts of livestock, home cooked casseroles and pasta dishes. This act of kindness made a lasting impression on Vince, one he would recall as an adult, years later.

San Pietro Avellana is surrounded by forests of beech and oak trees. Although the village has developed considerably since Vince's visit with his dad in 1957, much of the ancient town remains the same.

2. Together – Discovering Italy
Our First Trip

Lago Maggiore

We made our first trip to Italy together in 1990, during a six-week vacation, driving from Holland to Germany, Austria and Switzerland, spending a few days in each country, before entering northern Italy in Lugano on the Swiss border. Driving the excellent roads with stunning views of the Alps and over the high peaks of Saint Gotthard Pass was exhilarating for Vince who thoroughly enjoyed the European driving style. We headed to Lago Maggiore, where I visited with my family twenty-one years prior. On our way there, we phoned Vince's parents in California from a gas station pay-phone. We couldn't wait to tell them how beautiful Italy was and how thrilled we were to be in the "Old Country." As we waited for our phone connection, we watched a bride and groom pose for a photographer on a balcony across the street. When the international operator finally told us that our call was connected, Orry was delighted to hear Vince's enthusiastic voice as he told his parents about the beauty of the northern Italian Lake District. We both laughed at Orry's response when Vince described the women's gas-station toilets as *just a hole in the floor with a drain plate over it.*

"What!" Orry exclaimed. "It's been 50 years! You mean they haven't fixed those things yet?"

By early evening, we arrived at the West shore of Lago Maggiore, driving through the town of Baveno.

Feeling nostalgic, remembering my prior visit to the area, I wondered if the Hotel Alpi still existed. Although it was still there, it looked terribly dated and not as grand as I remembered it so long ago. With no reservations, we pulled into the driveway of a lakeside hotel in the resort town of Stresa. Since the lobby appeared attractive and welcoming, we crossed our fingers and hoped for an available room. Our modest room was wonderfully perfect, with a balcony and a splendid panorama of the lake and the Borromean Islands, we were thrilled to settle into such a lovely space. Lago Maggiore looked misty and romantic, an alluring backdrop for sharing an overwhelming feeling of love and happiness; happiness about being married to each other and about being in a special place at such a special time in our lives.

In the morning we woke up refreshed, energized and ready to explore our surroundings. Although we were operating on a micro budget, we found much to explore in Stresa that was affordable. I was eager to simulate with Vince the experience I had with my sister in Rome when she ordered a fresh Bufala Mozzarella sandwich for me. We found a typical, charming deli with outdoor seating facing the lake. I asked Vince to choose a table for us while I went inside to order the sandwiches. When the man behind the counter said, "*Prego,*" I replied by pointing to the fantastic rolls of fresh baked bread behind him.

"*Due, per favore,*" I said, "two rolls of bread, please."

The man instinctively knew that I was ordering *due panini*, two sandwiches even before I pointed to the ball of fresh mozzarella laying in a bowl of water and the hunk of *prosciutto*, a flavorful dry-cured ham. He acknowledged all my actions with a nod of his head. When he sliced the mozzarella, I watched the milk squeeze from the ball of cheese indicating its freshness, then he thinly sliced the prosciutto and placed it on top of the cheese inside the sandwiches, wrapped each panini in white butcher paper and reached across the counter to hand them to me. No mayo, mustard, pickles or lettuce. When ingredients are this fresh, they should not be tortured into complex combinations. Three bold, clean and natural flavors. The sandwiches were sensational! We savored every bite. Vince ordered coffee, which I must admit, even today is not my favorite drink in Italy, however, he loves the Italian-style coffee. *Of course he does. He's Italian!* Vince prefers a strong Espresso, occasionally even orders a *doppio,* a double, while I nurse my *caffè Americana con latte caldo*; American coffee with hot milk. (It is awful!) When I yearn for coffee, I order a cappuccino, although if you are visiting Italy, eventually you are bound to come across a piece of advice: *do not order cappuccino after 11 AM and definitely not after midday.* Italians consider cappuccino a morning drink.

In the afternoon we explored the enchanting town of Stresa. At our leisure, we took pictures, bought postcards and poked around in the delightful shops selling wine, ceramics, souvenirs and jewelry crafted from that gleaming, gorgeous 18KT Italian gold! On our wedding day Vince gave me a special gold necklace with a heart charm to symbolize giving his heart to me. Stresa seemed like a wonderful place to reciprocate that lovely gesture. We had so much fun going in and out of the jewelry shops looking for the ideal chain for my handsome husband until a beautiful box-style caught his eye. He wore it right out of the store looking even more like a "local" than before. When we stood by the ferry docks gazing at the lake, it made us both laugh when a tourist asked Vince for directions. He was beaming from ear-to-ear. The chain I bought for him that day has never left his neck!

A visit to Lago Maggiore is not complete without a visit to the Borromean Islands; a group of three impressive islands and two islets in the Italian part of the lake. Their name is derived from the Borromeo family, who acquired the islands in the early sixteenth century. Today, the Islands are a major local tourist attraction for their picturesque setting, a daily ferry operates between them and the larger lakeshore villages. We were certainly looking forward to exploring each island and boarded a morning ferry to Isola Bella right after breakfast.

Isola Bella; named for Countess Isabella Borromeo, was originally a largely barren rock until the late 1600s when Count Carlo III and his son Vitaliano VI built a predominantly fairy tale, Baroque-style summer palace. Vast quantities of soil were brought in to build up a system of ten terraces for ornate, tropical gardens. We toured through the palace, marveling at the impressive collection of family heirlooms, historic treasures, sixteenth century tapestries and paintings before entering the gardens through a grotto, complete with a unicorn statue ridden by the vain Goddess of Love. Isola Bella is almost fantasy-like, an exceptionally unusual island.

Our next visit was to *Isola Madre*; the largest and most diverse island, with an English-style garden, which was originally landscaped in the nineteenth century. The well-manicured foliage and lawns, expertly tended lemon trees and pergolas of ancient wisteria, free roaming pheasants and white peacocks created a magical setting as the exotic birds wandered among the amazing spectacle of azaleas, rhododendrons, hibiscus and camellias. Like any enthusiastic photographer, Vince chased after the birds in an attempt to capture that picture-perfect moment when a male proudly displayed his flamboyant plumage of prominent feathers to an impressive female.

Our favorite island was *Isola dei Pescatori*; the only inhabited island with a population of 215 full time residents. From the moment we stepped on the shore of the Island of the Fishermen, we felt a connection to "the old country." We spotted a woman dressed in black, wearing a head scarf tied underneath her chin, sitting in a chair feeding the ducks. Women in Italy typically wear black as an indication of being in mourning over the death of a loved one. Somehow, it was endearing to watch her. She reminded Vince of his grandmother and of his elderly Aunt Antemira.

We meandered through the unpaved, rocky paths in the fishing village, stopping frequently to take pictures, enjoyed a late lunch in one of the modest restaurants at the water's edge, we sat on a *terrazzo*, under a grape arbor that looked like it had always been there. Admiring the blue fishing boats tied up on the shore, it felt serene, as if time stood still here. Somehow, we felt *right at home*.

On our last morning in this beautiful region, we had one more excursion to take before we left. We took a gondola cable car to the top of Monte Rosa; Italy's second highest mountain, for an outstanding view of the Italian Alps. We couldn't have asked for a more crystal-clear morning, as the cable car climbed higher and the view before us became more expansive, we were awe-struck by the incredible scenery. Below, a glorious carpet of colorful wildflowers flourished in the meadows and among the rocks. Everything looked brilliant and blue, the enormous lake was barely indistinguishable from the sky. The largest part of Monte Rosa is in Italy. The eastern face of the mountain is in Switzerland. Both the Swiss and Italian Alps were visible at the top of the mountain and the view was truly breathtaking. We took pictures of Italy and Switzerland while standing in one spot. It was jaw-dropping! No wonder we were reluctant to leave Lago Maggiore. We shared unforgettable moments here and made ever lasting memories. We fell in love with Italy's northern lake district and deeper in love with each other. We vowed to return to this alluring part of Italy someday.

With our belongings methodically packed in our small car, we headed out on the last leg of our vacation. We planned to stop for lunch in Lichtenstein and have dinner in Munich, before flying home from Frankfurt the next morning. The Principality of Lichtenstein is adorable, enchanting, picturesque. There is no other way to describe this tiny country, the only one entirely located within the Alps. Once we arrived in the capital city of Vaduz, we chose an intimate restaurant to have a relaxing lunch with a menu featuring local specialties and outdoor seating for our favorite pastime of people watching. It was comical to watch busloads of Japanese tourists getting out of the bus, snapping pictures of each other before getting back on the bus and leaving. The young Japanese girls were delightfully entertaining as they posed in pairs and giggled, then ran toward each other to exchange cameras for another picture. Vince had me in stitches when he impersonated the girls by grabbing my camera and handing it to me as he said, "Here. You take a picture of me. I'll take a picture of you. Let's take a picture together. OK. We were here, we are off!"

The drive from Lichtenstein to Munich lead us through Bavaria's ultimate scenic landscape, around each bend in the road the view was more magnificent than before. Vince stressed the importance of arriving in Munich before nightfall to avoid reading street signs in the dark. We had a particularly special reason for wanting to have dinner in Munich. Two years ago, on our honeymoon, we ate at the Mathauser in Munich's historic center. The largest beer hall in Bavaria, the Mathauser seats more than 5,000 people! We had an outstanding German pork dish called Schweinshaxe; a giant crispy, oven-roasted ham hock served with a savory sauce. It was over-the-top delicious and an experience we wanted to duplicate on this trip, however, as the distance between us and the tranquil countryside increased, our yearning for Schweinshaxe faded and we became tense amid Munich's traffic, crowds and noise. All of a sudden, our surroundings were aggressive, hectic and loud. It was difficult to find a parking space and there were hordes of people everywhere! Our flight was not until the following day, so there was nothing to do but endure the situation. Although the Schweinshaxe was still outstanding, our dinner conversation was all about avoiding large cities on future vacations. We wholeheartedly agreed that the slower pace of the less populated, less travelled countryside with its hamlets and quaint little villages is where we preferred to visit. From here forward, our travel was limited to the quiet corners of the world where we can interact with the charming people who live there and feel enriched because we experienced their culture instead of their tourist crowds.

A Life Changing Trip

Vince and I did not return to Italy until nearly thirteen years later. Although we traveled often during those years, our destinations were always somewhere else. We were part of "Corporate America" with limited time-off from work. Each year we were faced with the difficult decision of where to spend our precious break from employment. As much as we loved Italy, we were also curious about life in other countries and eager to explore different civilizations.

The year 2003 was a difficult, turbulent year in our marriage. Due to the economic downturn in the Telecom Industry, Vince lost his job and could not find lucrative work. Several of our friends and colleagues with similar careers and educational backgrounds also found themselves suddenly unemployed. When they became available, competition for the same few job opportunities was fierce. Times were extremely tough, we argued often and disagreed about how to secure new employment. In spite of having little discretionary money, I felt strongly that if we could just change our surroundings for a while and create an incredible memory somewhere, our hearts would reconnect, our love would rekindle and we would return home rejuvenated and ready to tackle our unpredictable future with a fresh new outlook.

I saw a poster once of a quaint little harbor, I assumed, somewhere on the Mediterranean. The image just "spoke to me" and I dreamed of visiting there one day. Searching for a romantic destination for our temporary escape from reality, I came across that poster again. To my surprise, I learned that it was a travel promotion photo of Portofino; an ancient and sophisticated fishing village on the Italian Riviera overlooking a sea of indescribable beauty. That's it! Italy! Of course! We'll go to Italy.

I pulled out a map, located Portofino and from there as our starting point, put together a flexible two-week itinerary for us. Nothing concrete, just something vague to keep us headed in a direction toward a destination. I did not want to unpack and stay at a new hotel every night. I wanted to relax; travel unencumbered at a leisurely pace. Always the practical one, Vince was reluctant to agree to go on this trip due to our shaky financial situation. I pleaded with him and expressed what I believed this trip could do for us. It could change our lives by making us stronger. Thank God, Vince listened with his heart and finally agreed. So, with little cash and a few credit cards in hand, we were on our way.

Our vacation was off to an excellent beginning with the appropriate tone set immediately at the San Francisco Airport. Clearing airport security was a breeze, leaving us time to wander around in the duty-free shops. Ducati, an Italian sport-bike manufacturer, was sponsoring a raffle for a sporty red motorbike. When we filled out a ticket and dropped it in the slotted box, the Ducati representative gave us a black baseball cap with the red Ducati company logo embroidered on the front. We considered it a sign that our trip was *meant-to-be* and that all would be wonderful!

The eleven-hour flight to Milan was long and uneventful. We couldn't wait for our feet to touch Italian ground and for our lungs to fill with fresh air. We were looking forward to all the exciting opportunities that can come from a vacation with a flexible plan.

The most economical car we could rent at the airport was an Italian manufactured Fiat Punta. Vince was thrilled to be driving in Italy again and being among the best, assertive motorists in Europe. I admit it! I'm a horrible map reader. For me, there is nothing worse than reading a map to help Vince navigate through the big city traffic maze toward the highway leading to the countryside. For him there is nothing worse than trying to follow my unclear directions, nevertheless, somehow, we always arrive at our intended destination.

Once out of the airport jumble, we headed south on the *autostrada* (motorway) to the coastal town of Sestri Levante on the Ligure Coast of the Mediterranean Sea. It was a beautiful day and we were ready for our Italian adventure to begin!

Portofino

Although we were weary from the grueling long flight, we were equally excited to finally be on our way. The route we projected from Milan took us to Genoa along the Ligurian Coast, along the foothills of the majestic Apennines Mountains, dotted with beautiful rolling hills and charming medieval villages.

With wide-eyed enthusiasm, we pointed out the interesting sites to each other. Ancient defense walls surrounding villages that were built in the Middle Ages took our breath away. At a stoplight in town, we watched in awe, as an adorable couple riding a vespa with a child holding a puppy sandwiched between them, sped by us. We were already having a marvelous time. Everything seemed so *foreign* in Italy. Vince delighted in seeing the various European cars that are not available in America. We were confused and amused by the peculiar Italians who appeared to be driving in two lanes simultaneously, as if they couldn't commit to driving in just one. Vince jokingly commented that the Italian drivers consider a painted divider line in the road merely a *suggestion* of a lane. Then there were the roundabouts; a circular intersection in which traffic flowed continuously in one direction around a central island, to several exits. If you missed your exit, you stayed in the traffic flow until you approached the exit again. What an excellent concept! Roundabouts are more efficient than the four-way arterial stop signs we are accustomed to in California.

Before turning onto the coast road, we pulled into an 'autogrill;' a roadside gas station and restaurant, often with a bridge structure expanding across the autostrada providing access to travelers in both directions. Autogrills are no ordinary fast-food establishments. They offer an elaborate take-out menu with a wide variety of freshly prepared hot and cold food items. Everything looked tempting and delicious. The sandwiches we bought and ate on-the-go, thoroughly hit the spot.

We arrived in Sestri Levante before sunset. Once a quiet fishing village on a peninsula amidst two bays, this beautiful destination was slowly becoming an Italian vacation hot spot. We reserved a beachfront room for three nights at the Hotel Miramare on the shore of the *Baia del Silenzio*; the Bay of Silence.

The friendly hotel staff greeted us at the door, their warm welcome gave us an immediate favorable impression. A bellman promptly assisted Vince with our luggage and escorted him to our room while I completed the check-in process. When I arrived, the door to our room was wide open, revealing a stunning panoramic view of the bay. Vince handed me a glass of wine and lead me to the balcony. We were overwhelmed by the staggering scenery before us.

"Look at this," Vince said, "welcome to Italy, isn't it beautiful?"

Our hotel was located at the end of a crescent shaped beach. Adjacent buildings with gold, yellow and rust exteriors were aglow in the setting sunlight. Like a charmingly serene picture on a postcard, traditional fishing boats with mirror-like reflections in the water, were secured to their moorings. The Ligure Coast already seemed like a wonderful place to explore.

Standing on the balcony, captivated by the stunning view, Vince raised his glass and made a toast to our safe arrival and to our return to Italy. We removed our shoes, loosened our clothes and toasted to our love and happiness. As our bodies relaxed, our minds decompressed, we made another toast to our good fortune. When the wine bottle was empty, we stretched out on the comfortable bed and gave in as our excitement was overtaken by exhaustion and we fell asleep.

After a short power nap and a brisk shower, we were ready to survey our surroundings. Italy's business hours are a challenge to remember and difficult to adjust to. They vary depending on the nature of the business. Banks open at 8:30 and close for lunch at 1:30. They open again at 3:30, but only for an hour. Shops open at 9:00 and close for lunch at approximately one o'clock, then generally reopen from 4:00 to 8:00. Restaurants are open for two shifts each day. Lunch is served from 12:30 until 3:00 when they close to prepare for dinner. Dinner is served from 7:30 until 11:00, or occasionally a little later. To add to this confusion, Italy uses the military time system, which I find sometimes puzzling to this day.

Feeling somewhat re-energized, we walked to town in search of a restaurant specializing in local cuisine. Enchanting cobblestone streets lead us to the *centro storico*, the historic center where palm trees, cafes and trattorias lined a picturesque, seafront boulevard. We felt as if it was midnight, however, people were just beginning to fill the restaurants, indicating that it was much earlier in the evening. We found a cozy trattoria with outdoor seating facing the *Baia delle Favole*; the Bay of Fairy Tales, named in honor of Hans Christian Anderson; the Danish poet and writer, who lived in the area for a brief period during the 1800s. The Menu of the Day featured a dinner sandwich on *focaccia* bread; an Italian specialty flat bread, with fresh anchovies and sauteed onions. Fresh anchovies in Italy are not remotely similar to the salty, brown ones you buy in a can. They are sweet, firm, a bit tart with a delicacy almost impossible to find in California. I couldn't resist, without considering any other item on the menu, I promptly ordered the sandwich. The waiter suggested pairing with a fruity Bellini cocktail, made with peach nectar and *Prosecco*; the Italian version of Champagne. Vince ordered the *Caprese Salad* of fresh tomato and basil, with a glass of the house red wine. We also shared a plentiful mixed seafood salad. The cost of our entire heavenly meal was only 26€; the equivalent of $30. Our sensational meal was a perfect ending to our day!

Although the temperature in our room was perfect, the effects of jet lag made it difficult to sleep and we laid awake in bed for hours. With the windows wide open, a balmy breeze moved slightly through the sheer curtains and I could hear the sound of gentle waves lapping at the shore. With the sun just barely above the horizon, last evening's soft rainfall made everything look dewy fresh and somehow peaceful in the morning's breaking light.

Vince was standing at the window looking at the sea. When he heard me stirring, he turned toward me and said, "I love it here," walked over to our bed, laid down beside me and searched for my hand under the sheet. At 6 AM we finally fell asleep for several hours.

The sun was high and streaming brightly through our window when we woke up. Below our balcony, we heard the playful voices of people on the beach. Feeling famished and looking forward to a hearty breakfast, we showered and dressed quickly. In the lobby, we inquired at the front desk where the dining room was. The staff looked at us curiously and informed us that although the dining room was already closed in preparation for lunch, they would be pleased to serve us a cup of coffee. Vince and I looked at each other and burst out laughing.

"Wow! What time is it?" Vince said. "Do you mean that we slept the day away?" Nevertheless, we were fully refreshed, blissfully happy and eager to venture out!

At a local bakery, we ate a quick breakfast of cappuccino and pastries at the counter. At a neighborhood market, we bought a bottle of wine, water, bread, some fruit, and a few slices of salami and cheese to keep in Vince's backpack for an impromptu snack on our road trip to Portofino. After years of yearning to visit, I was finally going to that quaint little harbor I admired in the travel poster. *Today my dream would come true, I was going to Portofino!*

The one-hour drive along the Italian Riviera was a complete jaw-dropper. Every coastal village was more charming than the next. Among our favorites were Rapallo and Santa Margherita. As we approached Portofino, however, I was disappointed to catch sight of three imposing, cruise ships at anchor near the harbor's entrance. I feared that all those tourists would surely ruin the ancient charm of the quaint village. Not so! Portofino was everything I dreamed it would be and more enchanting than I can adequately describe. I handed Vince the camera and asked him to take my picture with the classic view of the harbor in the background so that my visit would be documented for all time. Posing with my arms outstretched, Vince clicked and said, "Well honey, you finally made it!"

I felt as if my heart would burst from happiness and utter disbelief. Was this real, was I *really* here? It is quite emotional when a dream comes true.

Standing in one spot provided a magnificent view of almost every angle of the snug harbor. I captured camera shots in every direction. The building facades were decorative and colorful. Vince pointed out the Trompe l'oeil paintings on the buildings, explaining it as an amazing art technique that creates an optical illusion. Trompe l'oeil painted windows, shutters and doors on exterior walls fool the eye in appearing to be three dimensional. The extravagant multimillion dollar mega-yachts in the tiny harbor did not impress me, but the adorable distinctive, typical Mediterranean-style, wooden rowboats with the dark blue hulls and bright blue interiors captured my heart.

We had lunch at a restaurant with an outdoor table in splendid view of the harbor entrance. Vince ordered seafood spaghetti, I the mussels in a garlic, white wine sauce. The house wine was poured from a bottle without a label, into a blue and white terra-cotta jug which was placed on the table. How wonderfully quaint! Both food and wine were outstanding. *Everything* in Portofino was outstanding! Following lunch, we peeked in the shops, bought postcards, souvenirs and a watercolor print of Portofino, which I would frame and proudly display in our home when we returned. We spent the afternoon exploring every nook and cranny of the village. Still sleep deprived, eventually we felt our energy level drop. Acclimating to the nine-hour Italian time difference was extremely distracting. In my heart, I wanted to stay in Portofino forever, but I knew it was best to return to the hotel for some well needed rest. In conclusion, Portofino was undoubtedly the most beautiful place I have ever been to.

Back in our room, we slumped on the bed where Vince dozed off, immediately, while watching TV. Preferring to sleep at night, I attempted writing postcards to fight the urge to catch a few winks. Ultimately, we lingered lazily in our room until evening, dining picnic-style on our bed with the food and wine from Vince's backpack. Later, we took a romantic stroll into town for a gelato and a glance of Sestri Levante at night. *Thank you, God, for an unforgettable day!*

The Cinque Terre

One of the most visited areas on the Ligure Coast is the *Cinque Terre*; the Five Lands, composed of five fishing villages clinging to a rugged portion of the Mediterranean coast. Centuries ago, the villages of Monterosso, Vernazza, Corniglia, Manarola and Riomaggiore were only accessible by sea or a dense network of mule paths which connected them to the Via Roma; the main road that leads all roads in Italy to Rome. Throughout time, these paths have been well maintained and today they provide hordes of hikers with breathtaking views of the sea-swept Cinque Terre. Although it is possible to reach the area by car, a regional train operates between them daily. Only residents are permitted to drive inside the villages. Tomorrow we scheduled a day-trip to the Cinque Terre. We planned to drive to Monterosso, park the car, and find the best way to visit the other villages from there.

We left early in the morning and drove inland toward the mountains where the winding road leads through the scenic, well terraced landscape Italy is renowned for. Thickly wooded olive, lemon and chestnut trees, vineyards and primitive stone walls overgrown with trailing ivy all thrived on the steep hillsides. When we reached the coastal headland town of Levanto, we stumbled upon a bustling farmer's market in the piazza. Even though it was raining softly, we were eager to walk around and be a part of the local crowd. We enjoyed engaging the Italians and trying to communicate in their language. We loved the full experience of buying at the market just like the neighborhood residents. I bought a colorful tablecloth, fancy embroidered dish towels, and a decorative bottle of *grappa;* a grape-based pomace liqueur. Vince struck up a conversation with a congenial vendor and bought biscotti, some dried fruit and hazelnuts. I found it comical and adorable when he took out a fist full of coins from his pocket, opened his hand, held them out to show them to me and said, "Can I afford this?" He took such pleasure in our new practice of keeping snacks and drinks in his backpack to satisfy a spontaneous urge to indulge.

When we arrived in Monterosso, we left the car in a public parking lot and paid for the whole day. A tunnel divides the village into two distinctly different parts; the new and historic. As the only sandy beach of the Cinque Terre, it runs along the coastline of the entire village. We found our way to the edge of the sea where we located the three-hour footpath to Vernazza. At first, it was effortless to walk at a steady pace, single file along the steep cliffs. At its widest point, the ancient path was not more than four feet. We stopped often to take pictures or comment on the unbelievable gardening skills of the Italians. As the sun became warmer, we removed layers of clothing, walked slower and stopped to drink water. By the time we reached the first scenic view point overlooking Vernazza, my blisters had blisters and Vince's shirt was completely soaked with perspiration. Notwithstanding our pain, we both agreed that the panorama was well worth our effort. We were awestruck! There was a tiny harbor filled with those adorable blue wooden boats, tied up to each other, several rows deep. We stood on a cliff catching our breath, gazing at the most picturesque of the Cinque Terre villages before we descended to the cafes with welcoming tables and brightly colored umbrellas in the piazza.

After a long, relaxing lunch and a heavenly gelato we finally felt fortified enough to do a little shopping. We bought postcards and a "floaty" pen; you know, one of those tacky souvenir pens with a photographic image or object floating in a clear window at the top. I have been collecting these silly little pens from my travels for years. I must have hundreds of them!

We wanted to explore the other villages, but did not know the best way to travel to them. Vince asked an idle waiter in a restaurant for directions to the train station. Unfortunately, the waiter did not speak English, although he was kind enough to ask if a colleague could help. His colleague didn't speak English either, however, being equally eager to help, he enlisted a third person. Vince and I were duly impressed by everyone's attempt to assist us! We tried communicating with each other, but under the circumstances, in the end, we all shrugged our shoulders and smiled until Vince finally said, "It's OK. Grazie, mille grazie." We waved and left the restaurant.

Eventually, we found the train station. To our relief, the agent at the window spoke English. We bought tickets to Riomaggiore, the most southern of the Cinque Terra villages. The train trip took only five minutes. Like Vernazza, Riomaggiore's tiny harbor was crowded with the blue rowboats. The pristine beach and picturesque wharf were uniquely framed by colorful houses stacked on top of each other, like towers. It didn't take long to explore this minuscule town overflowing with historic character. We took more pictures, bought more postcards and another gelato before taking the train back to Monterosso.

Our full day in the Cinque Terre had been dazzling and mesmerizing! We will never forget these stuck-in-time villages that cling to the steep terraced cliffs to form one of Italy's most spectacular stretches of coastline.

Tuscany

After a hearty breakfast, we checked out of the Hotel Miramare. It seemed as if the entire staff came to wish us a safe journey. Our time in Sestri Levante had been wonderful and now we were looking forward to exploring Tuscany.

At the base of the Ligurian Apennines Mountains, we drove south on the A12 highway, passed jagged peaks and marble quarries, where the natural marble with its gray and white hues was clearly recognizable. I had never seen a marble quarry and was amazed at how the stone was blasted off from the face of the mountain in enormous square blocks. There was so much to see along the way. We pointed out everything to each other so that neither of us would miss a thing. We drove by medieval villages that looked like they were carved right out of the hillsides and others that looked like they were wedged in between them, quite evident that Italian architects and builders are among the best in the world.

Two hours after leaving Sestri Levante, highway signs indicated our approach to Pisa. We saw the Leaning Tower from the road. Since Vince had never been there, we decided to take the short side trip. What a mistake, what a *horrendous* mistake! Pisa was dense with tourists, tacky souvenir stands, pushy people selling cheap umbrellas and gypsy women exploiting their children offering chewing gum in return for money. After a fleeting visit to the Leaning Tower, the Duomo and the Piazza dei Miracoli, we were back in the car headed for the fastest way out of town to the tranquil countryside. Our destination was San Gimignano near the town of Sienna, in the heart of Tuscany.

It was late September. The grapes had been harvested, the sunflower stalks turned back into the earth and the fields were freshly plowed. By the time we approached Tuscany, the light of day changed the brown ocher color of the clay into a glowing umber. First settled by the Etruscans in the third century B.C., San Gimignano was given its current name in 450 AD. Toward the end of the Medieval period, three walls encircled the town and seventy-two towers built by aristocrat families as symbols of wealth and power formed San Gimignano's dramatic skyline. Only fourteen towers remain today. Our first glimpse of San Gimignano was truly exciting. The towers were taller than any we had seen in the area. By now, we were dying to step out of the car. It had been a long day of driving and we needed to stretch, walk and definitely drink some wine.

We had a reservation at the Hotel La Cisterna in the historic center of San Gimignano. Vince drove up to the lobby's front door as if we had been to this hotel before. Our ample, attractive room was tastefully decorated and to our delight, included a balcony overlooking the *Piazza della Cisterna*. It was just before sunset, early enough to venture into town before dinner.

The town was energetic and oozing with charm. Flourishing terra-cotta planters spilling brightly colored geraniums decorated every window sill, passage, doorway and balcony. Age-old stone buildings with heavy wooden doors adorned with hand-forged iron work and period appropriate light fixtures suspended across cobbled stone streets gave us the surreal feeling of being in a town in the Middle Ages. The shops were filled with exquisite hand-painted ceramics, fine linens, tapestries and leather-ware crafted by local artisans. In addition, there were enticing trattorias, pizzerias and mouthwatering gourmet shops selling locally produced wines, olive oils, pastas and other delicacies. How we relish the Italian cuisine and artworks, my credit cards were already beginning to burn a giant hole in my pocket!

As the sky turned a radiant orange, lavender and pink, we noticed a crowd forming near a stone wall at the edge of town where the view of the *Val D'Elsa*; the Elsa Valley was especially amazing. *Enotecas*, wine bars were serving wine and bruschetta to outside guests sitting on the medieval wall or mingling nearby. When we asked if it was a private party, we were thrilled to learn that it was the perpetual daily observance of the setting sun! How utterly delightful, this was a ritual we wanted to join. I quickly found a vacant spot and jumped up on the wall to reserve a space while Vince ordered our wine. We watched a particularly glorious sunset that evening, what a lovely welcome to Tuscany.

Creamy-colored villas, rust-colored farmhouses and moss-coated castles, gently rolling hillsides, meticulously maintained vineyards, olive and cypress trees grown in arrow-straight formation distinctly describe the pristine landscape of Tuscany. Excellent wines, olive oils, cheese and meat products are produced and served to tourists who come by the busloads to enjoy this region of world renown fame. We were thrilled to be here and ready to wander through the cobblestone streets to peer in every corner.

The proprietor of a shop filled with luscious fabrics, welcomed us as if we were long lost family members. While we admired his intricately embroidered table runners and exquisite tapestries, he proudly told us that his name was Mauro and that all the patterns in his shop were his grandmother's original designs. To substantiate his story, he showed us a newspaper article with a photo of his mother and grandmother at the store's Grand Opening in 1906. We bought an embroidered table runner, colorful pillow covers and some handwoven linens. Vince took a picture of Mauro and me, smiling from ear-to-ear, holding my shopping bag full of treasures. On a return trip in 2007, we gave Mauro a copy of the picture. We were flattered that he remembered us. He even remembered what we bought!

Then there was Silvano Mezzetti, a talented artist who worked in the ceramic shop located next door to our hotel. Silvano hand-painted ceramics so artfully and with such skill that it took me forever to decide which pieces to buy. I immediately fell in love with a storage jar labelled 'farina' but I wanted it labelled *caffè*. *"No problemo,"* Silvano said, "I will paint it for you."

Honestly? Italian ceramics, hand-painted especially for me? Isn't that an intriguing idea? We followed him to his studio in the basement of his shop. There were stacks of blank ceramic pieces of all sizes and shapes. Silvano offered to paint any piece of my choice in any style or pattern I saw in the store. Unable to resist such an amazing offer and opportunity, we selected several pieces, including a sizable pasta plate to hang in our newly remodeled kitchen. Silvano would send the ceramics to our address in California. No problemo! I handed him my credit card and crossed my fingers while the bank authorized such a hefty purchase and was elated when Silvano handed me a receipt indicating the bank's approval.

Although it is important to visit the inspirational cities of Florence and Siena, Vince and I were completely drawn in by the more intimate side of Tuscany. Ultimately, that is where the experiences that linger in our minds, long after we returned to California, often occurred. What we remember best are the interactions we had with the hospitable and good-natured people who live there. Today, we still cherish Mauro and Silvano's beautiful works of art.

From San Gimignano, we headed to the excellent wine town of Montalcino where the internationally coveted *Brunello di Montalcino* is produced. We parked our car at a site with a two-hour parking limit, but there were no meters or kiosks to buy a ticket or pay for parking. When we asked a conspicuous police officer what we should do, we were amused by her answer. She told us to leave a piece of paper marked with our arrival time on the dashboard and pay for parking at the tobacco shop on our way out of town. We found the "honor system" truly charming.

Montalcino is a well-preserved hilltop town with the now familiar narrow, winding cobblestone streets and the customary potted geraniums that flourish in every nook and cranny. In the heart of town, we came across a trattoria with a lovely outdoor table tucked away on a side street. We ordered a light lunch of bruschetta with garlic flavored olive oil and an *insalata mista*, mixed salad paired with a glass of the famous Brunello wine. The wine was served on a silver tray in oversized, beautifully bell-shaped glasses with individual, handwritten paper collar labels around the stems that identified the wine variety and vintage. "Pallazzo" Brunello 1998; an outstanding, surprisingly affordable wine at 1.37€ per glass. As we savored our lunch, and revisited our lives, time past much too quickly and we continued on our journey to find the next hilltop treasure.

Pienza, an ancient gem of a tiny village, is a short distance from Montalcino. Driving along the surrounding stone wall, we noticed a strong red wine aroma in the air. As I looked around to see what the source might be, I caught a glimpse of two men wearing denim overalls and rubber boots pouring gallons of red wine from enormous green glass flasks out onto the street where the wine flowed to a trench at the bottom of the hill. To me, this was the epitome of old-world Italian charm and labor; emptying out the leftover vintage to replenish it with the new wine. I found it completely enchanting and I knew we should wander around this fable village, before continuing to Montepulciano. This turned out to be an excellent and timely decision.

Just a few narrow streets lead to the piazza in front of the Duomo di Pienza; the center of regular life in the village, where we arrived just in time to observe a wedding procession. Two little girls with flowers in their hair, dressed in pink, held a grapevine arch suspended over the bride and groom as they continued toward the church. An apparent entourage of guests followed, while onlookers applauded as they passed by. It was an incredibly romantic sight. We stayed until everyone entered the church and we heard the ceremony begin. On our way back to the car, we noticed a black Ducati motorcycle decorated with white lace and tulle parked at a local Trattoria, in all likely hood, the celebration site for the wedding reception after the ceremony. What a perfectly appropriate getaway vehicle for the euphoric couple. Vince and I looked at each other and smiled, realizing that we had been fortunate to be at the right place and at the right time to witness a storybook wedding procession in a medieval village of Tuscany. Pienza was the prettiest discovery of our trip.

I was not quite sure if I wanted to visit Siena this time. We had fallen in love with the humble hilltop towns and the slower pace of the country lifestyle and from what I read in the guidebooks, Siena was much more like visiting a crowded city. Nevertheless, no trip to Tuscany is complete without seeing the *Duomo di Siena*, the Cathedral of Saint Mary. Therefore, off we went and forty minutes later found ourselves standing in line to buy tickets to tour the Cathedral. It was unlike any other we had seen, with its ornately decorated exterior, it is one of the finest examples of thirteenth and fourteenth century Gothic architecture in Italy. The cathedral's gleaming black and white marble pillars and inlaid floors were truly extraordinary!

After our worthwhile visit to the Duomo, we walked to the *Piazza del Campo*, the Track of Champions in the historic center of the city where an important horse race called the *Palio di Siena* is held around the piazza every summer. We stopped for lunch at a pizzeria on the edge of the track. In Italy, ordering one pizza to share between two people is frowned upon by most restaurants unless the second person orders an additional dish. Typically, pizzas have a thin crust and are served uncut with a fork and a serrated knife. We each ordered a pizza. It was ridiculously delicious and, undoubtedly, the best pizza I ever had! I ate mine entirely by myself! After our plentiful meal, we felt compelled to wander throughout Siena's medieval streets. We walked for three hours and didn't miss a single passage! By the time we returned to the car, my leg muscles throbbed and ached. Nevertheless, we valued the experience and considered it "working off our lunch."

A forty-minute drive on the most beautiful scenic roads in all of Tuscany, brought us to Montepulciano; another wine town of equal fame. The superior *Vino di Noble*, the Noble Wine of Montepulciano is produced here. As soon as we arrived at the threshold of the ancient stone gate entrance to this superb medieval village, we were dazzled by the enticing, pungent smells of aging rounds of cheese, savory salumi, prosciutto and *cinghiale* (wild boar) sausage drifting from the gourmet shops. Friendly shopkeepers enticed us to enter for samples of wine and food products. Although, I was more than delighted to taste the myriad of Tuscan specialty foods, Vince preferred to buy *a little of this, a little of that* and a bottle of wine to wash it all down with when we returned to our hotel room because kicking off our shoes, loosening our clothes and spreading out a feast on top of our bed had quickly become our favorite dining style. It was a casual way to end a full day of exploring and sightseeing. With a backpack filled with delicacies, we walked up to see the famous *pulcinella* mounted on the clock tower; a statue of a classical character that moves to ring a bell when the clock strikes.

A trip to Tuscany must simply also include a visit to the exquisite town of Cortona where Francis Mayes; author of *Under the Tuscan Sun* found and bought her beloved "Casa Bramasole." Built on Etruscan tombs, Cortona is roughly 3,000 years old. We were intrigued to see the area Mayes so vividly described in her book.

Upon arriving, however, our foremost priority was to secure a room for the next two nights. We had no reservations. It was already mid-afternoon, Cortona was crowded with tourists and with no reservations, we were fortunate to eventually stumble upon an elegant and luxurious hotel at the edge of town. Situated inside Cortona's imposing ancient walls, the Hotel Villa Marsili dates back to the fourteenth century. We booked a superior room; quite an understated description of the beautifully furnished space with a heavenly king size bed and enormous windows overlooking the colorful Tuscan countryside. It was an unbelievable value for a four-star hotel and we were extremely pleased.

After a quick unpacking, somewhat settling into our lovely surroundings and enjoying the complimentary sparkling wine and appetizers, we were inspired to walk to the village. Cortona has two piazzas where people gather to mingle or watch children at play. It was a beautiful evening. Couples strolled arm-in-arm past the open shops and wine bars. The village generated an intimate, congenial atmosphere. We enjoyed a casual dinner of light-as-air tortellini and a salad followed by a long overdue spell of people watching and sipping coffee at an outdoor cafe. It's amazing how much we enjoy passing the hours that way. We stayed until the shops closed and found ourselves surrounded by locals who pulled up chairs to our table, ordered coffee, and initiated a friendly conversation.

"Buonasera, come stai?" "Good evening, how are you?" one young man said as he sat next to us. We enjoyed feeling like a local and stayed to see what surprises might unfold on such a lovely evening.

I thought I heard the bathroom light and the air conditioner shut off in the middle of the night. Feeling groggy, I rolled over in our comfy bed and fell back asleep. A few hours later, we woke up to discover that there was no electricity or running water in our luxurious, superior room. Vince went to the front desk to inquire. The hotel manager informed him that there was an electrical power-outage throughout northern Italy and no one seemed to know when it would be restored. In the dining room, a cold breakfast was served by candlelight from giant silver candelabra on long tables decked with white tablecloths.

"Come downstairs," Vince said, "you must see this. It is just wonderful. Everyone is un-showered, just looking like they're looking."

The attentive hotel staff strived to create the best of an undesirable situation. Fortunately, the power was restored by mid-morning.

After our candlelight breakfast, we spent the rest of the day touring Cortona. We hiked to the Sanctuary of Cristoforo and the Duomo Santa Maria Assunta where the highest hilltop provided staggering views of the valley below. I took countless pictures of antique windows, wooden doors, stairways, arches, bell towers full of character and stone houses. There is no element more timeless than ancient stone. We walked up and down the terraced, narrow streets until our legs hurt. It was invigorating, we were in high spirits and blissfully happy.

After a full day of wandering, we returned to our room exhausted. Exploring Cortona was amazing. Later in the evening, gratified by a delicious dinner, we talked about our memorable day. We felt a true connection to Cortona and the magnetic spirit of this glorious town left a lasting effect on our hearts.

Our time remaining in Italy was dwindling quickly. Since we scheduled to spend the last part of our vacation on the Amalfi Coast, we became acutely aware of the importance to adhere to our schedule. Reluctantly, we left the tranquil Hotel Villa Marsili immediately after breakfast. A forty-minute drive through the countryside lead us to the A-1 *autostrade* into Umbria, the Green Belt Region of Italy. The impeccably manicured, classic Tuscan landscape became more natural and rustic here. The rolling hills became more mountainous. We passed abandoned farmhouses, lovely ochre colored stone ruins, just waiting for someone to love and restore them to their former glory.

I daydreamed of what I could do with one, if ever presented with the opportunity.

Almost half way between Rome and Florence, right off the highway, we saw an intriguing and formidable sight unlike anything we had seen on our trip. It appeared to be a metropolis perched high on a rocky red cliff. Vince pointed out where it was evident that the modern-day city was built on the ancient ruins of the original city underneath. I asked him if he knew what we were approaching.

"I don't know," he replied.

"Try to identify it on the map and let's check it out." We took the next freeway exit and followed the winding road to the top until we arrived in Umbria's grandest hilltop town.

Orvieto is built on a massive hunk of tufa rock. We parked the car near the Duomo. What a sight! A magnificent cathedral with a colorful mosaic facade was the most beautiful cathedral I had ever seen. This one smaller and more time-worn charming than the imposing grand cathedrals of Florence and Siena. A pleasant piazza in front of the Duomo with a clock tower and a *pulcinella* was lined with bustling ceramic shops and enticing restaurants. We quickly found a modest *alimentare*, a combination deli, wine and general grocery store with an excellent choice of local products. We bought sandwiches and fruit for the remainder of our drive to the coast. Unfortunately we didn't have time enough to explore Orvieto in depth. We wanted to reach the treacherous Amalfi Coast before dusk. We quickly took a few photos, returned to the car and talked about coming back here one day. Orvieto seemed like a completely enchanting place.

The Amazing Amalfi Coast

Vince was pleased with the compact Fiat Punta assigned to us by the car rental agency. With enough pep and power, he could drive this little car with the same energy as the other Italian drivers on the road. Our hearts were light as we made excellent time on the road, munching on our snacks-on-the-run and talking about everything we had seen and done on our incredible adventure. As we approached the vicinity of Rome, I became somewhat concerned about avoiding the hectic city center, but luckily, we had no problems staying on the outskirts of town as we continued on our way to the coast.

Two hours after leaving Orvieto, we arrived in Naples. As usual, it was my job to navigate us through the freeway maze of frenzied rush-hour traffic, making sure that we followed the signs to Sorrento at the southern approach to the Amalfi Coast Road. However, there was so much going on around us, at lightning speed, that I could not read the signs fast enough to provide Vince with accurate directions. We missed our exit and were forced to enter the treacherous Coast Road to our hotel in Positano from the opposite approach. How terribly frustrating! I had hoped to spare Vince from making the unfamiliar narrow, winding drive until the following day when he was refreshed and relaxed. He had been driving the entire day. Nevertheless, due to the magnificent scenery, our frustration quickly subsided. It was a jaw dropper! (I wish there was a more impactful word to describe the beauty of the area. *Jaw-dropper* is even inadequate.) From the moment we turned onto the famous road, we were transfixed by the dramatic views of the blue Mediterranean Sea on our left and soaring mountains, lovely beaches and picturesque villages clinging to rocky terrain on our right. Most would find this a challenging drive, but Vince loved it and said, "Oh yeah. We can definitely have some fun here!"

The fifty-kilometer road, carved into rugged cliffs plunging dramatically toward the sea, is an unbelievable display of Italian engineering and ingenuity. We were astonished to find ourselves sharing the road with fearless riders on scooters, tour bus operators and daring Italian drivers known for their behind-the-wheel bravado. I hung on with white knuckles each time we were forced to stop on a narrow curve, prompted to drive in reverse with our side-view mirrors pulled in so that a tour bus could pass. This was truly our most exciting driving experience in Europe!

We finally arrived at our hotel, the Punta Regina located just off the main road, away from the tourist area in the beautiful resort town of Positano. From the moment we walked through the door, I was immediately pleased with this delightful boutique hotel. We were promptly greeted by the friendly staff and a concierge stood ready to escort us to our room even lovelier than the internet photos indicated. The large white marble bathroom was outfitted with terry cloth bathrobes and comfy slippers. While the concierge explained the special features in our room, Vince grabbed my hand in excitement and whispered, "Look at the terrace!" Our room had a large vine-covered terrace with an expansive view of the Mediterranean. I love watching Vince emanate such enthusiasm and happiness!

After a quick unpacking and somewhat settling in, we went outside to stretch our legs. What a spectacular spot in the world! It was *beyond* beautiful here. We made an eight o'clock dinner reservation at Ristorante da Vincenzo located just a few steps away from our hotel. We took pictures of the gorgeous surroundings, including one of Vince posing underneath the restaurant sign with his name; Da Vincenzo. Being on the Amalfi Coast, in Positano in Italy was unimaginable. *Somebody, pinch me!* I didn't want to take a moment of this evening for granted. I was blessed to be here, to experience this beauty with the one person who completes me.

Dinner was outstanding and reasonably priced. Although all meals on our trip have been delicious, this was *hands down*, the best meal of all. While Vince paid the dinner bill, I stepped outside to snap more photos. The evening temperature was balmy and perfectly wonderful. The lights of the boats at anchor and of the shops in the village below us, created a lovely romantic setting. Then suddenly, as if the evening wasn't amazing enough, a group of strolling musicians with mandolins stopped to play a lilting melody for the outdoor diners. I was speechless and filled with joyful emotion. What an unforgettable introduction to the amazing Amalfi Coast! Vince looked at me and immediately recognized my sentiment.

"I love you," he said as we walked back to our hotel.

I squeezed his hand, looked at his handsome face and vowed, "I love you more."

After a much-needed restful sleep and drinking several cups of coffee on our fabulous terrace, we planned our day. First, we were going on a tour of Pompeii, then visit Sorrento before driving the complete length of the Amalfi Coast Road from beginning to end back to Positano.

As a true fan of ancient archeology, Vince has always longed to visit Pompeii, the ancient Roman town that was destroyed in 79AD by the Mount Vesuvius eruption. Nearly 60 feet of ash and pumice buried Pompeii, largely sealing away and preserving the city's history until it was discovered in the 1700s. We took the audio-guided walking tour of the forum where Pompeii's two main streets intersect the religious and political centers. When the city was thriving, the Romans who lived here led a sophisticated lifestyle. Seeing the plaster casts of the buried victims on display in the "Garden of the Fugitives" was truly a moving experience. After spending almost four hours and only seeing half of this important World Heritage site, we both agreed that we were on a history-lesson overload. It was honestly overwhelming; we were tired and the sun was beginning to heat up. After a brief and casual lunch stop at a sandwich shop across the street, we headed for Sorrento.

The beautiful area between Sorrento and Amalfi is world famous for the *limoni*; lemons that grow in this region. Although the large fruit is a bit strange looking with a gnarly, knotty skin, the lemons are prized for their extraordinary flavor and health properties. We spotted lemon grove terraces climbing the steep cliffs everywhere. Two types of lemons produced here; the elongated, pointed shaped fruit known as the *Limone Costa d'Amalfi* grows along the Amalfi Coast while the more rounder shaped *Limone di Sorrento* grows along the Sorrento coast. Both varieties are bright yellow in color, have skins rich in oil, contain high levels of vitamin C and are intensely fragrant. It is quite an experience to drive with the windows down during harvesting when the sweet scent of fresh lemons permeates the air. Harvesting occurs several times a year and is still done by carrying fruit filled baskets up and down the ancient steps. The lemons are used for the preparation of seafood and as the star ingredient in the region's specialty desserts. Shops in every village sell lemon gelato, lemon chocolates, lemon flavored olive oils, vinegars and the famous Limoncello Liqueur. Roadside stands sell Granita; a slushy, frozen drink made from lemonade shaved ice. Locals say that flavors vary greatly depending on which type of lemon is used. Every conceivable product made from lemons is also readily available in this region. Besides beauty products and candles containing lemon extracts, artfully painted ceramics, delicately embroidered linens and other souvenirs depicting the unique fruit are plentiful. Even the ceramic tile mile markers on the Amalfi Coast Road are hand decorated with lemons. I must admit that lemons are my addiction. I love them *in* and *on* everything. Lemons! Lemons! I can't have enough of them in my diet, they add such a freshness to any dish.

Sorrento is elegantly gorgeous! The town is reminiscent of California's Palm Springs or Santa Barbara. Unlike the smaller villages along the Amalfi Coast Road, Sorrento exudes a resort feeling. Giant palm trees and expensive luxury hotels line the main piazza. Terra cotta pots overflowing with yellow lantana and red geraniums adorn terraces and door steps. The town was crowded with cruise ship tourists. After finally finding a parking space, we walked to the historic part of town. At a souvenir shop, we couldn't resist buying an Italian soccer shirt for Meghan; our niece and a Ferrari racing flag for Spiker; our nephew. We ordered a cappuccino at a touristy outdoor cafe. It tasted *terrible*, the only terrible cappuccino of our entire trip. We wandered to the harbor and looked for the ferry docks. Tomorrow morning we were taking a boat trip from Sorrento's harbor to the island of Capri.

After being among throngs of people for most of the day, we were pleased to be back at our hotel in Positano, to unwind and enjoy the amazing view on our terrazzo, sharing fruit and a bottle of wine before dining at a beachside Trattoria. The evening atmosphere was alluringly festive. It was as if everyone out tonight was celebrating a special time in their life. After our meal, we walked on the black sandy beach to the edge of the water. The Mediterranean Sea felt surprisingly warm.

October 1, 2003, Today is our anniversary! We awoke to a bright and sunny morning ready to celebrate fifteen years of wedded bliss! We exchanged anniversary cards which we brought from home. It is always so much fun to exchange cards with Vince. He diligently searches for *just the right one* and it shows on his face when he watches me read the printed message and the words he wrote especially for the occasion. Vince is the love of my life!

We caught the 11:15 ferry to the glitzy, glamorous island of Capri; playground of the rich and famous! As the boat pulled away from the shore, the excavated, exposed remains of a lower city became visible in the tufa cliffs, providing an unusual perspective of an ancient Sorrento. As we had seen in Orvieto, it was quite evident that current-day Sorrento was built on top of the archaeological bones of a former, primordial city. Vince pointed to the relics of the primitive dwellings and stairways leading to the shore. It was amazing to think about the people who existed here long before us.

It was a quick thirty-minute boat trip from Sorrento to Capri's Marina Grande harbor. As the ferry tied up to the dock, I was already immersed in the beauty of the island. Capri looked just like I imagined; an Italian Island in the sunny Mediterranean. The snug harbor was filled with privately owned, luxury yachts and on shore, I could already spot the souvenir shops, restaurants with outdoor seating under oversized market umbrellas and the swarms of tourists following their guides like sheep. In spite of the crowds, Capri was picturesque and enchanting. I couldn't wait to disembark.

After a quick bite to eat, we followed a large group of people to the *funicolare*; a cable car transportation to the town of Capri at the top of the mountain in the center of the island. The view was absolutely staggering! On this spectacular, sunny day, the Bay of Naples and Mount Vesuvius were clearly visible. I took a million pictures! We crossed the Piazzetta; a lovely square surrounded by quaint shops and cafes, to a scenic promenade along exclusive boutiques for the elite, magnificent hotels for the ultrarich and expensive restaurants where celebrities of the 1950s dined wearing summer hats and glamorous sunglasses. At a bakery with a tempting elaborate window display of decadent desserts, we bought fresh baked cookies studded with pine nuts. They were the best *pinoli* cookies in the entire world!

Capri overflows opulence and grandeur, yet we loved being here. With bright, colorful vines and flowers, fragrant lemon and orange trees, lush green gardens and views of the blue, blue sea the island's natural beauty is unsurpassed. Hand in hand, we continued our walk at a leisurely pace, stopping to take pictures until we reached the end of the promenade where the historic Punta Tragara Hotel clings to the cliffs. Originally a private villa in the 1920s, it served as the headquarters for the American Command during World War II when President Eisenhower and Winston Churchill were guests of the hotel. In front of the hotel's entrance is a large terrace with benches and telescopes overlooking the sea, the village of Anacapri; the only other town on the island, and the Faraglioni rock formation; Capri's most famous landmark. Vince pointed to a sailboat in a pristine anchorage below. We watched as the skipper and crew jumped from the bow into the emerald green water and swam to the rocky shore. As we turned to begin our walk back, Vince grabbed my hand and said, "What a beautiful sight. If we ever sail here, I will anchor our boat in that exact spot beneath the cliffs of this hotel."

We rode the *funicolare* back to the harbor. Before boarding the ferry, we bought postcards to send home and a tote bag with embroidered lemons for my mom. At a deli, we ordered a freshly prepared sandwich of prosciutto, mortadella, salami and cheese, by pointing to our meat selections and holding up fingers to indicate the number of slices we wanted. The man behind the counter must have thought we were crazy Americans; no Italian would ever put more than one type of lunch meat on a sandwich. A pleasant ferry ride returned us to Sorrento.

At a ceramic shop next to our hotel, an exquisite locally hand-crafted biscotti jar decorated with lemons caught my eye. To commemorate our wedding anniversary and the wonderful day we spent in this region where lemons are prized, Vince bought it for me immediately.

Tonight we were going "all out" for our anniversary dinner. Based on a recommendation from a friend in New York, we made an eight o'clock dinner reservation at Ristorante Il San Pietro di Positano. I felt so elegant stepping into a Mercedes taxi for the short ride to the seaside property which appeared to be chiseled into the cliffs. The entrance to Hotel Il San Pietro is at street level, an elevator brought us to the restaurant below. We walked among terraced landscape with flourishing gardens spilling over ancient stone walls before reaching the oversized, ornate glass doors to the dining room. The views of the Mediterranean were stunning in every direction. We were seated at a table by the railing with an unobstructed panorama. Oh, I really needed a moment to take it all in.

After studying the menu which offered a profusion of fresh fish choices, Vince ordered the John Dory and I the pear and pumpkin ravioli with mussels. Every mouthful was delicate and heavenly delicious. We shared a bottle of wine and toasted to our life, our love and to one day returning to the Amalfi Coast. It felt so surreal; sitting under a bright star-studded sky with my handsome Italian husband, eating an extravagant dinner and gazing out at the twinkling city lights of Positano. *Is this indeed my life?* It was all so romantic and magical.

In the morning, I asked Vince to go to the beach with me, one more time before leaving Positano, to collect seashells and beach glass and for one last look up to the village. Speedily, we found our way to the black sandy seashore. Although, there were no shells, when Vince showed me the pottery shards in the sand I almost squealed with excitement! How appropriate to find pottery shards tumbled by the waves of the Mediterranean Sea on a beach in Italy, where terra cotta is more widely used than glass. I quickly collected a few pieces to take home.

Inevitably, we were on our way. We chose the more scenic route leading away from this amazing area and back to the harshness of the bustling city and the autostrada. Driving from Positano to Salerno was Vince's last opportunity to experience the thrill of driving on this spectacular road. It was also our last chance to admire the stunning beauty of the Amalfi Coast.

Being unfamiliar with car-rental-return and airport-check-in procedures, we thought it was best to return the car a day early, check into a nearby hotel and take a taxi to the Naples Airport for our extremely early morning flight home. We booked a room at the Hotel Paradiso near the airport. I wanted to savor every remaining moment in the best country in Europe! Naples is one of the ultimate ancient cities in Italy, however, Vince and I were not the least bit interested in exploring or sightseeing. We wanted to unwind and prepare for the long journey back to California.

I repacked the contents of our luggage in a more organized manner at my leisure. For lunch, we ate the sandwiches and fresh fruit left over from Capri. We just didn't feel like going out for a meal. Later, we walked to a pastry shop to buy a bottle of wine and pan-pizza slices for dinner and croissants for breakfast in our room before leaving the hotel.

Our room had an expansive view of the Bay of Naples and Mount Vesuvius and French doors leading to a small balcony. When we opened them in the evening, the sounds of the city serenaded us while we shared our bottle of wine and pan-pizza on the bed. As the light of the most perfect full moon I have ever seen illuminated our room, our last evening in Italy was bittersweet and intensely romantic.

How we responded to Italy had newly defined us. We came back with a renewed outlook toward our future and everyday living. It was the outcome I had hoped for at the onset of this vacation. Experiencing *La Dolce Vita* had a significant effect on our life and we both recognized the change in us.

A Mediterranean Sailing Trip

Florence

The next two years were transitional years that seemed to fly by. Still unemployed but never idle, Vince finished the kitchen remodeling project that he started two years ago. Extremely pleased with the result, I was proud of my husband's handiwork and it was very exciting to finally adorn our freshly painted walls with the beautiful hand-painted ceramics we bought in San Gimignano and Positano on our prior visits to Italy. I loved the splashes of color they added to the space. Our unique, non-cookie-cutter style kitchen was gorgeous and a true reflection of *us!*

After eight years of racing as part of the largest one-design keelboat fleet on the San Francisco Bay, we sold *Ultimatum*; our beloved J-105 sailboat. Along with the expense and upkeep of owning a 35-foot race boat in a growing fleet, it became increasingly more difficult to find crew dedicated to an entire racing season. Therefore, the painfully heartbreaking decision to sell our pride-and-joy was made. Nevertheless, to compensate for being without a "toy," we bought a sporty Harley-Davidson motorcycle to occupy Vince's free time. Riding a motorcycle was a more cost-effective sport, notwithstanding it was much easier to jump on a bike for a few hours of riding than prepare the boat for a few hours of sailing. Not quite the same thrill, but even so, a great alternative way to have fun.

Eventually, Vince found lucrative work as a salesperson at Artistic Tile and Stone; a high-quality shop located in our home town of San Carlos. He enjoyed the customer interaction and the creative outlet it provided. In just a few months, Vince transformed his successful former career in technical sales to a new one in design sales. Completely committed to the new occupation, Vince immersed himself in learning everything about the products, consequently becoming an expert in selling granite and stone, he was quickly nominated as the store's top seller. I was extremely proud of my husband's ability to excel in his brand-new profession. It wasn't long before our lives were once again "care free."

In the fall of 2005, with Vince's sixtieth birthday approaching on October 6, I asked him how he wished to celebrate the milestone event.

"Let's go sailing in Italy," he replied casually. "Let's visit the 'old country' again, and (a long pause followed) I would like to go to Jerusalem."

Oh, my Gosh! My heart skipped a beat, my eyes grew as big as saucers and I was completely overwhelmed with joy. We started planning immediately, with Vince coordinating the sailing segment of our trip, I scheduled the land travel, together we created a sensational itinerary!

I had nervous butterflies in my heart and soul when my mother and her life-partner; Cornelis arrived promptly at noon to drive us to the airport. We were flying to Florence, where we would spend one night, before driving a rental car to Naples in the morning. In Naples, a ferry would take us to the island of Procida where a representative from Sail Italia; a charter boat company would meet us at the harbor. Procida was the starting point of our one-week bareboat charter vacation on a sleek and sporty 35-foot sailboat. Vince plotted a course to sail south along the coast to Amalfi. *Just the two of us!* I have only dreamed of sailing past timeless history; ancient castles and mighty fortifications on the Mediterranean and imagined it as a fairytale-like experience. Our vacation would continue in Israel, where friends would help us celebrate Vince's birthday. We truly planned a trip of a lifetime!

After flying in excess of twelve hours, we finally arrived in Florence. It felt amazing to be in Italy again! We quickly found the Thrifty Car Rental counter, loaded ourselves into a cute, little, blue Fiat Panda and headed for our hotel. Our reservation was at the Hotel Pendini on the Piazza della Repubblica in the historic center of town. The centrally located accommodations were highly recommended by our friends Bill and Susan, who stayed in the hotel a year ago.

I came well prepared to answer any question Vince could ask about navigating to our destination. I brought a copy of the hotel's email confirmation which included a map and driving directions from the airport, a copy of the driving directions posted on the hotel website, in addition, to a downloaded *Google-map* "suggested route" version on my mobile phone so that I could instantly refer to it, if necessary. Unfortunately, nothing could have prepared us for the onslaught fiasco of aggressive "big city" traffic we encountered immediately after exiting the airport. When we entered the first roundabout, among the speeding busses, taxis and scooters, I could not read the road signs quickly enough to direct Vince to the right exit. His driving was astonishing! Not at all intimidated by the charge of rush hour traffic, Vince stayed in the roundabout at the same speed as the other drivers until I felt dizzy from going around in circles. I was relieved when he finally pulled over and stopped along a curb, on a straight road.

"Let me have those directions," he demanded. I showed him everything I had. After looking over all the formats, he shrugged his shoulders and said, "Let's just follow the signs to the *Centro,*" the Center. In Europe, the directions to the center of town are usually marked by a white sign depicting a black "bull's eye." What a great idea! Vince jumped back into the rapid flow of traffic without blinking an eye. I was elated when we finally crossed the Arno River and saw the top of the Duomo di Firenze. We were approaching the historic center. Now, all we had to do is locate the hotel.

There are at least seven major piazzas in Florence, connected by a snarly mess of narrow one-way streets. It was difficult to determine if we were near the piazza of our hotel. At last, Vince stepped out of the car and asked a police officer for directions to the Piazza della Repubblica. The policeman pointed to a building on a city block *behind* us, across a crowded intersection on a one-way street. Without a word of warning, Vince picked his moment, threw the car in reverse and drove through the intersection to the hotel's front door. I covered my eyes. In an instance, the car stopped, my gentle-mannered husband stepped out, came around to open my door and offered his hand.

"We have arrived," he announced.

Phew! What a relief! The stressful part of our trip was now behind us. I was eager to check into the room and rejoice in the feeling of being in Italy again. The Hotel Pendini was on the third level of a historic building. Through a heavy front door, we entered a dimly lit hallway. The dark and dingy building's interior looked nothing like I expected. A sign at the opposite end of the hall directed us to the hotel lobby by way of an elevator built into an alcove. As we stepped inside the tiny elevator Vince said, "What have we got ourselves into?" However, I trusted Bill's recommendation and knowing that Susan also liked the accommodations, was assurance enough for me that this three-star hotel would at least be satisfactory to us.

When the elevator door opened, we stepped into the lobby where a member of the hotel staff greeted us with a warm welcome. Soon it became quite clear why our friends recommended this hotel. Someone checked us in immediately, while another staff member offered to help with our luggage. With registration out of the way, we were escorted to a large, comfortable room, tastefully furnished with vintage-Italian style antiques and sizable windows which provided a magnificent view of the Duomo di Firenze; *the Cathedral of St. Maria del Fiore* on the Piazza della Repubblica.

The history of the Piazza della Repubblica dates back 2,000 years. After the unification of Italy in 1861, Florence was declared the capital city and the historical center went through a major renovation. Buildings were demolished and new ones erected. The government's goal was to refresh medieval Florence with the stylish atmosphere of Paris. The triumphal arch known as the *Arcone* was erected in 1895. Cafes and trattorias bordering the piazza attracted artists, writers and intellectuals. Today the square is still lined with these popular eating establishments, although elegant shops and art galleries have cropped up among them. The square has become a theater to musicians, street artists and strolling romantics. How thrilling that it was all right outside our door! Since our visit to Florence was just an overnight stay, our location could not have been better.

We unpacked only what we needed for our short stay, loosened our clothes, kicked off our shoes and collapsed on the bed. We were severely jet lagged, although after a few hours of rest, feeling somewhat rejuvenated, we splashed water on our faces and were ready to do some sightseeing.

We had no interest in going to the Galleria dell' Accademia to view Michelangelo's astoundingly beautiful statue of David, carved from a single block of marble. There were "fake" copies of the statue on every street corner in Florence. We also skipped going inside the pink and green marble Duomo, which took 170 years to complete. On a walk around the showstopper facade, we were already appropriately impressed. Trying to find our bearings with our sightseeing focused on experiencing the local traditions and culture, we noticed that a stream of tourists seemed to be flowing in the same direction, as if they knew that something important was about to happen somewhere.

"Let's follow them," I said, "let's see where everyone is going."

Everyone was headed to the *Ponte Vecchio*, the Old Bridge over the River Arno. The ancient bridge, built in 1345, was the only one of six bridges spared by the Germans during their retreat on August 4, 1944. The Ponte Vecchio is as much a symbol of Florence as the red dome of the Duomo di Firenze. The picturesque, three-arched structure lined with jewelry shops and market stalls is the most popular place in Florence to watch the sunset as the sun bathes the bridge in glorious hues of orange and gold. Every person attending the ritual competes for the best spot on the bridge to capture the picture-perfect moment as the soft glow of shop lights and lamp posts along the river banks reflect in the water. The true beauty of this magical sight is difficult to verbalize.

The evening temperature was perfect for strolling arm-in-arm with my handsome Italian husband, meandering through the historic streets and piazzas taking pictures and window shopping. Everywhere, freshly made sandwiches, bruschetta, pasta dishes and aromatic sausages ready to be devoured were displayed in the windows of self-service eating establishments. Unable to show restraint, we shared a pizza and a carafe of red wine in an outdoor Trattoria, caffè and a *dolce* (dessert) in another. We were delighted to be in Italy again. Being here made us realize how much we have missed this fantastic country. We watched flocks of pigeons as they entertained children in the piazzas amidst the bustle of people walking by, stopping to admire a street artist's work, or gathering to listen to musicians play a familiar melody. It all created such a congenial and inviting atmosphere. We bought postcards and stickpin souvenirs and although in our hearts we wanted the evening to go on forever, we were completely exhausted and eventually, reluctantly surrendered to our need for sleep. It had been a long wonderful day in Florence; the best Renaissance City in the world!

It was nearly one o'clock in the morning, when we were startled awake by a crowd of people singing loudly as they walked across the Piazza della Repubblica. Vince called their drunken joviality a "happy noise" because they sounded as if they had just left a rowdy party. I didn't quite agree with Vince's assessment of their state. When the noise subsided, I walked to the open window to breathe in the evening's fresh air when suddenly, I was captivated by the stunning sight of a perfectly shaped crescent moon suspended in the night sky, barely above the top of the Duomo. I took a picture and hoped that my camera would capture the image as beautifully as my eyes perceived it.

Vince began stirring and by four o'clock, we were both awake. Too early to go downstairs for coffee and breakfast, we spent the rest of the morning lying around, feeling foggy and dazed waiting for the sun to rise. Trying to sleep any longer was impossible.

Procida

The sun came up long after we were awake and it looked as if it was going to be a beautiful day. Before eight o'clock we were already bound for the car rental agency at the Naples International Airport in Capodichino which, Vince estimated as a four-hour drive. Getting through the congested traffic in Naples was challenging, but returning the rental car went without a hitch. Sail Italia arranged for our transfer from the airport to the ferry dock. A man holding a sign with our name on it was waiting for us at the rental counter when we arrived. This is always a *good* sign. He introduced himself as our taxi driver; Gennaro Di Procolo. (How's *that* for an Italian name? He assisted with our luggage, lead us to his Mercedes taxi and drove to Pozzuoli on the Bay of Naples. The quaint seaside village of Pozzuoli is the childhood home of Sophia Loren; world famous Italian film actress. An ancient cobblestone piazza that uniquely rises and falls with its underlying volcanic activity formed the center of town; a bustling place and quite charming with narrow palm tree studded streets, lined with shops and fresh fish eateries. When we arrived at the harbor, Gennaro matter-of-factly handed us two tickets for the ferry, pointed to our departure dock, and wished us a *Buon Viaggio* before disappearing into the crowded flow of traffic.

We had more than an hour to settle in at one of the local Trattorias with an outdoor table overlooking the seaport to enjoy a bite to eat. Ahhh! Our favorite way to pass the time. I ordered prosciutto with melon while Vince ordered a crostini with Parmesan cheese and a carafe of the house wine; a *sparkling* red which we found unusual, but certainly drinkable. We asked the waiter to snap our picture. After all, we were just about to embark on a Mediterranean sailing adventure and this was the beginning; definitely a moment worth documenting.

The weather was ideal for a boat trip. We were the only passengers sitting on the top deck of the huge ferry. As we left the dock and Naples grew distant, the Isle of Capri and the distinctive outline of Mount Vesuvius came into focus. Both were like "old friends" and lovely reminders of our prior trip to the Amalfi Coast in 2003.

Procida's silhouette also appeared quickly. Vince recognized it immediately from the charts and photos he studied endlessly, planning for our trip. Through the haze, a large stronghold appeared on the highest point of the island. It looked like a desolate age-old fort, or a timeworn castle. Built at the edge of a cliff, it was an impressive sight. When we approached Procida's harbor, it was exciting to see the familiar blue fishing boats and the colorful wooden row boats that we first saw in Portofino. The Moorish influence was obvious in the town's architecture. Looking ever so charming, standing next to each other all in a row, the faded pastel colors of the buildings along the waterfront were reminiscent of ice cream flavors in subtle shades of pink, white, yellow and orange with brown or green shutters and blue doors; the same blue that matched the blue fishing boats.

As the ferry moved closer toward the dock, I noticed pennant flags suspended from rooftops across the narrow streets, brightly flourishing oleander trees and restaurants with wicker chairs. Scooters and small cars buzzing along the waterfront were a flurry of activity. There was a yellow church and a piazza with a children's merry-go-round in the middle of the square. Procida looked adorable and seemed like a friendly place with good energy. We loved it at first sight and couldn't wait to disembark.

Roberta; from Sail Italia, met us at the end of the ramp and welcomed us to the island. We squeezed into her tiny red truck and drove a short distance to the office where the check-in process took place. I was dying to see the boat, our home for the next week, but there were a few formalities to take care of first. In addition, Vince was required to attend an orientation meeting and a briefing later in the afternoon.

To my delight, I finally met Valentina De Candia; the excellent agent who made all our travel arrangements. We exchanged emails for months and in the process, developed a friendly relationship. Valentina had a completely delightful disposition, young with short punk-red hair, she spoke adequate English, smiled often and seemed genuinely pleased to meet us. After we hugged as if we had always been friends, she offered us a bowl full of chocolate truffles, handmade by her mother. They were outrageously delicious! The staff served ice water and potato chips while they processed our contract. As Vince filled out documents, I bought a polo shirt and a belt embroidered with the Sail Italia logo for him. He loved them and couldn't wait to wear them.

With the red-tape finally out of the way, we were escorted to our yacht; a gorgeous 40-foot Beneteau named "A Kind of Blue." On board, the Sail Italia staff presented us with a bottle of Limoncello on ice, two glass flutes and a hand written note wishing us "smooth sailing." What a warm and welcome gesture. We couldn't believe that this luxurious sailboat was ours for the next seven days. I felt my heart smile!

With our luggage already on board, we moved into the port-aft cabin. The other two cabins would serve as storage for our empty suitcases, extra linens, towels and large bottles of water. It was grand having so much space just for the two of us. I unpacked and stored our clothes in the drawers and hanging lockers provided and arranged our toiletries in the head so that we could easily access what we needed, even under sail.

When the shops opened in the afternoon, we wandered into town for provisions, although we only needed the basics. Under way, we planned to sample the local cuisine and sit idly with cocktails at cafes to soak in the wonders of Italy's southwestern coast. We bought fresh baked bread at a bakery, unlabeled bottles of homemade red wine, olives and fruit at an *alimentari;* a small grocery shop and prosciutto, salami, cheese and coffee at the local market. Vince ordered by pointing to the bountiful display of cured meats behind the counter, holding up his fingers to indicate the number of slices desired of this-and-that and raising the palm of his hand to indicate "stop" or "that's enough." He was extremely resourceful and comical to watch. Since our lack of language skills was quite evident to the other customers waiting for their turn at the deli counter, they anxiously helped us communicate. Enthusiastic as a kid, Vince wanted to buy a sample of everything. I finally reminded him that we were planning to eat some our meals on shore. Task accomplished; we thoroughly enjoyed our true "community effort" shopping experience in town.

On our way back to the boat, we stopped at an art studio in a cave-like dwelling on the ground floor of an ancient building to admire an oil painting of oranges and lemons arranged on a white tablecloth with a red border and another one of green figs, purple and yellow grapes and a pomegranate split in half. The exquisite, true-to-life detail reflected in the paintings appealed to us and the vivid colors were eye-catching. When the artist appeared, he introduced himself as Giuseppe Di Liso; an island native. Although he didn't speak a word of English, he welcomed us to his studio and demonstrated his artful skill of painting on plywood. Giuseppe was charming and quite an intriguing artist. As we studied his paintings, he asked us where we were from, when we replied that we were from California, he proudly pointed to a miniature American Flag taped to the back wall of his studio. Then, he showed us his door jamb where previous American tourists had carved their name, hometown, state and date of their visit into the old wood. Evidently, there were guests from Chicago, Maine and Nebraska. Ultimately, we could not choose which painting we liked best and bought both. Giuseppe was ecstatic.

We ate dinner in one of the waterfront restaurants. Procida is still an undiscovered island gem that does not cater to tourism; therefore, menus were written only in Italian. Vince and I have always enjoyed the challenge of trying to translate a menu. It is remarkable how much of the language we have learned this way. If our attempt to pronounce our selection was not understood, we pointed to it on the menu and waited in suspense until the meal was brought to our table. We have often been surprised, although never disappointed. Vince ordered four different seafood dishes for us to share. The smoked fish, grilled octopus and fried calamari were to-die-for and the seafood linguine was out-of-this world. We shared a bottle of wine and talked about the thrill of exploring the Amalfi Coast by boat.

After dinner, we stopped at a coffee bar for a *'rum bubba;'* a local dessert favorite. It is a luscious, yellow cakey pastry, drenched in an aromatic rum. We asked the man behind the counter if we could take it with us to eat on the boat. He nodded. With a silver server, he transferred the delicate dessert and placed it on a gold paper tray. Then, he gently wrapped the tray in purple and gold paper, sealed it with a gold sticker, tied it with curly ribbon and handed the pretty package to me. My eyes grew wide as if I had just been handed a precious gift. I couldn't believe how elaborately and carefully this 1.25€ dessert had been packaged. It was a true testament to the Italian character; *Savor the small things in life.* On deck, we ate and enjoyed the divinely delicious Rum Bubba in much less time than it took to wrap it.

Although Sail Italia cleared us to leave the harbor and Vince was eager to start sailing, he reluctantly decided that we would spend the first night aboard in the harbor. We were sailing in unfamiliar territory; it was late and he became increasingly more concerned that we would not reach the nearest anchorage before dark. Therefore, we would deviate from our original plan and set sail bright and early in the morning.

Once our heads hit the pillows in our cozy cabin, we were asleep within minutes. Unfortunately, though, I was restless and woke up intermittently throughout the night, recalling the exciting events of our day; remnants of exploring Procida, our grocery store shopping experience and meeting Giuseppe; the local artist kept running through my brain. Sitting outside in a waterfront restaurant earlier that evening, we seemed to interest some children who were obviously not accustomed to seeing tourists. They laughed and giggled as one of the congenial boys made his small fist into a make-believe microphone and held it directed at our mouths for a *pretend* interview. He asked us where we were from.

"*Buonasera, come stai. Di dove sei?*" "Good evening, how are you? Where are you from?"

We answered with the few Italian words we knew.

"*Si, si. Procida e bella.*" "Yes, yes, Procida is beautiful." Their adorable faces kept flashing before me and the sound of their laughter kept ringing in my ears.

When Vince also stirred, I looked at my watch to see that it was only three o'clock in the morning. We both craved a cup of good coffee, although neither of us took the initiative to make it. We stayed snug in our cabin and talked about our itinerary, but eventually, I rolled out of bed and attempted to brew coffee with the coffee-maker we found on the boat. I had never seen one like it and fumbled around with the strange two-part contraption, but for-the-life-of-me, I could not figure out how to use it. In desperation, using a paper towel as a coffee filter held over a glass pitcher worked like a charm. The coffee easily dripped into the pitcher without making a mess and it tasted surprisingly delicious. Later that morning, we asked Sail Italia to exchange the coffee pot for one we knew how to operate, however, there were no other styles available. With all the fancy, expensive espresso machines sold around the world, that quirky stove-top gadget is the one most Italians preferred. Nevertheless, Vince was determined to learn how to use it and by morning, his persistence and patience was rewarded with an excellent pot of espresso.

Italians typically don't eat an elaborate breakfast. Morning nourishment consists of a straight shot of caffeine, sometimes accompanied by a *cornetto*; a croissant. Our first meal on board was "our version" of an ample Italian breakfast, consisting of some of the outstanding, salty, nutty pecorino cheese and a few slices of prosciutto, spicy salami and the melt-in-your-mouth mortadella with pistachio, that we bought the day before. We shared a beautiful, fragrant peach that reminded me of Vince's father's homegrown variety; the best I ever had. Fresh blood-orange juice was the perfect pairing beverage to our scrumptious breakfast. Why doesn't food at home taste like this? With the sun peeking over the horizon, we savored our meal on deck as Procida woke up in a flurry of activity. With the morning's light indicating that it was going to be a glorious day for sailing, we intended to leave the harbor as soon as Vince finished his business at the bank.

Rush hour on Procida was quite an experience as a constant, chaotic flow of pedestrians, mini busses, scooters and tiny (sometimes dilapidated) cars dispatched down the narrow streets toward the waterfront. We walked up the main road to the center of town and each time we heard a motorist approaching, we held our breath while we flattened our backs against the wall until the vehicle passed. We found it entertaining and downright delightful.

Capri; Faraglioni Rocks

By eleven o'clock, we were finally ready to leave the harbor and begin our exciting sailing adventure. Vince commanded perfect instructions for me to release the bow lines while he released the stern lines and motored the boat out to sea. Determined to do my best to be an exemplary first mate, I followed his orders, stowed the fenders and kept a watchful eye out for the unexpected. Somehow, it all felt as if we were living in a fantasy, sailing the Tyrrhenian Sea; the part of the Mediterranean off the western coast of Italy. I captured our departure from the harbor on camera, notwithstanding that each image was already a memento of my heart and mind. The first spectacular sight, the stronghold on the cliff, was exactly the site I envisioned when sailing away from an ancient city somewhere in Europe.

When we were safely out of the harbor, Vince asked me to hold the boat straight, head to wind, so he could hoist the sails. The clanging of the rigging made me nervous, but once the boat settled into a proper heading and we were sailing smoothly, it was completely exhilarating. Vince was in his glory, constantly trimming sails, adjusting cleats or coiling lines. Sailing was his passion! The deep blue water of the Mediterranean was iridescent and the sun was already irresistibly warm. An ideal spot-on deck invited me to lower my blood pressure, stretch out and work on my suntan. Completely relaxed, I felt at peace and when my skipper changed into his sexy Speedo swimsuit, it marked the true beginning of our sailing vacation!

Unfortunately, there was not enough wind to keep the sails filled, plus we were fighting back a rising tide. Proceeding at only three knots, it would take forever to reach our first anchorage off the coast of Capri, near the Faraglioni Rocks. Other boats in the area also seemed to be struggling to sail in the light air. After more than ninety minutes of trimming sails for optimum boat speed but going nowhere, Vince acquiesced and finally turned on the motor while I was lazily asleep on deck. Startled awake by the sudden sound of the engine, I couldn't believe my eyes! We were on the southern coast of Capri, where the steep rocky cliffs plunged straight down to the ocean floor making it possible for us to venture close to the shoreline. The dramatic beauty of the Italian coast was undeniable and seeing the beaches and tiny fishing villages at close range was truly breathtaking. Soon we came upon the pink and orange structure on the cliff which we immediately recognized as the Punta Tragara Hotel, an indelibly ingrained sight in my mind. Instantly, I reflected on our visit here in 2003 where we stood in front of that hotel gazing at the yachts moored below when Vince declared that if we ever sailed in these waters we would anchor there. Now, here we were, two years later, preparing to anchor our boat. It was a "pinch me" moment for Vince. I also realized how lucky we were. How did a young eleven-year-old immigrant girl from Holland, raised by her hardworking single mother and grandmother get here? How did she become so fortunate to live this opulent lifestyle?

Vince established the ideal location to drop our anchor. When the boat was settled, he turned off the motor and put on his snorkel gear. He always swam over the anchor to visually affirm that the boat was secure. Soon as he jumped into the brisk water, he bounced back up like a cork.

"The water is crystal clear," he announced. "You can count the grains of sand on the bottom. There are no fish, but the water is as clear as a bell."

I couldn't resist, hurried to put on my snorkel and mask and cautiously, lowered myself partially into the water from the swim ladder. The refreshing temperature took my breath away. I needed a few minutes to adjust before I released my hand from the ladder. It was exhilarating to be in the water, feeling jubilant and daring, I snorkeled around the boat. Although we saw only a few harmless, minute jelly fish, we didn't care, we were in the Mediterranean, laughing and splashing, acting like utter children. How grand!

After a playful swim, we rinsed off, changed into comfortable clothes and relaxed on deck. Absorbed in the beauty of our surroundings, our life in California seemed like a million miles away. Vince opened a bottle of wine and we nibbled on fresh fruit, sliced salami and toast with marmalade. In the late afternoon, when the sun ducked behind a cloud, we grabbed two blankets from our cabin and took a dreamy nap on deck. In the evening with no desire to eat at any of the restaurants on shore, we made sandwiches for dinner and dined onboard our beautiful yacht. Nothing could be better than this!

Two monster-size, commercial cruise ships, en route to Amalfi, sailed by. We couldn't imagine being a passenger among such a multitude of tourists. As we watched the sun turn the sky from brilliant orange to bright shades of pink and purple before it dipped below the horizon, I felt that God must have painted this seafarer's sunset for us. "Red sky at night is a sailor's delight." In the distance, a vintage luxury yacht at anchor looked particularly romantic with her deck lights reflecting in the water and in conclusion, I wrote in my travel journal: "Today was an absolutely spectacular day!"

Still suffering from jet lag and unable to sleep through the night, we woke up hours before sunrise. Vince suggested going on deck for a breath of fresh air. The imperious cliffs of Capri appeared prehistoric against the moonlit sky. The enormous granite, illuminated by the moon and stars, seemed almost magical. However, as Vince observed closer, he realized that their natural beauty was enhanced by inconspicuous spot lights suspended in the hillside's indentations. Again, Italian engineering is truly amazing! In the distance, the lights of the vintage yacht were still aglow and the other sailboats with brightly shining mast lights appeared to have their own guiding stars. It was an idyllic, tranquil setting. In the darkness of night, we seemed to be anchored closer together and I was comforted by the company of the other boats.

We returned to our cabin and slept until 8 o'clock. I hoped that by now we were fully acclimated to the local Italian time. The morning was cloudy and gray, so we had our coffee and a light breakfast in the main salon. The town of Anacapri was shrouded in mist and barely visible. Our boat was equipped with an inflatable dinghy tied up on the fore deck and an outboard motor affixed to a wooden board at the stern. Vince was compelled to take the dinghy for a test drive, although at first, I was reluctant and suggested that we save the experience for a brighter, sunnier occasion. Nevertheless, encouraged by Vince's enthusiasm, I agreed in spite of the weather. He lowered the dinghy into the water and in a matter of minutes, attached the outboard motor to the stern, offered his hand to help me on board, turned the dinghy away from the boat and headed to the Faraglioni Rocks. As we approached the imposing stone giants, they appeared even larger and at their base, the water was even a deeper blue. While I photographed our excursion, Vince skillfully navigated the dinghy between the rocks and through the narrow passage of the arch. In hindsight, I was grateful that I agreed to go. It would have been a shame to miss getting so close to these massive stones.

When we reached the boat, it started to rain, but just as we hurried to close the latch hatch, the rain stopped and the day became sunny and warm.

Amalfi

Ahhh, Amalfi! Today we planned to sail to Amalfi. I was nearly giddy with excitement just hearing Vince mention the romantic name of this ancient town on the famous Coast Road. At the end of our trip in 2003, we passed through Amalfi on our way to the airport, stopping only to take a picture, since we didn't have time to explore. For that reason, we were particularly looking forward to arriving at this next destination.

Rather than hauling the dinghy on board and storing it up on deck where it encumbered Vince's forward vision, he decided to tow it behind the boat like we did on previous sailing trips in the Caribbean and South Pacific. Tilted up and locked into position for towing, we also kept the motor attached to the dinghy. When everything was shipshape and secured, Vince weighed anchor with the use of the windlass and appointed me to take the helm. We quickly cleared the other boats around us and raised the sails. Once we were properly trimmed and sailing smoothly, Vince dropped his Speedo and with a playful smile on his face, did a gleeful little dance. *Adorable! I loved my naked skipper!*

Unfortunately, again there was not enough wind to sail. After several frustrating hours of perpetually trying to catch a breeze, Vince lowered the sails, turned on the motor and locked in the autopilot. What a marvelous device to have on board! We affectionately nicknamed the instrument "Auto." With "Auto" automatically steering to a predefined course, we were free to enjoy the scenery. Inclined into a comfortable position with our arms around each other in the cockpit, we let our "electronic crew" do the work. Suddenly, Vince pointed to a winding road which snaked through the landscape.

"Look. There is the Amalfi Coast Road!" he exclaimed. Was that *honestly* the magnificent road we toured two years ago?

"Oh, my goodness! It looks so different from the water," I replied. Standing on deck, it was quite thrilling to view the picturesque narrow highway from a different perspective. The expansive panoramic view was unobstructed. I remembered how the busses pulled in their side-view mirrors to pass on a curve. From this distance, we clearly saw how congested the traffic was and realized how fortunate we were to be on the boat.

We continued along the coast, past volcanic, mountainous terrain, lush vineyards, olive groves and lemon orchards typical of the Italian countryside. Charming villages among illustrious villas of distinction, ancient churches and the remains of medieval castles spilled down the hillsides and scattered among them, ruins of magnificent Saracen towers still stood watch for invaders. When we neared Positano and Ristorante Il San Pietro where we celebrated our fifteenth wedding anniversary just a few years ago, Vince directed our course to a shining white village on a distant shore.

"That's where we're headed," he said, "Amalfi! We will be in the harbor in about two hours."

Suddenly, I noticed by the look on his face, that Vince was becoming concerned about executing a "Med-tie." In the Mediterranean, boats dock with the stern instead of the bow tied to the quay and although Vince thoroughly studied the process in the navigation guide, we had no first-hand experience docking that way. While cruising to the harbor, we formulated a faultless plan and talked through the maneuvers. It seemed like a complex undertaking that I hoped we could accomplish without a problem.

Not knowing what obstacles we might encounter inside the harbor, I attached fenders to both sides of the boat as we approached, when a sporty gray and white inflatable speedboat, flying a large Italian flag, rushed out to meet us. I alerted Vince that someone appeared to be heading our way and suggested that he donned his swimsuit while I took over command of the helm. Within minutes, the speedboat pulled up alongside and a handsome man with a gorgeous tan, wearing fancy Hollywood-style sunglasses welcomed us and inquired in a thick Italian accent, "Ciao, Capitan! Do you want to come into the harbor?"

"Si," Vince answered.

"Do you want to stay for the night?"

"Si. Grazie."

"OK, come, follow me."

The speedboat made a wide turn behind us and as he jetted out in front, the handsome Italian arched his arm forward and shouted again, "Follow me!"

Vince and I looked at each other.

"Oh my God!" I exclaimed. "Welcome to Amalfi!" We followed quickly, positively relieved that someone would assist us in the docking process. Vince slowed our boat speed down considerably when we entered the harbor where two men stood on the dock with lines in hand, ready to toss them to us.

"Vince, he wants you to go over there," I shouted, indicating where the men were standing. Vince turned the boat toward them, proceeded, then cautiously backed the stern into the slip.

"*Buongiorno,*" muttered the men as they stepped on board, focused on the job at hand. In what seemed like an instant, one secured our stern lines while the other controlled the helm. It was quite hectic as the experienced men exerted quickly with accuracy and precision and although I was oblivious, Vince paid heed to everything they were doing. At our bow, the man with the sunglasses stood in his boat signaling for my attention.

"*Signora,*" he called as he picked up a long, thick rope from the water, handed a looped end to me and pointed to a cleat.

"It is beautiful here," I commented as I reached for the rope.

"Yes, it's not like America!" he retorted.

Suddenly being aware of where we were, I choked up with emotion, tears filled my eyes and I was wholeheartedly captivated by the breathtaking beauty of Amalfi. Before me, jagged mountains sloping toward the sea made a dramatic backdrop for what appeared to be an imposing monastery built below the ancient remains of a castle. Picturesque, white buildings among pastel cream-colored houses piled high on a rocky shore surrounded a predominant church boasting an extraordinary majolica dome. On the cliff above the harbor, the ever-present traffic on the Amalfi Coast Road proceeded at a snail's pace as it entered the resort town through a tunnel dug into a giant granite boulder.

Vince and the harbor crew were still busy tidying up lines and making crucial adjustments ensuring that we were safe and securely tied up to the dock. Nevertheless, I wanted him to stand on deck with me to share this overwhelming moment of realization that we were in world renown Amalfi. Eventually, the men vacated the boat, tipped their hand in a saluting wave as they disembarked.

"*Ciao. Buonasera.*"

"*Grazie!*" Vince retorted and waved back. "*Prego. Arrivederci.*"

Vince finally stepped out of the cockpit and came to meet me on the bow. "I just completed my first Medtie," he said with a lofty little attitude.

"I am very proud of you," I responded, "but honey come here. Come, look at this. Look at Amalfi. Can you believe how spectacular this is?" Amalfi honestly looked like the magnificent, classic Mediterranean coastal town I always imagined and I needed a moment to take it all in.

The Med-tie made it convenient to step from the boat to the dock by way of a plank. We had not been on land since we left Procida, therefore, it was wonderful to feel surefooted. The man with the sexy Hollywood-style sunglasses walked toward us and introduced himself as Giulio; the Harbor Master. Vince asked how much we owed him.

"No, you don't pay now," Giulio said in a melodious masculine voice with that to-die-for, irresistible Italian accent. "You pay later. How long you stay?"

"One night," Vince answered.

"OK, no problem, you pay tomorrow." That was easy, formalities were taken care of and now I couldn't wait to explore the village.

We showered and dressed quickly for the short ten-minute walk along the waterfront. Upon entering the village, the impressive ninth century "in your face" massive Cathedral of St. Andrew, wedged smack dab in the tiny main piazza with a Roman fountain, captured our attention immediately. It was unlike any other cathedral we had seen before. The uniquely Arab-influenced exterior literally looms over the historic center inciting us to climb the sixty-two steps to the immense medieval bronze doors. The Duomo of Amalfi, as it is most often referred to, is the religious heart of Amalfi and Saint Andrew is the patron saint and protector of the village.

As we expected, the village was dense with swarming tourists, which made it difficult to walk through the narrow street, lined with a plethora of souvenir shops. Nevertheless, the throngs of people inspired us to sit with a cup of coffee and a cannoli until the crowds dissipated. We stood waiting until a table became vacant in one of the outdoor cafes on Piazza Duomo where people-watching was prime. Once we were seated, we noticed a woman meticulously placing several large flower arrangements on the Cathedral steps. Just as we wondered what was about to occur, a beautiful bride and groom entered the piazza with a photographer. The woman who placed the flowers on the steps seemed to direct them, while she arranged the bride's veil until it draped, flowing delicately down the stairs. We were delighted to watch the romantic couple pose for several photos as I quickly found a spot among the other onlookers also eager to snap their picture.

After a long overdue spell of people-watching, we bought a few provisions for the boat before heading back to the harbor. On our private boat away from the masses, we sipped wine and watched the launch boats ferry the myriad of tourists to their cruise ships and countless busses return tour groups to their grand hotels.

Hours later, when we thought the town was safe and quiet, we meandered back to Amalfi, this time to enjoy the genuine charm and beauty of the most famous village on the Italian coastline. We dined at a cozy Trattoria, visited an antique stationary shop where a man created a sheet of paper from wood pulp, the way paper was made hundreds of years ago. We strolled through the narrow main street, past souvenir shops and the typical grocery markets displaying long braids of garlic and red peppers by the front doors. We walked all the way to the edge of town, through a splendid arch in a charming red palazzo which seemed to mark the entrance to real-life Amalfi; a friendly, humble neighborhood where the locals lived undisturbed.

Eventually we found our way back to the Piazza Duomo where the lights of the cafes and shops washed the ancient village square in an amber colored hue. With only a few locals and a handful of tourists mingled around the fountain or gathered on the steps of the Cathedral, the evening was filled with romance. The intoxicating balmy air enticed us to stay in town a little longer, to linger somewhere leisurely with a gelato or a final cup of coffee. I took pictures of the elaborate street lights; like beautiful chandeliers mounted on posts, they lined the famous Coast Road on the outer edge of town and near the water along the wharf leading the way to the harbor.

When we arrived back at the boat, we climbed on board and stood silently on the bow for a parting look at Amalfi by night. My amateur photographs would not do justice to the image of this evening that would perpetually remain in my memory.

Waking up to a sun-drenched morning, I stood on the companionway to peak through the top hatch to greet the day. The parking lot in town was still empty, an indication that Amalfi was not yet overrun by tourists. On the beach I caught a most endearing sight of a short and stout, bald, elderly gentleman wearing a speedo, belly hanging over his waistband, wading in the water up to his knees, reading a newspaper with his back toward the sun. It was quite a comical, completely adorable sight.

"*Buongiorno,* my love," Vince said affectionately as he approached me with open arms for a morning hug.

"*Buongiorno,* Bunny," I replied, "it's a beautiful day, come look, isn't it gorgeous here?" I don't know how I derived at the nickname 'Bunny,' however, it is how I occasionally refer to my husband. When I moved over so that we could stand on the companionway together, Vince also poked his head through the hatch and gazed in every direction when something caught his eye as he pointed to a path in the mountainside above the Amalfi Coast Road.

"Hey," he said, "look, there's a donkey trail up there." To our astonishment, a young workman was leading several donkeys carrying baskets laden with sand to a path on a higher ridge in the mountain. Several minutes later, the donkeys returned with empty baskets, only to go up again with another load. This typically old-world Italian way of accomplishing this task was charming to witness.

Today we planned to continue our journey to Positano, although not without taking one last stroll into the village before the tourists arrived. We hurried to the cafe in the piazza facing the Cathedral, ordered a cappuccino and—Ahhhh—cherished our last few moments in Amalfi. The simple pleasures of being in Italy; sipping coffee in a piazza while soaking in the morning sunlight is always a beautiful moment. Suddenly, a black limousine entered the town square from a narrow side passage, moving slowly, without making a sound, it seemed almost ghost-like. Four men wearing dark suits and white gloves walked solemnly behind and when the next car appeared, it became clear that we were observing a funeral procession. The morose motorcade stopped at the Cathedral's massive staircase; the four men opened the hearse to remove a miniature coffin covered with an enormous spray of flowers. Several people followed as they carried the ceremonial chest to the bronze doors at the top of the staircase. We watched until everyone entered the cathedral and the cars drove away. Coincidentally, during our brief visit to Amalfi, we witnessed two ceremonies marking life's contrasts of events; a bride and groom celebrating a new *beginning* and a family grieving a life *ending*.

When we returned to the boat, Vince was stir-crazy and eager to settle our bill with Giulio which was surprisingly reasonable for an overnight stay in

Amalfi's harbor. I released the bow lines; Giulio released our stern lines and Vince steered us out of the harbor. As we waved goodbye, Giulio shouted, "*Arrivederci!* Say hello to America!"

Positano

It was a short cruise under power to Positano. Much to my complete delight, Vince decided not to hoist the sails. The coastline was truly spectacular between Amalfi and Positano. With "Auto" driving the boat, the crew was free to relax in the cockpit and marvel at the splendid scenery. This part of the Amalfi Coast is world renown for the luxurious hotels, expensive restaurants, and prominent villas one more extravagant than the next scattered among the quaint villages.

Soon, the recognizable church with its dominant majolica dome uniquely distinguishing Positano from other villages on the coast, came into view. There were no docks at this waterfront and securing a mooring was outrageously expensive. Nevertheless, we cruised through the harbor in search of a suitable location to anchor. Ultimately, Vince selected an area near the South end where we would be sheltered from the wind and an onslaught of ferry boat traffic. I always breathe a sigh-of-relief after the anchor has been set, the motor has been turned off and we are settled, because it is only then that we can relax and enjoy our environment.

The temperature at this beautiful anchorage was slightly warmer than Amalfi, with deep ink blue water and crepe-y clusters of flourishing bougainvillea climbing the meticulous hillsides. We swam to a beach of tiny black pebbled sand; like coarse ground pepper, a rough stony shore ideal for topless beach glass and shell collecting. After hours of frolicking like children in the sea and sun, we returned to the boat famished and ready to explore the village.

All "dolled up" but yet dressed for comfort, we prepared the dinghy to venture to shore. What a total disaster! Vince stepped from the boat into the dinghy. As he held it in position with one hand, he offered me the other to come aboard, however, the swells in the sea made it difficult for me to judge when to take the initial big step into the dingy. In spite of Vince's urging not to think about it and *just do it*, I was apprehensive. When I finally took the "leap of faith," I landed in the dinghy with the thud of a fifty-pound sack of potatoes! My butt was wet and became more drenched from the spray of the sea as we motored to shore. Once there, Vince asked me to step off into the shallow water while holding the dock-line which was tied to the bow, then wait for a wave to push the dinghy ashore. In theory, that sounded like a simple undertaking, however, it was easier said than done! Just after I stepped off into the shallow water, a strong wave hit the back of my legs, I lost my balance and fell *end-over-tea-kettle* into the salty water. When Vince saw my predicament, he came to my rescue, but to no avail. He was also thrown off balance into a breaking wave and emerged just slightly short of being soaking wet! Here we were, in full view of everyone on the beach, getting tossed around like paper dolls in the tide. Eventually, Vince stumbled to shore holding the dinghy's dock-line, when a kind gentleman ran toward him to offer assistance, although, by then we were in control of our conspicuous, nightmarish circumstance. Vince walked up the beach to secure the dinghy, regardless, I could not explore Positano in my wet clothes. Furthermore, my shoes squished water when I walked. I pleaded with him to take us back to the boat where we could dry off and change our clothes. We were a mess!

Back on board, we gained composure, fixed ourselves up and tried it again. This time Vince motored to a stationary, commercial dock where, although I could step off onto a stable walkway, the dock was too high for me to reach. With the outboard motor in idle, Vince grabbed my waist and tried to lift me up as we bounced against the sea wall. His strong grip was painful, I pleaded with him to stop. I felt completely defeated. My self-esteem was shot and I truly felt incapable of doing anything. However, my determined husband would not hear of that, at last, he grabbed the dinghy's dock-line, bolted over my head and jumped up onto the wharf. I honestly don't know how he managed it! He guided the dinghy to a staircase that belonged to a private boat launch. Yet he didn't care, it was the only place where I could easily disembark. Thank God. Vince was my hero!

For a few moments, I couldn't even look at my husband. I was so embarrassed that I had been so awkward and clumsy. Vince sensed how humiliated I felt and put a comforting arm around my shoulder.

"Where do you want to eat, Treat?" he asked, trying to console me.

We chose the first restaurant with an available outdoor table facing the sea. We ordered wine before perusing through the menu, it was just what we needed to break the ice. Our feet were wet, but the sun was shining and it was a lovely day.

"Here's to us," Vince said, "let's just enjoy being here. We made it!" My sheepish disposition gradually vanished and I began to indulge being with my husband in Positano, on the Amalfi Coast. After all, how lucky can two people be?

After a relaxing lunch, wine and light hearted conversation, we walked up the winding road to the top of the village to Ristorante da Vincenzo where we had been in 2003. It was just as we remembered and we were delighted to know that the restaurant seemed to be thriving. We loved the feeling of familiarity. We bought several souvenirs for family and friends and a gelato and postcards from the quaint little shop we knew around the corner. At the South end of town, we wandered to the most recognized view of Positano; the beach and the church of Santa Maria Assunta, where we took a "selfie" (a self-portrait) with the shimmering, blue Mediterranean coast in the background. As we gazed out to sea, Vince pointed to our boat at anchor. Suddenly he noticed that the winds had grown stronger, he became concerned about getting stranded on shore and suggested that we head back down to the dinghy on the beach. I dreaded boarding that darn thing again, however, unfortunately I had no alternative.

Happy to be back on the boat, safe and sound, we shared a bottle of wine while Vince cooked a delicious pasta dinner with the seasonings we bought in Amalfi. We ate in the main salon where we were sheltered from the weather, by the time we finished eating, the constant wind was blowing much harder. Becoming exceedingly anxious, I focused on cleaning the galley and washing dishes, while Vince kept a constant watch on the distance between our boat, the shoreline and the other boats anchored nearby. I tried making journal entries and writing postcards, but the persistent howling wind was distracting and wearing down my nervous.

Soon, the night sky turned dark and ominous and although the stars were out and the moon was bright, it was eerie outside. Vince often made vigilant walks on deck to ensure that our windlass was holding and we were not drifting. Our anchor chain which was stretched out to its maximum length. Suddenly, we heard a loud, frightening sound that Vince could not identify. He jumped up on deck and discovered that the bow line of one of the small local wooden boats was completely entangled with our dinghy line. In the strong wind, the unfortunate small vessel must have broken loose and now it was banging into the side of our yacht. In the darkness, Vince tried desperately to untwist the two wet ropes while I held a flashlight directed at the tangled mess.

In the process, our dinghy with the outboard motor attached flipped over. What a horrific situation! In his anguish, Vince had no choice but to cut the wooden boat loose. As we watched the little boat drift out of sight and into the darkness, we felt remorseful and without saying a word, Vince pulled the dinghy close to the transom where he was able to turn it upright. What a relief to see that the motor was still attached.

With the stress of the entangled boat behind us, I prepared to hunker down in our cabin in the hopes of getting some rest, however, Vince had another idea.

"Let's move the boat," he said.

"What?" I replied in shock. "You mean re-anchor, in this wind?"

"Yes, we must. Tomorrow morning, someone will be looking for the fishing boat. If we move from here, maybe no one will ask us any questions."

Without further discussion, Vince started the motor and I reluctantly took the helm while he raised the anchor. As a novice sailor, I was petrified of moving the boat in this terrible weather when the howling wind and the sound of the running motor made it nearly impossible to hear Vince's instructions. I relied on his hand signals to do what he ordered. I feared that if Vince fell into the water, I would not be able to save him, nevertheless, as always God was watching over us as we re-anchored the boat under extremely dangerous conditions.

Before the break of dawn, the windstorm finally subsided, we were exhausted and fell sound asleep.

Our Seventeenth Wedding Anniversary

At eight o'clock, we were still fast asleep when the noise of an idling motor wakened us.

"*Buongiorno!*" Someone shouted.

Vince stepped on deck to find two crusty looking men standing in a metal boat holding on to our lifelines.

"*Scusi, signore. Buongiorno,*" they said again and apologized for waking us. One of the men spoke Italian, the other a bit of English. It seemed that they had lost a fishing boat in the gale last night and wondered if we had seen it. Vince shook his head, shrugged his shoulders and wished them luck in finding their boat as he pushed them off the railing.

"Grazie!" said the friendly men as they waved and moved toward the next boat for questioning. "Today will be sunny and windy, but tomorrow will be a beautiful day. *Grazie, grazie mille.*"

Oh! We felt completely awful for denying what we knew.

I enthusiastically anticipated celebrating our anniversary today! During breakfast, we exchanged greeting cards and discussed how we should spend the day honoring seventeen years of wedded bliss. Since I arranged and coordinated the travel details for this trip, I assigned the task of planning the day's agenda to Vince. It was indeed a bright and sunny day and I was looking forward to doing whatever he planned for us.

While I straightened up the salon and took a long leisurely shower, in preparation for going to shore, Vince made several attempts at starting the outboard motor. No matter what he tried, it just would not start, evidently when the dinghy flipped over during the windstorm, the gritty salt water that seeped into the motor ruined the engine. Painstakingly, Vince rinsed it several times with fresh water, but the damage was already done. Ultimately, with nothing left to do, we detached the inoperable motor from the dinghy and mounted it to a storage location on the boat, where it stayed for the remainder of our trip.

By mid-afternoon we were all dressed up with nowhere to go, pondering our options for getting to shore. Although our yacht was equipped with a ship-to-shore radio, we didn't know who to call for a launch service. We watched as water-taxis appeared to be shuttling passengers to the beach from other boast around us, until out of desperation, Vince tried to attract their attention by ferociously waving his arms. Eventually when one of them came within shouting distance, he jumped at the chance to shout out, "Can you take us to the shore?"

The driver acknowledged our plea and replied that he would return to pick us up in an hour. Mission accomplished! The cost of the short one-way trip was a well worth 4€ per person. With no wind on the beach, the weather was gorgeous, quite warm and perfect for celebrating!

The first order of business was finding an *Enoteca, a* wine bar with great atmosphere and a table facing the sea where we could unwind, share a bottle of wine and enjoy watching the tourists. We had not eaten lunch and although it was much too early for dinner, nibbling on appetizers seemed like a wonderful idea. We ordered focaccia bread with anchovies and pancetta, luscious purple grapes and a much-needed bottle of crisp white wine. What a life! The sun was low and the sky was becoming those glorious streaks of orange and red. When the wine was served, we finally made a toast to each other.

"Happy anniversary, honey, not a bad place to celebrate, is it?" I teased.

"There could be worse places," Vince replied, "happy anniversary, Treat." 'Treat' was his endearing nickname for me; a bit unusual, but I love it. We spent the entire late afternoon in this magnificent spot, relaxed and unhurried, until the sun fell far below the horizon and the first star appeared.

When it was time for dinner, I was caught by surprise, when my sentimental husband pointed to a lovely waterfront restaurant and announced that he had made a reservation for us there. The Maître d' led us to a table with a white linen tablecloth, a vase filled with beautiful flowers and a panoramic view of the beach.

"Perfetto. Grazie, signore," I heard Vince say to the Maître d' as he nodded his head to show his gratitude. Vince pulled out my chair and as he helped to scoot me in place, I became aware of how romantic the restaurant was. I felt like a princess.

While we studied our menus, a group of musicians unpacked and tuned three mandolins and an enormous harp in preparation to play near our table. I have always loved the harp and regard the graceful, medieval instrument, quintessential to playing Mediterranean music. I was thoroughly looking forward to being serenaded by the group.

"Honey, you chose a splendid place to have dinner," I said, "this couldn't be more perfect."

Just as I finished speaking, the music began and, as if on cue, Vince raised his glass in a toast.

"Happy anniversary, Treat," he said again, as we clinked our glasses everyone sitting around us applauded. Completely puzzled, I turned to look at Vince, who was grinning from ear-to-ear. To my amazement, a bride and groom entered the room, followed by the wedding entourage. Ahhh! That explained it. For a fleeting moment, I imagined that the flowers, the music and the applause had been for us, but when it became obvious that it was all for the wedding party, I realized that our fortunate timing to share in their celebration, was priceless. We both laughed out loud, appreciating that once again, we were at the right place at the right time. I felt completely happy deep down to my toes!

On the beach, we noticed groups of people boarding quaint local fishing boats with drinks in their hands. The boats decorated with strings of old-fashioned Christmas lights fastened to the mast head, draping down to the bow and stern, lend a fairytale setting as they drifted off into the sunset.

"Look," I said to Vince, "I wonder where they are going."

After the wine and appetizers were served, we were suddenly startled by a clamoring noise, difficult to distinguish. It sounded like the loud voices of demonstrators, although we also heard music and laughter. Suddenly, a conspicuous, merry group of locals carrying rudimentary signs marched down the hill toward the restaurant playing tambourines, percussions, an accordion and a grinding organ. The epitome of a local hometown marching band stopped directly in front of our table.

"Oh my Gosh!" I exclaimed as I snapped pictures of the adorable, free-spirited group. "What is going on? What are they doing here? What do the signs mean?"

"Happy anniversary, Treat," my husband replied.

"No way! Vince, you didn't arrange this," I said, as I quickly searched for my dictionary to translate the meaning of the homemade signs. I was so excited. Just then, a waiter came to our table.

"Good, eh? Do you like?" he asked as he nudged his head toward the band.

"Who are they?" I asked. "What are they doing here?"

The waiter explained that the restaurant was hosting a fish festival on a private beach on the other side of the ferry docks. The uproarious marching band was promoting the event with the intent of luring guests to the party boats for transportation to the festival. Ahhh! Again, for a brief moment, I was under the mistaken impression that the band was for us. Our timing to share in the festivities was perfect and priceless. Vince asked the waiter to bring our dinner courses at a leisurely pace so that we could linger in the evening's joyous atmosphere.

After our meal, we shared a decadent dessert, ordered coffee and limoncello and took a dreamy walk along the North shore cliff for a view of Positano at night.

The only word I can use to describe what we saw on the beach below is: *magical.* It was magical to see the twinkling lights of the village on the cliff side, while on the secluded beach below, the fish festival was in full swing. The lights of the party boats illuminated the festive scene while the enticing smell of fresh fish grilling on an open fire lured hungry guests to sit at the dining tables arranged on the sand. Everyone was drinking and laughing and it certainly seemed as if the whole world was celebrating something special tonight!

Finally, Vince suggested that it was time for us to head back to the water-taxis for our return trip to the boat although I didn't want this evening to ever end. Feeling somewhat despondent, I started my slow descent down the rocky path toward the beach, when I was completely startled by a dazzling display of fireworks that lit up the sky. At first, I couldn't believe what I saw, but then, there it was again, another explosion of brilliant color and light. What a tremendous surprise! Was this 'truly' happening?

"Oh, my God! Honey!" I exclaimed. "Are you kidding me? Wow!" The enormous bursts of fireworks kept coming, one more beautiful than the next, with loud booms and hissing sounds enhancing every explosion, I could barely contain my excitement.

"Happy anniversary, Treat!" Vince said with that familiar juvenile twinkle in his eyes.

"Oh, sure," I replied. "You had nothing to do with this. Nice try, honey. Nice try!"

"Sometimes it just pays to be lucky," Vince retorted as we hugged and kissed and laughed about the entire evening's fantastic, lucky timing of events and circumstances.

The fireworks continued until we reached the beach where our water-taxi was ready and waiting to take us back to the boat. While I changed into more comfortable clothes, Vince offered another limoncello before we went to bed. We sat curled up on deck, gazing at a moonlit Positano until midnight when the last fireworks marked the end of the fish festival. It had been an extraordinary day and an anniversary celebration that we will *never* forget!

Capri; Marina Grande

Positano was a rough anchorage. The boat was unsettled, all night long, which made sleeping difficult, however, in spite of a restless night, I woke up refreshed and filled with energy. I was still reeling from our amazing anniversary and during breakfast, I couldn't stop talking about the unplanned, lucky coincidences that made our day extra special. The old adage of "being at the right place, at the right time" certainly applied to our seventeenth anniversary.

Fortified by a hearty breakfast quenched by several cups of Italian-style coffee, Vince was antsy to weigh anchor and begin sailing to the Marina Grande; Capri's main harbor located on the northern side of the island. He set our heading, while I took some last-minute pictures of Positano and before long, the romantic, alluring village was in the distance and our conversation turned to the adventures we anticipated in Capri. Unfortunately again, there was not enough wind to sail, although the lovely sunny weather was pleasant and the scenery was outstanding.

After traveling under noisy engine power for more than four hours, our arrival to the glamorous harbor, on our own boat this time, was a blatant contrast to our arrival on a ferryboat from Sorrento in 2003. From the moment the harbor came into view, I felt as if we were among the swanky *Lifestyles of the Rich and Famous!* There were the typical cruise ships at anchor near the marina and on the other side of the seawall, Vince pointed to several sleek luxury yachts with enormous tall masts.

"Look at those! They're monstrous! There's a lot of money here," Vince remarked. Indeed, there were some mighty expensive yachts in this harbor with every vessel measuring in excess of 80 feet in length.

"We'll probably be the smallest boat here tonight," I replied.

Wondering what the procedure was for securing a slip in the legendary Marina Grande, Vince slowed our boat speed down considerably before asking me to take the helm, but no one came out to meet us or guide us to the docks. As Vince prepared the stern lines, I kept an eye out for a dockhand or harbor master signaling us toward a vacant slip. Making slow circles in the confined area near the harbor entrance, in near proximity of commercial boat traffic, was daunting. Relieved, I finally heard someone on shore whistle at us and point to a dock in the front row of slips. Vince backed the boat in position while I threw the stern lines in a neat little bundle to the man standing on the dock. Looking like professional sailors who had done this a million times before, we completed our Med-tie perfectly, without a problem. Vince was a proud skipper and complemented me on my boat handling. I was pleased that I had been helpful. After everything was in order and the excitement of our flawless docking performance faded, we were ready to go to town.

Oh, my goodness! Like Amalfi, Capri was literally swarming with hordes of tourists who arrived on ferries, tour buses, cruise ships and private yachts. It was exasperating fighting our way through the hectic crowd to buy a ticket before waiting in an enormous long line to board the *funicolare* to the main piazza at the top of the cliff. Nevertheless, the ten-minute ride through the island's natural lemon gardens is the best way to arrive at the center of the City of Capri. It was a brilliant day and the exceptional views at the top were worth fighting the crowds to get here.

In spite of the multitude of people, we were thrilled to be back on the island. Vince remembered exactly which bakery made those scrumptious, over-the-top delicious pinoli cookies we discovered on our first trip. He walked right into the shop and bought a half dozen to devour as we window shopped on the glamorous Via Camerelle; Capri's world-famous walkway. Few places we have been, boasted such a high concentration of expensive designer shops and artisan showrooms. Vince bought a delicate Murano glass pendant for me and for our mothers. We enjoyed a lovely late afternoon lunch at a posh restaurant and by the time we returned to the marina, the hordes of day-tripping tourists were nearly gone.

Capri was most tranquil before dusk, when the stark beauty of our surroundings was much more prevalent and the island looked like a picture postcard. As usual, we opened a bottle of wine, prepared a few appetizers and positioned ourselves in a comfortable spot on the foredeck. It was "cocktail hour" on the boat and Vince loved relaxing on deck to watch the other boats come into the harbor before nightfall. He found it particularly entertaining to watch novice boaters approach the dock in preparation for a med-tie because more often than not, they completely botched the operation and we have shared many laughs observing the hilarious mishaps that often occur. Since the Marina Grande is considered the playground of the elite, we anticipated some world class yachts coming for the evening such as *Strangelove;* a sexy, sleek 60-foot sailboat and the 108-foot power boat from London that were already here. Basking in the marina's vibrant activity at twilight, we suddenly noticed that everyone around us seemed to be looking toward the horizon. Quite curious to see what caught their attention, we climbed on the Bimini top just in time to see one of the largest privately owned yachts in the Mediterranean, preparing to anchor near the seawall because she was too big to enter the harbor. The dark blue hulled, 240-foot, four-masted sailboat was the most luxurious yacht I had ever seen.

Our sailing adventure was almost over. Sadly, we were scheduled to return to Procida to end our charter tomorrow. Impulsively, Vince suggested having a romantic parting dinner at one of the cozy restaurants on the Via Camerelle. What a wonderful idea! The restaurants along the waterfront would surely be overcrowded with local boaters and since I was also looking forward to riding the *funicolare* at sunset, I wholeheartedly agreed to dine at the top.

As we walked toward town along the docks, past all the luxury yachts that now filled the harbor, we peered inside the lavish salons. Nearly all, had an elaborate lounge, adorned with a large screen television. On-board, teak tables were elegantly set with white linen cloths, flowers and formal dinnerware. Uniformed crew pampered guests serving cocktails and hors d'oeuvres from large silver trays, while personal chefs prepared scrumptious gourmet meals fit for an admiral. Still, something about that kind of life did not appeal to me. I wouldn't trade *A Kind of Blue* for a mega-yacht.

At the *funicolare* station on top of the cliffs, the magnificent sea view enhanced by the brilliant colors from a glorious sunset was ideal for taking pictures.

The restaurant we selected to celebrate our final dinner on the island, was located under a graceful old magnolia tree, with an inviting courtyard overlooking the exclusive shops on the famous walkway. A properly attired waiter welcomed our arrival, ushered us to a frontside table and offered us a glass of Prosecco. As we sipped our sparkling celebratory drink, he opened a bottle of wine that we didn't order and asked how we arrived in Capri. We readily talked about the highlights of our sailing adventure and revealed that we were at his restaurant to commemorate the end of our trip. While the waiter listened with genuine interest, he handed Vince the wine cork before presenting us with the complimentary bottle of wine. We were stunned by his kind and generous gesture. As an entree, our waiter suggested a grilled local fish, prepared with roasted potatoes, green olives and lemon. The fish was cooked to perfection, an excellent pairing for the bestowed bottle of wine; a 2004 Gewurztraminer from the local St. Michelle Eppan winery. Our meal was delicious, the wine heavenly and the service impeccable. Every aspect of our last evening on Capri was unparalleled, thanks to our waiter who made it truly extraordinary.

By the time we returned to the Grande Marina, the crowd of the "rich and famous" who wined and dined on their private vessels, congregated on the docks and socialized on their decks. Boisterous men wore light colored slacks with navy blue blazers, smoked fat cigars, sipped aperitifs and made exaggerated hand gestures as they engaged in swaggered conversation. Alluring women wore slinky gowns, glittery jewelry and smoked long cigarettes in sexy, elegant holders. We wondered who these "Captains of Industry" were as we walked past the affluent crowd, toward our modest sailboat. On deck, the mild evening temperature was perfect for savoring one last romantic moment under the stars with a limoncello nightcap. Although Capri was the most extravagant and opulent destination we have ever visited, our trip to the Amalfi Coast would not have been complete without a stop at this ultra-glamorous island in the Mediterranean.

In later years, we embraced opportunities to share further explorations of Capri on subsequent visits with family and friends. With pleasure, we escorted fellow travelers on leisurely strolls along the exclusive designer shops on the Via Camerelle for an afternoon of world-class window-shopping. We brought them to our favorite bakery for the best pinoli cookie in all of Italy and eagerly pointed out the breathtaking views from the top of the cliffs with the hope that their visit to Capri would be an experience of a lifetime.

On an early autumn vacation in 2007 with our closest friends Bob and Karen and Stan and Carole, we rode a chairlift three kilometers from Capri's historic center to the charming town of Anacapri on the highest part of the island. At the foot of Monte Solaro, much quieter and less touristy than her famous sister-city, Anacapri is the only other municipality on the island and a welcome breath of fresh air after spending time in bursting-with-life Capri. We spent hours exploring the more modest ceramic shops and relaxed on a park bench with a lemon granita, before eventually riding the chairlift back to the hectic tourist mobs. Saturated with the color, fragrance and essence of the Mediterranean, Anacapri left an enduring impression on our hearts.

A few years later in the spring of 2012, we hosted a sailing trip along the Amalfi Coast for our twenty-year-old niece Meghan and her girlfriend Alison. The seductive girls attracted admiration from young Italian men everywhere we traveled. Meghan and Alison wholeheartedly embraced the experience of being in a foreign country and immersed themselves into the Italian culture at every opportunity. With genuine enthusiasm, they sampled the local food and wine and made an effort to speak the language. The girls proactively showed an interest in their surroundings by taking the initiative to explore on their own. Vince and I truly enjoyed watching them seize every moment of their Italian adventure. It was an unforgettable adventure for all of us.

Valentina

We were fast asleep at four o'clock in the morning, when an obnoxious, noisy group of German speaking men stomped across our deck, as they docked their boat. They were giddy, clumsy, loud and oblivious that they had so rudely awoken us. Exasperated and seething with anger, we glared at them through an open hatch. The rookie sailors had obviously been drinking. Fortunately, after they secured their boat, the crew stumbled into town and we were able to fall back asleep for a few more hours.

Today was shaping up to be "Vince's Day!" Our adventure was almost over and although it was the experience of a lifetime, due to the constant lack of wind, the sailing conditions had been less than favorable. Nevertheless, today the weather looked promising and we anticipated an excellent day for sailing. Knowing how eager Vince was to leave the docks, I stowed our gear and kitchen equipment in preparation for a long sail, however, we appeared to be tightly wedged into the harbor by the mega-yachts. Reluctant to navigate in such a limited area, we waited until someone on the port side boat appeared on deck. Eventually, Vince got his opportunity to announce our departure when a disheveled looking man emerged, holding a cup of coffee and a newspaper.

"*Buongiorno!*" Vince called out as he approached the neighboring boat. "*Parla Inglese?*" "Do you speak English?"

To our relief, the reply was in English. When Vince expressed concern for potentially damaging our boats as we left the dock, the man immediately confirmed our lack of space and offered to fend us off. When Vince fired up the engine, I released the stern lines, while other yachtsmen suddenly appeared on decks and docks to watch Vince flawlessly, skillfully maneuvered through the maze of magnificent yachts without a scratch. My heart burst with pride as I realized that all who witnessed were duly impressed with my husband's ability to get out of such a tight spot.

Once we cleared the marina, we raised the sails like professionals, set our heading for Procida and engaged the autopilot. We sailed past *Phocea,* the four-masted beauty anchored on the other side of the jetty. As we looked back at her, she was even more elegant and impressive then she appeared at first glance. The wind was excellent for sailing and the temperature ideal. We cruised smoothly for hours at the comfortable speed of six knots. It was exhilarating to feel the wind in my hair and the motion of the boat as I watched Vince, clearly in his element and finally sailing the blue waters of the Mediterranean. In my heart, I thanked God for this moment.

When the Procida harbor was in sight, Vince instructed me to contact Sail Italia on the VHF marine radio to announce our approach. I located the proper Channel 16 and held the button on the mouthpiece down as I called out.

"Sail Italia, Sail Italia. This is 'A Kind of Blue'…over."

I made several attempts, but was unsuccessful at getting a response. At last, Vince entered the harbor unescorted.

Inside the marina, we were puzzled to find no one there to assist us with the final docking process. After making several tight turns of the boat and a few more attempts at trying to reach the charter office on the radio, Vince eventually tied up in a random vacant slip. Soon as I was able, I jumped on shore, marched to the office to declare our arrival and found Roberta on the telephone. She was surprised to see me, but smiled and motioned for me to take a seat while she completed her conversation. From a glimpse at the clock on the wall, I suddenly realized that we had arrived during the afternoon hours when businesses close for lunch, clarifying why no one was at the docks to guide us in. We completely forgot about that wonderful Italian mid-day custom of shutting down in the afternoon. Vince and I have become firm believers that if Americans observed this practice, there would be less stress in our society.

I returned to the boat, informed Vince of the situation, suggested that we take showers and relax until it was time for our debriefing. It was good to know that we were at our final destination with not much to do except unwind, drink the last of the *vino* left on board and pack for our departure tomorrow morning. I was looking forward to having a quiet, relaxing dinner tonight at one of the familiar restaurants on shore.

At the appointed time, Vince went through the debriefing procedure with Valentina. With candor, he confessed that sea water had somehow gotten into the outboard motor and damaged the engine. Empathetically, Valentina reminded us that we were responsible for the repair or replacement cost. Contractually, towing the dinghy with the motor attached was not allowed. She would obtain the required estimates, submit the necessary documents and bill us accordingly. It was what we expected.

Valentina was warm and engaging. We enthusiastically told her of our amazing experiences in Amalfi and how Giulio came out to meet us. We described our unforgettable anniversary celebration in Positano and the countless luxury yachts we saw in Capri. Valentina informed us that the yachts were owned by business tycoons and millionaires who were attending a week-long Trade Commerce Convention in the region. Together we talked with Valentina as if we had known each other for years. She was born and raised on Procida, a single mom raising her three-year-old son named Ciro. She and Ciro lived with her parents and her brother. Valentina's eyes sparkled as she spoke of Ciro and her family. Her dad was retired and her mom was an avid cook, well known by the locals for preparing copious amounts of food for nearby festivals and social events. To our dismay, our delightful conversation was interrupted by a business matter that Valentina needed to tend to. We hugged and kissed and made a vow to stay in touch.

In the morning, we were scheduled to take the first ferry to Pozzuoli. I packed our belongings while Vince made sandwiches for our long road trip from Naples to the airport in Florence. When I felt that we were organized and ready to have our last dinner on shore, we went to Trattoria da Giorgio; the same waterfront Trattoria where we ate our first meal after arriving on the island at the start of our adventure. Some of our tastiest local dishes have been served there. It seemed like an appropriate place to end our sailing trip.

It was raining when we walked back to the boat after dinner. Since we anticipated a strenuous day of travel tomorrow, we prepared for bed early. The subtle rain falling on our deck sounded romantic and seemed somehow appropriate for our last night on board. *A Kind of Blue* had been the quintessential boat for us, being just the right size to handle, her layout was comfortable and spacious and she sailed well. We will remember her fondly.

Almost tucked into our berths, we heard an unexpected knock on our door. It was Roberta, holding down the hood of her foul weather jacket to shield her face from the rain with one hand, she was holding a large brown paper bag in the other.

"*Scusi, signora Di Lorenzo,* for you, from Valentina," she said as she pushed the bag toward me. I reached out to take it from her and wanted to invite her in for a chat, but she turned quickly and disappeared.

"*Buona notte, Roberta.* Good night and grazie!"

I shouted and hoped that she heard me.

"What is it?" Vince asked.

"I don't know. It's from Valentina."

When I opened the bag, we were completely bewildered. In the bag was a jar of cured tuna, one of strawberry jam and three more of fruit preserves. Evidently, all were homemade by her mother. We looked at each other, deeply touched.

"You're kidding me?" Vince said, slightly emotional. Valentina's incredible act of kindness reminded him of his childhood visit with his dad to "the old country." Instantly, he remembered the bestowals from the heart; modest gifts of homemade delicacies from family and friends. I wanted to run to the Sail Italia office, find Valentina to express our appreciation for her remarkable gift that meant so much to us. Unfortunately, the office was already closed and by the time it opened in the morning, Vince and I would be on the ferry.

The additional weight of the jars was more than we preferred to carry on our continuing journey to Israel. Nevertheless, it was important to bring these beautiful gifts home and Vince was willing to leave less meaningful items behind to compensate for the weight of the jars. Valentina's heartwarming gesture taught me something valuable about my husband and the beautiful, benevolent Italian culture.

Throughout the years, our relationship with Valentina has blossomed into a genuine friendship. We stay in touch through emails and internet social media. We returned to Procida two years later, to embark on another bareboat charter vacation. Although Valentina no longer worked for Sail Italia, she and Ciro met us at the marina when we arrived. It was great to see her again and a pleasure to finally meet her son; an adorable boy with impeccable curly hair and the warm, sweet personality of his mother. To our surprise, Valentina brought cookies and jam for our sailing trip and a lemon meringue cake large enough to feed our crew for several days. Her mother's homemade desserts were scrumptious! Our friends were astonished by Valentina's generosity and thoughtfulness.

On each succeeding trip, we watched Ciro grow up and develop into a handsome teenager. Eventually, Valentina met her Prince. She fell in love with Daniele De Pinto; who worked as a mechanic on the ferries. A few years later,

Daniele and Valentina were married in one of the sixteen churches on Procida. They spent their honeymoon in Paris. Giuseppe was born the following year. With a new husband, a father and a baby brother for Ciro, Valentina's family was complete and our dear friend's life is now happier than she ever imagined.

We felt a melancholy tug at our heartstrings the next morning when the ferry pulled away from the dock and Procida faded into the distance. We knew that we were leaving a very special place. Procida is a testament to the Italian "sweet life." Precisely on time, Gennaro met us in Pozzuoli when we disembarked. As the meticulous chauffeur, he stood waiting next to the car, with the trunk and door open, ready to store our luggage. He drove us to the Naples airport where we were eager to rent a car and begin our journey to Florence.

It was more than a four-hour drive to Florence. When we reached Tuscany, we couldn't resist making a quick excursion to San Gimignano to visit Silvano's ceramic shop and Mauro's linen store. In typical Italian style with a kiss on each cheek, we were warmly greeted by both as if we were old friends. They seemed genuinely happy to see us. We bought an exquisitely painted ceramic fish platter for Vince's brother from Silvano and handwoven linen napkins for friends from Mauro. In a deli around the corner, we bought cookies for Vince's mom and a bottle of limoncello for his cousin. It is nearly impossible to refrain from shopping in Italy, where a superabundance of remarkable handcrafted items is at such an affordable price.

The drive from San Gimignano to Florence was easy to navigate, because, for once, I was able to follow our route on a huge paper map without a problem. To eliminate the stress of driving to the airport early in the morning to return the rental car before our seven o'clock flight to Tel Aviv, we planned on returning the car the night before and staying at a nearby hotel. Taking a taxi to the airport after a good night's rest, seemed much wiser.

We had another reservation at the Hotel Pendini, where we knew the staff was friendly and spoke English. I was also hopeful that they would accommodate my request to ship home a box filled with the myriad of gifts and souvenirs we accumulated. As expected, they were more than happy to assist and provided a large enough box to fit everything that we would not need for the duration of our vacation. In our hotel room, I reorganized the entire contents of our luggage while Vince offered to tackle the formidable task of buying gelato. He had an undeniable craving for the Italian specialty dessert and promised to bring it back to the room. It sounded heavenly.

As I opened the window for some fresh air, I caught a glimpse of my sweet husband, strolling by the many street artists performing in the piazza. It was dreamy watching him stop to listen to a talented music group playing a familiar gypsy-style tune. When the infectious music stopped, a crowd of admirers cheered "bravo" and applauded. Vince looked up and saw me standing at the window and waved ardently. He raised up a finger as if to say, "Wait a minute," picked up two of the band's compact discs and held them up to show me, shrugging his shoulders suggesting the question of whether he should buy them. When I readily gave him the OK hand signal of approval, he paid for the CDs and beaming with enthusiasm, returned to the room.

"What a beautiful evening!" he exclaimed as he walked through the door. "It is so festive in the piazza. Did you see me?"

"Yes," I answered. "Did you see me? I was pointing to the gelato store behind you. Where is the gelato?" I teased, as he handed me the CDs. In all his excitement, Vince completely forgot about his promise to bring back gelato. Of course it didn't matter, because the music he bought would remind us of this evening forever and the image I have of him holding up the two discs when I stood at the window, is one of my dearest memories.

We completely loved our evening in Florence, although sadly, it was our last evening in Italy and marked the end of our amazing sailing trip.

3. Yearning for Italy

When Vince and I were not in Italy, we were filled with a powerful longing to be there; away from our deadline driven lives in the San Francisco Bay Area. We yearned to be in a world that seemed simpler, more genuine. From that first magical Italian vacation in 2003 onward, the misty vistas of the central Apennines, the fresh-from-the-farm cooking and the comforting intimacy of the Italian culture became our benchmarks for judging the quality of life everywhere else. By now, Italy was in our hearts.

Without realizing it, we made seamless, subtle changes in our California life-style as I began cooking with an Italian flair and gradually changed home decor to compliment the ceramics we collected. I gained an insatiable interest in books about life in the Italian countryside. I daydreamed about living La Dolce Vita somewhere in Italy. When family and friends came to visit, they tolerated countless viewings of photos and slideshows of our vacations and we talked endlessly about our Italian experiences. We never love Italy more than when we can share her history and mind-blowing beauty with loved ones.

I have always considered it fortunate that Vince and I have acutely compatible travel styles. We absolutely love immersing ourselves in the local culture. We seek out where the locals go to gather and mingle. We want to eat where they eat, sample the regional delicacies (street vendor food is one of our favorite ways to do this), drink the local wines, attend the open-air markets and go to the neighborhood festivals. We thoroughly enjoy wandering to an undetermined destination, unescorted, to discover the churches and piazzas not known to the average tourist. However, by taking vacations with friends, we learned that not everyone shares this way of globe-trotting. Not everyone is comfortable with the unfamiliar and even the well-traveled often don't venture out in a quest for unusual experiences. They want everything to be the same as it is at home. We can still recall the time we were in Mallorca with traveling companions who suggested going to an *Irish Pub!* Vince loudly declared that he did *not* travel to Mallorca to sit in an Irish Pub and suggested going to a local bistro for beer and tapas. The authentic Spanish food was amazing and our friends loved the experience.

One year, we enticed our friends Bob and Karen, Stan and Carole, to join us on another sailing adventure along the Amalfi Coast, followed by a road trip to Tuscany's Chianti wine region. Bob and Vince are best pals who have known each other for more than 45 years. We were delighted to show them the unparalleled scenic beauty of the innermost Italy we had fallen in love with and we looked forward to exposing them to the foreign culture we talked so much about.

Bob considers himself a wine connoisseur, therefore, he was particularly eager to taste the Italian wines. When it came time to buying the provisions for our cruise, I was excited to take Karen and Carole to Procida's bakeries and markets to select from the wonderful deli meats and exceptional quality seasonal produce. Bob perused through the wine shops, studying the labels, noting the vintage and vintners. With great consideration, he chose a pricey array of, what he determined to be, excellent wines. Stan, who was also in search of fine wines, explored on his own. Vince and I prefer the local or house wines (*Vino delle Casa*) served from a ceramic pitcher or a bottle without a label.

The women and I were still grocery shopping when we ran into Bob and Stan along the waterfront. Enthusiastically, Bob showed us his selection of wines. He offered to serve a wine-tasting on the boat, then buy more of the wines we liked best. Stan was also looking forward to tasting the red and white wines he chose. As we completed our shopping in one of the small, family run markets I had discovered on our previous visit to Procida, Karen pointed to some dark, dusty bottles of wine tucked away on a bottom shelf.

"Look at 'those' wine bottles," she said as if she meant that no one in their right mind would ever buy those.

"Oh, Wow!" I exclaimed. "Dusty bottles of wine! Vince's favorite!"

Everyone was surprised at my comment. I quickly grabbed five bottles (it was all I could carry) and paid 6€ for all! I was ecstatic! Bob looked at me as if I was crazy. We walked back to the boat together, although I hurried out in front. Vince was standing on the transom and reached out a hand to help me board.

"Where have you been?" he asked.

"Look, honey! Look. We found dusty bottles of wine, with no labels. Your favorite!"

We were all impatient to taste the variety of wines we bought. We tasted Stanley's moderately priced wines first. Then we tasted Bob's expensive wines. All were exceptionally good. Then we tasted my low-budget, homemade wine. Vince and I watched Bob as he swirled his glass, sniffed the wine and took a sip.

"Joyce, where did you buy this wine?" he asked. "I want to buy a few more bottles for our trip." We all chuckled. My 'no label' wine was the winner. Bob and I went back to the little grocery store on the waterfront and bought the remaining bottles on the shelf.

In the piazza in front of the church, a percussion band of street musicians was just warming up to play. Their instruments were made from wooden barrels of all sizes. (Only in Italy!) We were exhausted from our journey, but couldn't resist lingering to listen. It was another typical evening in the rural "old country."

We spent the latter week of travel with our friends, on a road trip to Tuscany's Chianti wine region, where we stayed in charming San Quirico d'Orcia; a small medieval village in the Elsa Valley. Our hotel was the Palazzo del Capitano, an exquisitely restored, notable mansion of the fourteenth century. We had guest house accommodations; three superbly decorated bedroom suites located on three levels. Vince and I stayed on the third floor in a room with a large terrazzo.

The view overlooking quaint terra-cotta rooftops covering sand colored stone houses on cobblestone streets was right out of a Tuscan travel magazine; remarkably picturesque and quite charming. The six of us gathered there for cocktail hour with wine and cheese before dinner. While the sky blushed a rosy hue, we discussed what tomorrow might bring. Frankly, we enjoyed not having a concrete plan, allowing for spontaneity. After dinner, Vince and I returned to the terrazzo with a Limoncello night cap. It was terribly romantic, looking at the stars together, as my husband identified the constellations for me. I adore him especially when he points out the Milky Way, Orion's Belt and the Big Dipper. We relished having a moment all to ourselves, with our delusions of grandeur and fantasizing about owning a vacation home in Italy one day. In our next lifetime, we would own a home just like this one; a home made of ancient stone, with a beautiful terrazzo and views overlooking the rooftops of a charming Italian village.

Relaxing in an outdoor cafe, watching people and trying to spot the blatant "American Tourist" has always been one of our favorite ways to pass the time. We enjoyed whispering lighthearted comments to each other about the men wearing front pleaded khaki pants and a fanny-pack around their middle and about the women wearing bright, white (obviously new) athletic shoes, baggy cropped pants and a sweatshirt. We became expert at spotting the American Tourist by their attire from a mile away. Another telltale sign was the behavior. The naive, thoughtless or arrogant individual who wants everything like it is *at home* in the "good ol' USA." There is the tourist who orders a hot chocolate at a coffee-bar, or the one who complains about the minestrone soup not being creamy, like the kind *at home,* obviously not knowing that there is no set recipe for this delicious, rustic soup of true Italian origin. Minestrone soup is made from whatever vegetables are in season or left over from the meal before, often with the addition of beans, pasta or rice. We have seen travelers insist on getting a glass of water with ice or coffee refills at no charge because that is how it is *at home.*

Nevertheless, most Italians are somehow able to maintain their sense of humor. They grin and bear the "ugly American Tourist." We experienced this first hand in San Gimignano. Bob, often orders a glass of milk, which perplexes the server who is not accustomed to an adult requesting a drink typically served to children. Although an earnest attempt is always made to accommodate his unusual request, it is never like the cold glass of milk served in restaurants *at home.* Some waiters served warmed milk in a cup and saucer, frothy milk in a tall glass with sugar, tepid milk in a pitcher with a separate cup and a cookie. However, the most comical and best strive was made by a waiter at a local bakery in San Gimignano who brought Bob his glass of milk followed by an offering of a piece of candy.

"For the bambino," the waiter said with a smile. Bob had such a quizzical look on his face. It took him a moment to understand the joke while we all laughed at the waiter's unique sense of humor.

Several years ago, we sailed with the same group of friends from Calabria to the Aeolian Islands.

Calabria is the southwestern region of Italy, which forms the "toe" on a map of the country. It was an extremely strenuous trek from San Francisco to our hotel in Tropea; an ancient village, uniquely positioned high on a cliff above the Tyrrhenian Sea. We stayed at the hotel Residenza il Barone, located within walking distance to the edge of the historic district of Porta Nuova, where the panoramic vistas were breathtaking. We had a clear view of an active, smoking volcano on the island of Stromboli in the distance and perched on top of an isolated volcanic plug, was the Chapel of Santa Maria dell' Isola. We felt like we had stepped back in time. The harbor of Tropea was the most spectacular we had ever seen. The sheer, steep rock face that separates the harbor from the village became a dramatic canvas at twilight, when the golden rays of a setting sun bounced against the magnificent stone, spreading a glorious color as far as the eye could see.

After a brisk exploration of the village and a quick casual dinner, we were completely exhausted from our long journey. When our bodies were horizontal, we literally collapsed on our bed and fell sound asleep. A few hours later, however, I awoke when I felt Vince reach gently for my hand under the cover. I looked at his face. After just a few hours of sleep, his eyes were open and he looked relaxed.

"Bunny? Are you OK?" I asked. "Why aren't you asleep?"

"I love it here," he whispered. "I really love it here."

"I know. Honey, I love it here too." Italy is in our heart. We were very happy to be back.

Vince's favorite island in the Aeolian Island chain was Salina for its laid-back atmosphere and unsurpassed natural beauty. We spent several nights in Salina's Santa Marina harbor where we met Silvio; a warm and colorful character who spoke some English and owned the coffee and granita stand in the main village. Every morning, when we walked to his stand for the best espresso and iced coffee in the area, Silvio would often sit with us and talk about life on the island. He was born and raised on Salina and all the locals appeared to know him.

One rainy afternoon, we found ourselves "boat locked," with not much to do, so I asked Silvio for a suggestion of how we could spend our time. He proposed taking a bus ride to the western side of the island, along Salina's beautiful seashore, to the sleepy town of Pollara on the edge of the steep slopes of an extinct volcano. Pollara dates back to the 1500s. Its beautiful beaches were the setting for the 1995 award winning film "Il Postino." Silvio said that the weather would be better in Pollara. He suggested taking an easy hike down through the main part of the village to the beach for a visit to the unique cemetery where everyone entombed there were descendants of the first family who settled in Polara; *la famiglia De Lorenzo*.

De Lorenzo? "No way!" I cried out in disbelief. "Silvio, that's my name, my husband's surname is Di Lorenzo."

"Impossible!" Silvio replied. I showed him my California driver's license as proof that although my last name was spelled slightly different, it was still an amazing coincidence. Vince and I considered it serendipity.

No matter how often we visit Italy, her magic is always intoxicating. From the moment the pilot announces our initial descent, we are thrilled to be back, feel the excitement in our souls and simply cannot wait for the plane to touch the landing strip in Rome. Not surprisingly, we are not the only ones who feel this way. More than forty-five million travelers from all over the world visit the "boot country" each year. What *is* it about Italy that made the whole world fall in love with her or anything having to do with her? Perhaps it is because the Italian brand is world renown and unfailingly associated with quality; quality of sports cars, music, fashion, cuisine, leather goods and ceramics. The Italian economy is in worse shape than the American economy, Italians smoke more than Americans, they spend less on health care, yet they live healthier, happier and consequently longer lives. Is it, perhaps, because they follow the Mediterranean diet, live passionately, are largely debt-free and consequently live with less stress? Whatever it is, Italians have found the secret to cherishing and living *'La Dolce Vita,'* the sweet life. Italy has completely captured our hearts and we can't get enough of her.

Our First House Hunting Trip

Our lives sustained some significant changes during the first two years following my mother's death. Exactly two months to the date of my mother's death, we lost Cornelis. Although he and my mom were not married, he had been a significant member of our family. Eighteen months later, on January 10, 2008, suddenly and sadly, we also lost Orry; Vince's dad and my beloved father-in-law. Family and friends came to pay their respects, lend support and honor the life of a truly remarkable man. Orry touched many souls. Our lives would never be the same without him.

Later that summer, Vince and I became mortgage free. What a triumphant milestone! We celebrated by hosting a mortgage burning party at our home. Again, family and friends came, this time, to celebrate our joy. It was a wonderful event.

In December 2009, at the age of sixty-four, Vince retired from a sales career that spanned over forty years. We were proud and elated that he finally reached those "golden years" when he can kick up his heels, do as he pleases or just enjoy being idle. Retirement! Isn't that what it's all about? I was envious and couldn't wait to reach the same point in my life in just a few more years.

We began to devote more time to our Italian house hunting project, considering every region in Italy as a potential place to buy a part-time residence.

Abruzzo, the region where Vince's father was born, seemed affordable, however, since we had not explored the area, we really never considered living there. Campagnia, the region of the Amalfi Coast might have been our first choice, but much of the area is crowded with tourists throughout the year. Lombardy, where we spent glorious vacations at Lago Maggiore and Lake Como, was a spectacular region to own a holiday home, but buying in the same neighborhood where celebrities also live, was much too expensive. Tuscany, with its magnificent villas, manicured olive orchards and rambling vineyards, seemed a bit too formal. Lastly, we loved Calabria for its splendid beaches, crystal blue water, serious sunshine and bountiful fresh seafood, but we knew we would miss the changing seasons. Therefore, following careful thought and consideration, we ultimately focused our attention on Umbria; the green belt region in the heart of Italy.

Umbria seemed ideal for us, with lush vineyards and ancient olive orchards covering the landscape for as far as the eye can see. Among lakes, woods, green slopes, and undulating terrain cultivated by man for centuries, picturesque medieval villages adorn the hilltops. Furthermore, Umbria's amazing cuisine is simple, varied and extraordinary with the prized black truffle as the gastronomic glory of the region. The high-quality olive oil that is produced in the area is world renowned for its organic health properties. Award winning Umbrian wines includes the famous classic whites of Orvieto and the full-bodied reds of Montefalco. Outstanding pig meat delicacies such as *cinghiale*, prosciutto and sausage-type specialties from the Umbrian village of Norcia, have earned high esteem throughout Italy for excellence in quality. Umbria is also the home of *umbricelli* (a thick egg free pasta), exquisite chocolate from Perugia, savory cakes and flatbreads made with cheese or cooked *al testo*, under the ashes. Throughout the year, there are countless festivals and celebrations in even the most remote Umbrian villages. The heart of Italy would certainly offer us a casual but superior quality of life.

With a location for our vacation home determined, Vince and I were energized by our new dream. Enthusiastically, we became self-educated on Umbria and the Umbrian lifestyle. We spent hours at the computer scanning Italian real estate websites, printing volumes of interesting property listings and reading articles written by ex-pats who had taken the leap of faith, been through the buying process and were now enjoying living the "Italian Dream." Dinners at home became happy occasions to share our latest findings, discussing the pros and cons of each. In due course, our conversations turned to making an exploratory trip to discover if we could comfortably assimilate with the locals and adapt to the Umbrian lifestyle and culture. It seemed as if one day, our dream could become a reality.

Orvieto; Casa Flavia
"Let's Assimilate!"

In May 2010, we were ready to rent a small apartment for a few weeks in Umbria. As the only Umbrian town slightly familiar to us, we decided to make Orvieto our home base. We were looking forward to establishing a temporary household and living like the locals. Optimistically, we hoped to form relationships with the neighborhood merchants by shopping primarily at the weekly markets and local stores for groceries and essentials. Although we would cook most meals "at home," we planned to patronize only the nearby restaurants. I found an ideal apartment in Orvieto's historic center and quickly booked a short-term rental. The apartment was named *Casa Flavia*, for the landlady's young daughter. It was our first time renting and operating from an apartment. I couldn't wait to receive the keys from Roberta; our host!

Our vacation started off on a positive note at the car rental agency in Rome, when the Alfa Romeo Vince reserved on-line was not available and we were offered a sexy, black, 6-speed manual transmission, BMW instead. Vince was beyond thrilled! Once we left the maze of airport traffic and reached the countryside, we stopped at an Autogrill for a snack-on-the-go. Autogrills really are the zenith of roadside convenience stores for their large variety of fresh takeout food selections. This one had an entire roast pig, head and all, displayed on a platter, ready to be sliced for sandwiches or carved into luscious hunks to be devoured by hand. I was salivating, but Vince, concerned about the growing onslaught of rush house traffic, was anxious to continue on our road trip and I concurred. An hour and a half later we took the exit to the winding road up the mountain to Orvieto. We reached Piazza Cahen; the main square by the *funicolare* and as agreed in our last email exchange, I called Roberta to let her know that we had arrived.

Roberta was evidently younger than I anticipated. She was friendly and greeted us with a warm welcome and a plate of homemade cookies, what a sweet and charming gesture. She instructed us to leave our car in the main parking lot, indicating that spaces marked in blue required that a paid ticket from the parking meter should be left on the dashboard, yellow spaces were for the Handicapped and white spaces were free of charge. We parked in a white space, transferred our luggage to Roberta's car and drove up the Orvieto's main street; the *Corso Carvour* toward the historic center of town. Orvieto was as quaint as we remembered. As Roberta drove to *Casa Flavia*, we passed a multitude of adorable restaurants and shops. We were very excited to be in Orvieto again, even though, the town was jam-packed with tourists.

The apartment was conveniently located in the center of town, on a side street, a block from the Corso Cavour. We entered the building through a heavy, arched door leading to a common entry way and walked up two flights of stairs to the front door of the apartment. Our first impression was favorable, although somehow, it was not quite what either of us expected. It was nicely decorated with an iron framed king-sized bed, a very basic twin bed, wardrobe, fully equipped kitchen, comfortably furnished sitting room with a television and dining area. The large bedroom door led to a sunny, private patio with a bistro table and two chairs. The brightest part of the apartment was the bedroom while the living room was dark and without windows. Nevertheless, the space certainly served our purpose and at a minimal daily rate of $105, we absolutely could not complain. After taking care of formalities with Roberta, we unpacked and finally felt as if we had arrived!

Motivated to find our bearings, we wandered into town. There were many shops and restaurants located literally around the corner from *Casa Flavia*. Also nearby, was the magnificent Duomo that I deemed my favorite cathedral in Italy, since he first time I saw it. The fourteenth century cathedral with gold mosaics, a rose window and three enormous bronze doors is one of Italy's Gothic masterpieces. I was ecstatic to have eleven days in Orvieto to admire the Duomo to my heart's content.

Establishing a favorite coffee bar for "people watching" with a cup of caffè or a glass of wine was a daunting task, but an extreme priority for us. There were a myriad to choose from. However, we narrowed it down to two different cafes on the colorful Corso Cavour. Our criteria was based on friendly service, a pleasant atmosphere and a steady stream of local patronage. From the moment we sat down at Cafe Barrique, a tailless calico cat walked over from a doorway across the street, jumped on Vince's lap and made herself quite comfortable. Oblivious and caught by surprise, Vince looked at me and said, "Perfect." He welcomed the cat with a loving scratch under its chin. Happy and content with the cat on Vince's lap, we sat outside drinking coffee for quite a while, gazing at passersby and poking fun at those who we thought were conspicuous "Americani." Already feeling right at home, we were engrossed in a surrounding that literally oozed history and lust for life.

Eventually though, we gave in to the jet-lag that overcame our weary bodies when our energy level diminished. Vince nudged the cat to vacate his lap and paid our bill at the counter. We immediately realized the pleasant convenience of sauntering back to our neighborhood apartment for a short rest before dinner.

The first day of international travel is always the most difficult as we adjust to the new time zone, but we managed to nap until eight o'clock in the evening, splashed water on our faces and feeling somewhat refreshed, ventured out again in search of a place to have dinner. Based on the prefixed menu, complete with photographs posted at the entrance, we chose a restaurant located a short block from Casa Flavia. The name of the restaurant was *Locanda del Lupo*; Country House of the Wolf. For a mere 18€ per person, approximately $21, we were served a mouth-watering, delicious 3-course meal including ½ bottled water and ½ liter of red wine. We shared a plate of pasta with a spicy tomato-based *Arrabbiata* sauce and one with olive oil, ground sausage and crispy *pancetta* (Italian bacon). Our second course was a substantial portion of a variety of cheeses and cured meats including prosciutto, salami and blood sausage. Unable to eat it all but compelled not to waste the delicious food, I layered the left-over meat and cheese between two slices of bread, discreetly wrapped them in a paper napkin and stuck the package in my purse for a late-night-snack. With our tummy's happy and full, the last course of succulent wild boar stew, perfectly roasted potatoes and a liberal green salad, were consumed slowly. The portions were large enough to feed an army. This restaurant was truly a sensational discovery, an excellent value and a fantastic first meal in Orvieto.

When we finally climbed into bed for the second time, neither of us had a problem falling asleep. Unfortunately, we were wide awake again at two o'clock in the morning as the jet-lag persisted. Frustrated by sleep deprivation, Vince made an effort to watch TV while I tried making journal entries. Eventually, we both tried reading, hoping our drowsiness would turn into a deep slumber. However, nothing worked and we remained restless for the next five hours waiting for dawn to break. At the first sign of daylight, I fumbled my way through an attempt to make coffee, but I couldn't figure out how to ignite the gas stove. Regardless of feeling punch-drunk, by seven o'clock we were both showered, dressed and raring to go. Vince insisted taking a walk until Cafe Barrique opened.

"Let's assimilate!" he said, "the brisk morning air will do us good."

Orvieto was gorgeous in the morning when the town was quiet and only the locals were stirring. The beautiful piazza in front of the Duomo in the historic center of town, was my favorite place and I took full advantage of being able to snap some tourist-free pictures before the streets filled with sightseers. We wandered around until the shopkeepers gradually opened their doors and the insatiable aroma of freshly brewed espresso drifted from the coffee bars to the streets. We headed straight for Cafe Barrique. Vince ordered a double espresso for himself and a cappuccino for me; still the only coffee I can tolerate drinking in Italy. We watched the town come alive with energy. It was wonderful not to be pressed for time!

Around the corner from Cafe Barrique, we noticed a small pizzeria with people waiting in a line that extended beyond the front door. The man behind the counter was taking giant rectangular trays of freshly baked pizzas out of an oven and selling them by the slice to the hungry crowd. There were trays of pizza with cheese and tomato, pizza with thin slices of potato, garlic and rosemary, others with spinach and artichokes and thinly sliced onions and sausage. Savoring the idea of fresh pizza for breakfast, we joined the waiting crowd. We couldn't wait for our turn at the counter and eagerly pointed to several different types when it was our turn to order.

"Uno, per favore," Vince said as he pointed to each one.

The man cut the piping hot pizza with a metal spatula, scooped out the slice and placed it on a sheet of butcher paper on top of the glass counter.

"Prego," he said, as he pushed the slices toward us. Each slice cost only 1€. The pizzas were extraordinary, they were delicious! After we ate all four slices, we bought more before finally walking back to Cafe Barrique for another jolt of caffeine.

By early afternoon, we had enough vivacity to take a drive. The Umbrian countryside was stunning. Absolutely drop dead gorgeous! Verdant landscape, covered with brilliant green hillsides sprinkled with red poppies and wild flowers were as far as the eye could see. I have always admired paintings and photographs of the extraordinary splendor of Umbria when the red poppies are in bloom. Now, here we were, seeing it firsthand. I was not disappointed. On the contrary, anything I had seen before, paled in comparison to the true beauty before me.

We stumbled upon Baschi; another fairytale-like, adorable, medieval village, this one near the autostrada. Enticed to walk through the narrow, picture-perfect, cobblestone streets, the enchanting hamlet, meticulously adorned with potted gardens of flourishing geraniums spilling over entry way and window sill looked like a postcard in every direction. Below the village, near a railroad track, we spotted a dense field of glorious red poppies. We tried desperately to reach the field on foot, but we could not get close enough to literally stand in the middle of all those fire-engine red flowers to pose for a "selfie," a self-portrait taken with the camera held at arm's length, aimed at ourselves. The poppies were a spectacular sight! We drove deeper into the countryside, wandering leisurely, taking pictures at a whim, until Vince thought we were due for some wine.

Back in Orvieto, we stopped at a neighborhood market to buy our first groceries "like a local." It was so much fun pretending to be a resident, buying perishable goods to store in our own refrigerator and household items such as dish soap, laundry detergent and other products that we typically would not buy as hotel guests. Novice users of the Italian language and not familiar with Italian brand names, we selected items based on our *best guess* of what was depicted on the label. We enjoyed filling a shopping basket and paying with the correct amount of paper money and coins. Oh my gosh, did we have a good laugh when we discovered our mistakes as we unloaded our groceries at "home!" The tube with a picture of bright, shiny white teeth, which I thought was toothpaste, turned out to be denture adhesive. The box I mistook for laundry detergent was fabric softener and the aerosol can of what I just knew was hairspray, was in fact a can of spray-on hair coloring.

After storing our groceries and a couple of quick refreshing splashes of water on our faces, we walked to our favorite coffee bar, this time for a glass of wine. Italians drink wine only as a pairing with food. Therefore, wine in any establishment is served with tidbits such as nuts, chips or crusty bread. This custom makes it very easy to spend a lovely part of the day unwinding, engaged in delightful conversation with a few glasses of wine and some nibbles.

As we sipped our wine and talked about our first day of experiencing life as Orvietani, I knew that Orvieto had cast a spell on us and that we had fallen in love with the town. Cautiously, with trepidation, I approached the subject of a meeting with a real estate agent in town. I wasn't sure if Vince was ready to take that first step yet. Maybe he wanted to acclimate for a few more days.

Although, by now, we had certainly done our due diligence and thoroughly researched almost every aspect of the buying process. An initial conversation with a credible agent, however, would provide us with the "real-time," local knowledge we lacked to pursue, or abandon, our dream of owning a secondary home in the boot-shaped country. To my surprise, Vince was responsive to my idea of talking with a professional and experienced mediator.

We ordered more wine. Again, we reviewed in detail what we required in a home, yet this time I felt nervously adrenalized and could not stop smiling as we exchanged thoughts and ideas. I knew that *this time*, our discussion was a precursor to the one we would have with a real estate agent. Vince's eyes twinkled as we agreed on our list of critical 'Must Haves.' As part-time residents, apartment style living in a secure building made the most sense. We preferred a fully restored dwelling in a stone building, in a vibrant medieval village near Orvieto and within walking proximity of shops and restaurants. We desired an apartment with a balcony or space large enough for outdoor dining overlooking a scenic view, required no restoration, renovation or repair, radiated history and exploded with Italian charm. We needed basic furniture, enough space for overnight guests and a garage for ultimately storing a car. A few hours later, we had enough courage to walk into an *immobiliare;* a real estate agency. We concurred, that Vince would lead the conversation, since my perpetual zealousness sometimes runs away with me. We were extremely optimistic.

Since we spoke only a mere handful of Italian words, we entered a Coldwell Banker real estate office hoping that agents representing an American owned company would be able to communicate in English. We were greeted by Mandy, a friendly English woman who worked as the office administrator. She introduced us to Vanessa; one of the sales agents. Maria Laura; the office manager was on an appointment with clients. Mandy initiated the discussion by inquiring about our goals, and how we intended to use the property. It seemed illusionary, sitting in a real estate office in Italy, listening to Vince verbalizing our aspiration of acquiring a home here. Already, I envisioned us living in the area. In spite of our modest budget, Mandy was encouraging, asked many questions and took copious notes. She reflected on her similar dream, which led her to the agency she now worked for. Mandy bought her home three months ago in Porano; a *borgo* near Orvieto. A borgo, we learned, is a medieval self-sufficient community, smaller than a village or town. As we continued to reveal our dream of owning an Italian home to Mandy and Vanessa, Vince became apparently more comfortable and consequently somewhat animated as he outlined our requirements. I adored watching him take charge achieving our wonderful goal. At the conclusion of our meeting, Mandy committed to setting up a meeting with Maria Laura for an initial briefing of our requirements so that she could select a few properties for us to see.

After a discussion that lasted for more than two hours, Vanessa left Mandy to close the office for the evening as I grabbed a few property listings. Much to our amazement, Mandy invited us to see her home in a newly built subdivision of Porano. We jumped at the chance to see the interior of a resident's home. She offered to drive us, first to her home for a quick tour, then to visit a neighborhood coffee bar in the medieval section to experience the social ambiance of a small village. It was an eight-minute lovely drive to Porano, on a pretty country road along woods and meadows. A brilliant rainbow appeared over Orvieto just as we passed a panoramic observation spot. Naturally, we considered it "a sign" of encouragement, seized the moment, and captured it in a photograph. What a surprise!

Castle Rubelo, built in the twelfth century, with its three lofty towers of remarkable architectural value and the adjacent historical church of San Giovanni Battista mark the approach and impressive entrance to the village. Mandy informed us later that nowadays, the castle operates as an extravagant Bed and Breakfast. Porano was an attractive village in a wooded setting with a pleasant atmosphere, boasting one restaurant, a coffee bar, a pharmacy, several flower shops and an alimentari. Mandy's home was a three-story townhouse in a corner building with an outstanding view of Orvieto; which she claimed as the best in all of Umbria. In the midst of renovating, with stone counter tops and ceramic tiles from England, Mandy was obviously proud of her lovely home. Before taking us back to Orvieto, we were her guests at the coffee bar in Porano's compact medieval center. We ordered coffee and sat at a bistro table outside, imagining and anticipating our own social gathering with friends, if we found our dream home here.

Vince's tenacious determination and his insatiable craving for coffee paid off the next morning when he figured out how to ignite the stove in our rented apartment. With a stovetop drip coffee maker, we were finally able to brew a satisfying cup of American-style coffee and spend the morning being lazy, writing postcards, watching the local news on TV and rehashing our conversation with Mandy. We looked forward to our meeting Maria Laura and touring properties with her. In the hopes that Mandy would be able to schedule an appointment for us today, we limited our plans to only exploring in the local area.

Before the inevitable swarm of tourists arrived, we walked to town and discovered a bustling open-air market in Piazza del Popolo. Vendors selling colorful flowers and plants, beautiful farm fresh produce, eggs, cheese, salumi and other Italian delicacies along with household items and clothing crowded the piazza. I was ecstatic! We bought *porchetta* sandwiches from a rotisserie truck; an elaborate mobile kitchen displaying a freshly roasted pig with the severed head arranged on the side. Porchetta is no simple pork roast, it is instead a savory, fatty, moist boneless pig stuffed with herbs and placed on a spit to roast very slowly over a wood burning stove for hours. The aromatic pork smelled divine and the crispy golden crackling pig skin looked delicious. Vince ordered *due panini*. We watched with mouthwatering anticipation as the man in the truck thinly sliced the succulent, lean meat, placed it in the middle of a freshly baked, crunchy bread roll, sprinkled it with salt and pepper and wrapped it in butcher paper.

"Prego," he said as he handed the sandwiches to us. "*Buon appetito.*"

Oh my Gosh! We took a bite and looked at each other with wide eyes. It tasted heavenly!

"Is this not the best sandwich you ever tasted?" I asked Vince. "This is to-die-for!" I was truly in my *happy place*. Being in the market and eating the local street food, vividly reminded me of my childhood in Holland, when going to the *markt* (Dutch for market) in Rotterdam with my mother and sister, to dine on French fries out of paper cones and fried fish from paper wrappers was a joyful weekly routine.

Moseying through the market eating our sandwiches, Vince and I bought prosciutto, cheese and dried figs for our afternoon road trip to Deruta; a small nearby village world renown for the ceramics that are hand produced there. Before heading out, we stopped at Cafe Barrique for coffee. Beginning to recognize us, the barista proactively greeted us when we entered this time.

"*Buongiorno. Prego*?" he said, asking for our order.

When the barista served our coffee, Vince referred to him by the name on his shirt tag, trying to initiate a friendship.

"Grazie, Paolo."

Paolo nodded and smiled.

As usual, we sat outside in clear view of the foot traffic on the Corso Cavour where, within a few minutes, the calico cat from across the street, jumped on Vince's lap. It felt nice to be recognized by the local merchants and cats. It is the feeling of assimilation we were hoping for.

Excursions to Deruta and Todi

Deruta is world famous for the production of hand painted Majolica earthenware. Majolica originated in Italy during the Renaissance. I have been curious about the artists who meticulously and painstakingly create these exquisite works of ceramic art that I have coveted for years. Since the town was a short scenic drive from Orvieto, we seized the opportunity to visit the artists at work in their studios.

The highway exit to Deruta is distinguishable by an enormous blue and white ceramic star manifested on the road at the southern end of town. Just the mere sight of it made my heart beat faster and even though the guidebooks warned against buying from the glitzy factory shops located near the highway, I begged Vince to stop and let me out of the car so I could begin my shopping spree. There were numerous factories and mega-stores featuring pottery in all sizes, displaying the extra-large pieces outside, as if their inventory was overflowing and the shops were busting at the seams. I could hardly contain my enthusiasm. However, just a few minutes later, when we reached the historic center at the top of the hill, I was grateful for my husband's sensible restraint.

With its origins dating as far back as the fourth century B.C., we entered historic Deruta through the enchanting arch of the Porta di San Michele Arcangelo. It was as if we walked into a perfect model for a movie set; an enchanting fairytale village like you see in the movies. We were immediately dazzled by the beautiful ceramic tiles decorating a red ochre wall, the backdrop for windowsills flanked by wooden green shutters, boasting flourishing geraniums trailing from earthenware planters. Colorful, handcrafted table tops, large olive oil casks and tall vases spilled out of countless shops worthy of any art gallery. There was an abundance to choose from. How was I ever going to decide which pieces I wanted to add to our collection at home?

As we began our methodical visit to each shop, we were awestruck by the artisans who created the most intricate patterns imaginable, each stroke painted by hand. It was overwhelming and incomprehensible how anyone can do such elaborate, delicate work with a paintbrush. Vince was intrigued by the colorful, glass-like, kaleidoscope of geometric patterns, although the designs that attracted us the most, depicted lemons, grapes and other fruits, reminiscent of our visits to the Amalfi Coast. I was especially drawn to motifs that encompassed color combinations of dark blues, bright yellows, oranges and greens. After perusing through the majority of the family run shops and studios, we decided to purchase ten pasta plates. Now all we had to do was choose the dish style, the artist, and ultimately, the pattern. A leisurely wine lubricated lunch break to discuss our options was definitely in order.

It was indeed helpful to be away from the myriad of pottery while we debated about our choices during lunch. Nevertheless, we narrowed our decision down to an artist named Luca, owner of the studio-shop named after his mother; *Majoliche Artistiche Fanny*. Luca was an exceptional artist, but what differentiated him from the others, was his offer to collaborate on the creation of a one-of-a-kind, customized pattern which we could design. From the large array of finished ceramics in his shop, Luca inspired us to pick-and-choose the parts of each pattern we loved the most, to incorporate into our own specialized design, inscribed with our names on the bottom of each piece at no extra charge. That offer piqued our interest tremendously.

We chose a deep-dish plate with a scalloped edge; perfect for serving pasta dishes, hearty soups or stews. Vince commented that food served on a dish with a white center surrounded by a colorful border would look more enticing. What a wonderful idea! Our challenge to create a personalized, unique pattern was off to a good start. We liked a yellow cluster of grapes on an urn and a lemon from a pattern on a jug. We also chose a blossom from a gigantic plate and the "viney" leaves from a bowl to balance out the final the design. Luca suggested colors in shades of yellows, golds and greens on a dark blue background. The final result was absolutely stunning and truly defined "us!" The back of each dish would be inscribed: *"Dip a mano a Deruta per Vince e Joyce Di Lorenzo."* (Painted by hand in Deruta for Vince and Joyce DiLorenzo.)

We also bought a serving platter in a complementary pattern. The total cost, shipping included, was only $550; a fraction of what it would cost at home for custom designed imported Italian ceramics. I was thrilled and couldn't wait to host a party with our new dishes.

Happy with our purchase, we had good cause to celebrate, consequently Vince suggested taking a scenic detour to Todi before returning to Orvieto. Several guidebooks described Todi as the quintessential Umbrian hilltop town.

From the road, the panoramic view of the medieval town, fortified by three walls, was quite magnificent. We drove along the ancient exterior wall, past the splendid domed Renaissance Church of the Santa Maria della Consolazione, up the winding tree lined road to Todi's main square; Piazza del Popolo. Unfortunately, the weather became cloudy and less than ideal for taking pictures of the sweeping vista across the Tiber Valley. Nevertheless, we donned our rain jackets and wandered through the narrow streets to explore Todi. When the rain turned into a heavy downpour, we ducked into a coffee shop, ordered cappuccino and waited for the weather to improve. Eventually, my chivalrous husband ran through the rain for the car, picked me up at the door and we left Todi rather abruptly. I must admit, that neither of us felt an immediate affection for this *quintessential* Umbrian hilltop town. Maybe it was the rain, or maybe it was because we didn't find Todi foot-traffic friendly since most of the streets leading from the piazza were steep and dark. Or, maybe it was because the historic center lacked the typical, colorful geraniums spilling from windowsills and doorways. However, we agreed that one day we would return to explore Todi to the fullest. Perhaps then we would make a connection with this ancient town recommended by so many guidebooks.

At Clasa Flavia, I removed the layers of bubble wrap from the gorgeous serving platter we bought in Deruta. Just to look at it again made me smile, it was a beautiful work of art. Quickly, we refreshed ourselves and walked to Cafe Barrique. It was high time to relax, enjoy a glass of wine and spend a long bout of people-watching. As if on cue, the calico cat jumped on Vince's lap, the rain stopped and all seemed perfect in the world. We were content to be in Orvieto, feeling as if we belonged here.

When we finished our wine, we walked toward the Piazza del Duomo to wander through some of the ceramic shops on the way, however, we didn't see anything that compared to the quality of the dishes we bought in Deruta. We also stopped at a local Umbrian specialty meat shop and tasted cinghale prosciutto for the first time. *It was out of this world!* We bought three hunks to take home. When we entered the piazza, we were stunned by the magnificent beauty of the Duomo. In the glow of the setting sun, the gold inlay sparkled like starlight. We stayed in the piazza to watch the *pulcinella* on top of the clock tower strike seven-thirty.

Searching for a place to have dinner, we stumbled upon the Trattoria del Moro; an intimate family run eating establishment located on one of the adorable side streets in the heart of Orvieto. It was another outstanding choice of restaurants! We shared a divine plate of the cured Umbrian meats as our appetizer, followed by a pasta dish. Vince chose the wild boar stew and ordered a cheese lasagna for me. The lasagna was an absolutely delicious dish of light and fluffy, white ricotta cheese, drizzled with white truffle oil between two layers of the most delicate flat lasagna noodles we had ever tasted. The rich and flavorful wild boar stew was served over *pappardelle* pasta; a thick, ribbon shaped noodle. We ended our meal by sharing a crisp green salad and a *panna cotta*; a cooked blend of thick cream, egg and honey topped with a raspberry sauce. The entire to-die-for meal, including a liter of wine, set us back only sixty dollars.

Spello

We slept late this morning. I loved waking up in our apartment, where I could roll out of bed, stumble to the kitchen to make coffee while Vince watched the local news on Italian TV. This is what it would be like if we had our own home here.

The weather forecasted another rainy day, perfect for a long road trip to explore another village. Today we were going to visit Spello, located in east central Umbria, approximately a ninety-minute drive from Orvieto. Our friends Bill and Susan Young who had visited Spello the year before, highly recommended a day of sightseeing in this two-thousand-year-old Roman settlement.

It was almost noon by the time we arrived. In contrast to being in Todi, in Spello we immediately felt the hospitable energy exuding from this town. Every door step and entryway was loaded with a profusion of terra cotta planters brimming with fiery red geraniums, hot pink petunias and other trailing flowers. Window sills displaying container gardens were also plentiful as we realized that we were surrounded by colorful blooming exhibitions everywhere we looked. As we wandered through the enchanting narrow streets and admired the charm of this lovely village, we noticed that many windowsills and balconies were tagged with numbered markers. We soon discovered that Spello has long been passionate about flowers. Each May, the village organizes the *"Finestre, Balconi, e Vicoli Fioriti"* (Flowered Window, Balcony and Alleyway competition). The winner is chosen based on color combination, beauty and healthy aspect of flowers throughout the duration of the contest. What a marvelous time for us to visit this jewel-box of a village.

We had lunch at Osteria da Dada; a small tavern located on one of the tree-lined piazzas in town. We were literally jam-packed into a corner of the busy restaurant, sitting on wooden benches around a picnic table. All the guests were friendly and good-natured and no one seemed to mind the lack of space. There was no menu and a lone waitress served everyone in the cozy dining room.

Almost immediately after we were seated, mouthwatering, homemade Umbrian food was brought to the tables in abundance. We just "dug in," sharing and passing plates of bruschetta *mista* (mixed bruschetta). Although they were just crusty slices of bread, perfectly toasted, slathered in olive oil and topped with a mixture of diced farm-fresh tomato, garlic and basil, it was simple, superb quality food and extraordinarily delicious. Next, came heaping bowls full of fluffy potato gnocchi with a pesto sauce, followed by a second dish of a flat, ribbon-shaped *tagliatelle* pasta with a meat sauce. Then, came platters layered with the typical Umbrian cured meats; savory salumi, out-of-this-world prosciutto, luscious *capocollo* and a silky rich mortadella. As each platter was placed at the head of the table, we served ourselves before passing them to our adjacent guests. No wonder this is known as "family style" service. This manner of sharing food, induced light-hearted conversation and made us feel as if we were surrounded by family. We critiqued each scrumptious dish as the platters of food and carafes of house wine made the rounds. It was a wonderful way to experience this sensational meal.

Just when we thought that we couldn't eat another bite, we were served a crisp mixed green salad. As in most European countries, to aid in the digestion of the meal, Italians consume a green leafy salad as the final course. When the dishes were cleared from the table, a healthy shot of limoncello, grappa or an herbal liqueur called *Amaro* was offered as an additional *digestivo*. This memorable meal was inexpensive and a memorable event.

Bella Orvieto

We spent the next few days anxiously anticipating Mandy's phone call regarding our meeting with Maria Laura. We left our schedule open so that we would be available at a moment's notice. Our unencumbered agenda provided the perfect opportunity to explore Orvieto on foot. After a slow-paced morning at Casa Flavia, we slipped into our rain jackets and walked to the pizzeria at Piazza del Popolo for breakfast. While Vince was tempted by two different types of pizza, I pointed to a slice with anchovies and onions. As we stood on the street corner, captivated by the pleasure of eating our "breakfast" out of hand from a flimsy paper napkin, the cue of locals waiting for the fresh baked deliciousness grew longer. It was fun mingling with the neighborhood bustle. To our surprise, we suddenly heard someone call out my name.

"Joyce. Ciao, Joyce."

It was Roberta; our landlady, riding in a car with another woman. As they drove past us, Roberta waved ferociously. I was amused that we were recognized and greeted so heartily by a local. It was as if we had just run into an old friend and affirmation that we would love living in this overtly amiable Italian culture.

With pizza in hand, we meandered through the narrow side streets leading out from the Corsa Cavour to the Etruscan Museum on the Piazza del Duomo. For a small museum, it featured an impressive selection of artifacts which fascinated us for hours. After thoroughly exploring the museum, we wandered up and down Orvieto's cobblestone streets both in town and along the surrounding ancient defense walls. We crossed nearly every piazza, peered through the windows of nearly every church and palazzo. We took a million photos of every nook and cranny that was as pretty as a picture.

By the time the shops began to close for the afternoon, the rain became torrential. We dodged into our favorite coffee bar for shelter. Paolo was behind the counter. He acknowledged us with a nod and a smile and without an exchange of words between us, he instinctively began making a *doppio* espresso for Vince and an American-style coffee with milk for me. We were "regulars" now and Paolo was familiar with our orders. We sat at a table in the back of the bar, drinking coffee while I leafed through the real estate booklets I had collected along the way and Vince buried himself in an abandoned English newspaper. It was a comfortable way to wait out the rain in a friendly venue.

When the rain turned to a drizzle, we walked to the Conad; our favorite supermarket in town, to stock up on a few items for lunch and impromptu snacking at Casa Flavia. A small shop called *Sapore di Umbria*; A Taste of Umbria with an interesting display of local wines, dried spices and the typical variety of colorful pastas, looked like a lovely place to buy some wine. I immediately recognized the gleam in the shopkeeper's eye and that sexy tilt of her head, slightly to one side, as she spoke to Vince. She was outwardly flirting with him! Her "come hither" approach was obvious and therefore humorous. While she barely made eye contact with me, in her eagerness to assist my husband in selecting a good wine, she opened five different bottles for him to taste. Orvieto's premier wines are the delicious, semi-sweet, white Orvieto Classico, which is produced in the region between Orvieto and Lago di Corbara. Although Vince prefers a full-bodied red wine, Orvieto Classico became my personal favorite and at a cost of only 4€ a bottle, we could afford for me to become an alcoholic! Vince bought two whites and a red. The shopkeeper, smiling sweetly at Vince as he paid for his wine, offered him a discount. After we left, I mentioned her flirting and teasingly asked Vince, "Why are your girlfriends always so ugly? Can't you choose an attractive girlfriend?" Of course, I honestly was only kidding. Throughout our time in Orvieto, we became friends good with Patrizia. Every time we came into her shop, she greeted us warmly, or if we just passed by on the street, she waved as if we were Orvietani.

At Casa Flavia, it was a tremendous luxury to kick off our shoes and relax for the remainder of the afternoon. Vince prepared a beautiful plate of appetizers while I tried to operate the clothes washing machine. It was wonderful not to be in a hurry and to engage in the normal household activities as if we were at home. We drank wine, munched appetizers, made love sweet and slow, took a nap and watched television. It was a perfectly fabulous afternoon.

In the early evening, Roberta's husband Mauro stopped by on his way home from work. To our delight and relief, he spoke English and asked if we had questions about the apartment or the vicinity. It was a little cold in Casa Flavia and we did not know how to work the heater. With simple instructions from Mauro, that minor issue was quickly resolved. In addition to being more comfortable, a warmer temperature would help to dry our laundry indoors.

With more rain in the forecast, the clothes line suspended in the patio outside was useless.

Mauro was extremely cordial and a wealth of information. He suggested looking at property in Orvieto Scalo; a busy subdivision at the bottom of the hill where he and Roberta owned their home. Orvieto Scalo is conveniently positioned near many community services, yet real estate prices were reasonable. Although we appreciated his suggestion, Orvieto Scalo seemed too hectic and industrial for us.

When it was time for dinner, we were looking forward to trying the small eating establishment which we discovered a few days ago in an out-of-the-way courtyard near Orvieto's town center. *Trattoria Da Carlo* looked cozy and the daily handwritten menu that hung on a chalkboard near the entrance was quite charming. As we opened the door to enter, we were struck by the intimacy of the cozy dining room with a seating capacity of only ten guests. It looked like some one's living room. A lively waiter welcomed us and guided us to one of the vacant tables. The menu included items we recognized, however, there were also many dishes that we had not seen offered anywhere else. Not able to translate all the Italian descriptions, we opted for being surprised when Vince ordered the appetizer course. The waiter brought a large white plate with a meticulously placed, luscious stack of alternating grilled mushroom caps, sliced fresh tomato and mozzarella on a bed of peppery arugula, drizzled with a thick balsamic vinegar. Every mouthful was a beautiful bite of freshness and it was gratifying to know that we were also eating healthy. As an entree, Vince ordered the *baccala;* a dried, salted codfish, reconstituted in a flavorful broth and served in a light lemon butter sauce. It was divine! I selected the Italian meatballs which were served as three, good sized portions of precisely shaped balls of flavorful meat, smothered in a rich tomato sauce, topped with a nutty grated cheese. After consuming these delectable dishes, we shared the traditional green salad. All courses were accompanied by an exquisite local wine. At the end of the meal, the jovial owner/chef came over to our table and offered us a complimentary glass of grappa or limoncello. This was always a welcome gesture. He introduced himself as Carlo, his mother Teresa took the orders and Antonio was the waiter. Everyone was extremely cordial and hospitable. By the time we left the Trattoria, we felt as if we were leaving long-time friends.

We spent the day as true Orvietani. It had been lovely, just the way we hoped it would be. Without a doubt, Orvieto embraced our hearts and today's events were affirmation that we had truly fallen head-over-heels in love with this town.

Civita di Bagnoregio

Our long-awaited call from Mandy finally came and we were super ecstatic! We were scheduled to meet Maria Laura tomorrow morning at a coffee bar in Porano, before viewing several homes that might be suitable for us. After our brief conversation with Mandy, I was too excited to stay indoors. I felt like jumping or dancing! However, Vince was not quite as energetic. He preferred to relax and read a book, but since I could not contain myself, we agreed to meet at the Piazza del Duomo in a few hours. Even so, in less than an hour after we separated, we were in the car on our way to Porano for a preliminary drive to the coffee bar where we were to meet Maria Laura in the morning. Furthermore, we cruised around to reconfirm our favorable assessment of Porano's ambiance and character. Once again, the typical unspoiled, glorious landscape, dotted with Cypress trees and charming historic buildings bewitched us. We couldn't wait to see the properties that Maria Laura had selected and arranged for us to see.

From Porano, we continued on our drive to Civita di Bagnoregio, a tiny borgo of less than twenty full time residents not yet discovered by the masses, but more by the word-of-mouth sightseers who seek out the hidden gems of Umbria. We had no idea what an extraordinary, unique and (as Vince refers to it now) *magical* place we were about to discover. We parked the car at the appointed lot and walked to the edge of a cliff marking the path to Civita. The initial view was a jaw-dropper.

Civita di Bagnoregio, founded by the Etruscans over 2500 years ago, perched atop a volcanic pinnacle surrounded by a deep Grand Canyon-like gorge, has the appearance of an eroding island in the middle of the Tiber Valley. The only way to the massive stone, twelfth century Romanesque arch leading into the medieval hamlet, is via a steep ½-mile long foot bridge. The earth that once connected Civita di Bagnoregio to the more vibrant town of Bagnoregio, has long worn away. With the quickened pace of further erosion, and buildings continuing to crumble and fall into the canyon, Civita is known by the locals as *il paese che muore*, the "dying town." We had never seen anything like it and were eager to explore the village. The journey on the steep footpath was surprisingly easy as we reached the top in less than twenty minutes. Inside the gate, Civita's tranquil beauty was romantic and we were immediately captivated. In every picturesque corner, scrambling ivy covered warm colored stone walls and potted geraniums and begonias draped from balconies. The feeling that we had just stepped back into the Middle Ages was overwhelming. As we meandered through the cobblestone streets, we were inspired to take pictures in every direction. This place was an artist's dream.

Soon, we arrived at Piazza San Donato; the small, unpaved village square, where the church of San Donato was built upon a pagan temple in the eighth century. The church was the cathedral of Bagnoregio until 1699. We continued wandering to the edge of town, where we stumbled upon Antico Frantoio; a rustic bruschetteria set in a cave with an authentic 1500-year-old stone olive mill. Although, the menu was limited to bruschetta, it seemed like a perfect place to stop for a bite to eat. We sat at a charming, rustic table with a crimson red tablecloth, ordered a carafe of the house wine and a selection of the bruschetta. The chef placed sliced artisan bread on a simple wire grate over hot coals in the fireplace where he grilled the slices to perfection before creating the artistically assembled bruschetta at a small wooden counter. Our first course selection was three bruschette, individually topped with spinach, white beans and artichokes. They were delicious! The second course was topped with tomato and sweet basil and the third with a variety of Umbrian cured meats and cheeses. Although all the bruschette were quite tasty, the one with artichokes was my favorite.

In the main dining room, we heard laughing, singing and gleeful conversation spoken with that undeniable New York accent. A group of Americans who appeared to be having a party, sounded like a fun bunch. Vince and I enjoyed every intimate moment of our lunch, as we talked about how wonderful it would be one day to host such a gathering of family and friends. By the time Vince poured our last glass of wine, the party group was also finishing their lunch and getting ready to settle their bill. A distinguished looking gentleman walked over to our table.

"I apologize for my noisy friends over there. I hope that we didn't disturb you," he said.

"No, not at all," Vince responded. "It sounds like you were having a wonderful time."

"Yes, we were. We live here," the gentleman explained. "I mean, we live in Virginia, but we have a second home here. Our friends from the U.S have been staying with us for a few weeks. We were having a little going away party for them because they are leaving tomorrow. We know the owner here. Where are you folks from?"

Vince explained that we were from the San Francisco Bay Area and considering buying a part-time residence in Umbria, when his wife overheard our conversation.

"Do it!" she said, as she walked over to our table. "Do it. Buy a home here. You won't regret it. We bought ours eight years ago and we have just love it." Vince asked many pertinent questions about the buying process. Our informative and encouraging conversation lasted quite a while, before we parted and the couple wished us good luck.

During the drive back to Casa Flavia, we felt immensely motivated and inspired and, more than ever, looked forward to our meeting with Maria Laura tomorrow.

Our Search Begins

Both Vince and I were up-and-down all night. Anticipating our meeting with Maria Laura was a severe sleep deterrent that kept us awake until four o'clock in the morning, only to wake up two hours later. We tried to remain relaxed until eight o'clock when it was finally time to meet with our agent and begin the search for our Italian dream home. It felt surreal and so exciting!

Maria Laura was a tall, slender, beautiful young woman. Originally from Argentina, she spoke English with a unique and lovely accent. After brief introductions and an in-depth discussion over coffee to reconfirm our property requirements, we were finally on our way to view the first listing. I was so excited. We had never been inside an Italian residence before.

The dwelling was a semi-detached townhouse located in the historic center of Porano. It was an owner-occupied home, fully furnished, with two bedrooms, a kitchen, a bonus room that served as a laundry room with a washing machine, a ½ bathroom and a full bathroom with a tub and a bidet. At the front entrance was an attractive patio, furnished with a table and six chairs, which functioned as a shared outdoor space for two units. The property appealed to me, although Vince wanted a home with a view and was strictly opposed to sharing the outdoor space with neighbors.

The second property was located in a newer subdivision of Porano and even though it included a garden and garage, the home didn't resonate with us and we left almost immediately after a quick walkthrough.

Maria Laura informed us that the third property was a townhouse located in her neck of the woods. Much to our surprise, we discovered that Mandy was her neighbor. The apartment was similar to Mandy's home with a spacious living room window that provided an outstanding view of the Duomo di Orvieto gleaming in the distance, however, the space was undergoing a complete interior renovation and although that offered a new buyer the opportunity to choose paint colors and finishes, we preferred a less contemporary home in a more historic setting.

Vanessa hosted the tour of the last property on the agenda for the day. Massimo; a young, energetic agent from immobiliare, owned the listing and accompanied us. We enjoyed the congenial interaction between Massimo and Vanessa. They were obviously friends in addition to being business collaborators. Massimo described the property as a unique apartment in a restored church in a medieval village. We were crazy excited to see it.

The charming hilltop village of Lubriano has a population of less than a thousand full time residents and has been inhabited since prehistoric times. Walking from the community parking lot to the apartment, we promptly noticed that there were no shops or eating establishments in the vicinity. When Vince inquired to that point, Vanessa indicated that there was a wildly popular restaurant at the opposite end of town, highly recommended for the superbly delicious *bistecca alla fiorentina*; the famous Chianina beef steak, slightly similar to an American Porterhouse steak. The Italian variety of large, white oxen are primarily raised in Tuscany's Val di Chiana and are considered among the oldest breed of cattle in the world.

The heavy wooden door which led into a common entrance to several apartments in the restored church, was quite impressive and the unit itself was gorgeous. Massimo told us that the exquisite, honed Rosso marble floors were original and the same marble used to construct the columns of a church in Siena. The 2-bedroom, 2-bath, ground floor apartment with a dining room and a living room was quite large, had plenty of natural light and was full of the character we desired. There was an oversized stone fireplace and high cathedral ceilings. Nevertheless, the over-our-budget price did not include an installed kitchen, a suitable outdoor space for entertaining or panoramic views from any corner of the apartment. With all of its attributes, this was not the property for us and we looked forward to continuing our house hunting tomorrow.

When we returned to Casa Flavia, Vince prepared a delectable plate of cheese and sliced meats for our lunch. We also had half of a porchetta pannini and a sun-ripened tomato to share. While I tossed a load of laundry in the washing machine, Vince set the bistro table outside on the terrazzo. By the time I joined him at the pretty lunch table, the bottle of red wine he opened had been breathing and was perfect for drinking. Needless to say, we discussed the properties we had seen and although we loved something about each one, we agreed that none had captured our hearts, that we learned a lot and were eager to view more listings tomorrow.

We stayed outside, enjoying food, wine and conversation until the load of laundry finished washing. While we hung our clothes to dry on a line suspended in the sun, we smiled at each other, recognizing how "wholesome" it felt to do a house chore in Italy, as if we already lived here.

In the late afternoon, we strolled down Orvieto's main street just as the village lights were beginning to illuminate and the shops were beginning to re-open for the evening shift. Vince stroked and petted every friendly cat that crossed our path. We walked all the way to the end of town where the road signs point to the Autostrada. On the way back, we stopped to buy our first gelato. Gelatoria Pasqualetti; a tiny little place on the Corso Cavour, with a wooden bench outside the door, serves the most delicious, decadent gelato we have ever had anywhere! Continuing on our evening stroll with our Gelato in hand, we passed by Trattoria da Carlo. Carlo, Antonio and Teresa happened to see us and came out to say hello. We hugged as if we were long-time friends. A few minutes later, we came upon Il Sapore dell'Umbria, where we saw Patrizia busily arranging a new display of wine bottles at the entrance of her charming store.

"Ahhh, Vincenzo e Joyce," she called out when she saw us, "*Buonasera, come stai?*" We approached her with an Italian-style greeting; a kiss on each cheek.

"*Va bene?*" she asked. "Is everything going OK?"

"*Si, molto va bene.*" "Yes, very well," Vince replied. Somehow, we were able to communicate to her that we were window shopping and enjoying the evening.

When we walked by the immobiliare, Vanessa and Mandy waived to us. We felt an amazing sense of "belonging," we felt at home in Orvieto.

Strolling toward Casa Flavia, we stopped at a shop that specialized in beautiful, Umbrian handmade products. I couldn't resist the rich Italian leather goods and purchased a handsome hand-bound journal for Meghan and bars of artisan bath soaps made from olive oil and citrus for Carole and Vince's mother. The fragrant bars smelled lovely on the nightstand next to my bed. Even though it had been a very insightful day, we were anxiously looking forward to what tomorrow would bring.

We woke up refreshed and eager to start our second house hunting tour. Following our routine of eating pizza for breakfast at the tiny bakery on the Piazza de Popolo and sipping coffee at Cafe Barrique, our spirits were high as we discussed the three properties we were going to view today. They sounded intriguing yesterday when Vanessa described them to us. All were located in the small town of Bolsena, located a twenty-minute beautiful drive from Orvieto, on the West shore of Lake Bolsena. Since the listings were represented by Massimo's agency, he would accompany us. We were thrilled to visit a new area.

When we reached Bolsena, we headed directly to the historic center where the ancient Fortress Rocca Monaldeschi dominates the town as an imminent reminder of the powerful family that ruled this region during the fourteenth century. Bolsena earned religious significance in 1263 when a priest named Peter of Prague, stopped by while on a pilgrimage to Rome. The priest found it difficult to believe that Christ was actually present in the consecrated Host. While celebrating Holy Mass at the church of Saint Christina, blood began to seep from the Holy Host and trickled over his hands onto the altar. The priest went to see Pope Urban IV who resided in Orvieto at the time, to tell of his story. The Pope listened to the priest's account of the "miracle of Bolsena." After all the facts were ascertained, he ordained that the linen cloth, bearing the stains of blood, be placed in the Cathedral of Orvieto where it is still respectfully enshrined and exhibited today.

Bolsena seemed like a lovely village with steep stone alleyways leading to the lakeshore, where tree lined avenues created a resort-like atmosphere, encouraging visitors to spend time at the lake's beaches. There was also a picturesque piazza where people sat in sidewalk cafes. We immediately liked the vicinity and were motivated to see the properties on Massimo's agenda.

Unfortunately, since the first apartment was too contemporary for us without hesitation, Vince suggested that we move on to the next one. The second one was amazing! Located in a medieval building in the historic center of town, it was full of the original character we were looking for. We liked the apartment from the moment we walked through the door. Plenty of natural light illuminated the entire unit and the living room window provided a spectacular view of Lake Bolsena. The partially furnished unit consisted of a bedroom, an eating area, a living room and a sufficient sized bathroom. There was also a tiny kitchen in addition to a spacious bonus room. Some of the spaces were delightfully quirky. The bedroom, for instance, was a loft-style platform, built almost directly under the ceiling. There was no door and the mattress was placed on a concrete podium surrounded by four heavy posts encircled by mosquito netting. Massimo told us that homes in the Middle Ages were typically warmed by rising body heat from the farm animals that were kept in the stables below the living quarters. The stable had been restored into a bonus room; a cave like chamber with stone walls which were painstakingly covered in umber colored plaster. We loved this enchanting bit of history and already our imagination ran wild with the endless possibilities that the transformed stable provided. It could easily function as a charming guest room, wine cellar or lounge. As we continued to walk from room to room, I noticed that Vince was thoroughly looking at every detail. Under his breath, I repeatedly heard him say, "Very nice, very nice." Being careful not to reveal my extreme enthusiasm, I wondered what my husband was thinking.

Everything about the apartment was perfect, except it lacked the all-important outdoor space we longed for. However, the living room window which, could potentially be replaced by a door leading to the outside, overlooked a small terrazzo. According to Massimo, the terrazzo actually belonged to the community of Bolsena, despite the fact that a neighbor appeared to be using it as a private patio by decorating it with potted plants, outdoor furniture and a grill. Laundry hanging out to dry on a portable wooden rack also indicated that this community space was privately occupied. Nevertheless, I must admit, that it looked like an adorable place to sit and read a book on a sunny afternoon.

We had one more property to inspect. The last apartment was occupied by the owner and her twenty-two cats! Massimo warned us that although the home was large, brimming with rustic character and priced within our budget, it needed minor restoration and smelled of cat urine. Oh my God, that was an understatement! Upon our approach to the front door, the place reeked so profusely that Vanessa refused to enter. She was allergic to cats and couldn't bare the horrific odor. As we walked through the home, adult cats and small kittens appeared from every nook and cranny. We assessed quickly that even though the living room had a magnificent view of the lake, this apartment required more renovation than we were willing to manage. Furthermore, Vince determined that the odor of cat urine would be impossible to remove from the old wood finishes.

After seeing all three properties, Massimo suggested going somewhere quiet to discuss our evaluation of each of the homes. It was easy to summarize our viewpoints, because both Vince and I readily agreed that the first and last properties were not ownership contenders for us, but the apartment with the loft-style sleeping space tugged at our heartstrings. We loved the location and were fascinated by its historic character, but we were apprehensive about compromising the outdoor space we longed for, this early in our property search. Vanessa and Massimo conversed in Italian, then turned to us to suggest seeing a townhouse in Lubriano that, although it was in need of some tender-love-and-care, met most of our key requirements. It even promised to have a small garden and a spectacular view of Civita di Bagnoregio. Keeping an open mind, we were intrigued and agreed to see it.

Located a short drive east of Bolsena, Lubriano is bordered by high cliffs at the South end of town, overlooking the Valley of the Badlands and Civita di Bagnoregio. The townhouse was a corner, semidetached dwelling on a pleasant street, not far from the apartment in the restored church we had seen yesterday. The residents adorned their entry ways with brightly colored, flourishing potted blooms which was always a heartwarming sign and a hopeful indication that the interior might be as pleasing as the exterior. Alas, we were dreadfully disappointed to discover that every room was dark and dingy, smelled of musty mold and in serious need of total renovation. The walls were covered in torn, discolored wallpaper and loose plaster hung from the ceilings. The obvious water damage in the bathroom was a primary concern and the kitchen needed a complete replacement. Massimo explained that the Dutch owners returned to their homeland, leaving the apartment vacant for more than thirteen years. On the positive side, this place was a diamond in the rough, with the potential to be an amazing, beautiful home with a lush garden and a magnificent view of Civita di Bagnoregio. Nevertheless, it was not a project we dared to confront.

After our agents brought us back to Orvieto, Vince and I returned to explore the area between Lubriano and Bolsena. We planned to eat lunch in Lubriano, at the restaurant that had Vanessa recommended. As potential home owners in the region, we deemed it important to scrutinize the area in search of a harmonious connection.

No one spoke English in the restaurant. The Italian menu was still a language challenge Vince and I enjoyed. We pondered each item's description for a word we recognized, ultimately Vince ordered the Chianina beef steak and, based on Vanessa's recommendation from yesterday, I ordered the bistecca alla fiorentina steak. The waitress looked at me perplexed, verbalized something in Italian that I could not understand, then made a hand motion as if to say, "Just one moment. I'll be right back."

She went to the kitchen to return with an enormous cut of meat on a plate and asked, *"Questo?"* "This one?"

Oh, my goodness! No, I definitely did not intend to order a steak large enough to feed six people! Grateful that she showed me what I was about to order, I quickly changed my selection to the carpaccio and arugula salad. My salad was fresh and flavorful. Vince's delectable, melt-in-your-mouth steak was fork tender, cooked to perfection and tasted amazing.

Even though we thoroughly enjoyed eating lunch at an unhurried pace in this delightful local restaurant, Lubriano, somehow seemed lackluster and didn't touch our hearts. Unfortunately, it was not the quaint, sought-after village that we longed to call home.

We drove the most scenic route back to Orvieto, stopping often to take pictures in the ideal twilight of the day. The blue water of Lake Bolsena looked like a shimmering mirror while the fields of red poppies, still brilliant in color, began to lower their heads slightly. Umbria's magnificent scenery was truly beautiful beyond compare.

Happy to be back in our comfortable Casa Flavia, Vince loosened his clothes, opened a bottle of wine and invited me to relax with him on the sofa.

"Saluti, Treat, here's to us," he said as he raised his glass to make a toast. "Here's to us and to finding our home in Italy."

"I'll certainly drink to that," I replied.

It was truly sublime to sip wine together as we exchanged thoughts about our grand dream of living here. Our conversation became primarily focused on the quirky apartment in Bolsena and as we talked, our passion and voices rose with enthusiasm. We were extremely enthralled by that apartment, because so much about it genuinely suited us. Before we finished our bottle of wine, Vince suggested making a follow-up appointment to view the apartment for a second time. What an excellent idea!

"It would be good to view it again," he said, "let's see if Vanessa can schedule it for tomorrow." I crossed my fingers and felt my heart pounding in my chest as I listened to Vince make the appointment. I couldn't believe it. *This was getting serious!*

Later that evening, we felt as if we were walking on air when we wandered down the Corso Cavour, deciding on where to have dinner. We stopped at one of the ceramic shops near the Piazza del Duomo to buy a handmade serving dish decorated with lemons by a local artist. Although we loved it at first sight when we discovered it a few days ago, we refrained from making such a pricey purchase.

"Here," Vince said, smiling from ear-to-ear as he handed me the wrapped package, "this is for our Italian home." Oh, how I loved that surreal sentiment. From my husband's lips to God's ears.

When we reached Trattoria da Carlo near the center of town, our favorite Italian chef and his mom were outside tending to their hungry customers.

"Hello, my friends!" Carlo shouted and waved. Unable to resist such a warm greeting, we stepped inside the dining room, seated ourselves and helped ourselves to menus. Soon, every table was occupied with demanding guests and gradually our pleasant dining experience became a bit noisy and hectic. We noticed that Antonio was off duty, leaving Carlo and Teresa working feverishly to compensate for being severely understaffed. As usual, the food was delicious and we savored every morsel.

When I woke up early the next morning, Vince was already stirring.

"Good morning, my love," he greeted. "That apartment in Bolsena kept me awake last night."

"Me too," I replied. "I think it is just perfect for us!"

"I want to take another look at the bathroom," Vince reiterated, "and I want to get an idea of how to cut through a 16-inch-thick stone wall to replace the living room window with a door to the terrace." Obviously, my loving husband had given this serious contention.

At ten o'clock, we met Vanessa in the parking lot behind the real estate office, while Massimo agreed to meet us at the site. We arranged to follow Vanessa in our own car so that we could continue our exploration of Bolsena after viewing the apartment.

Massimo was already inside, waiting to greet us when we arrived. I held my breath, wondering how we would feel walking through the front door, this time as potential buyers. I hoped that our mind's eye hadn't exaggerated the apartment's charm, only to disappoint us. Oh, on the contrary! Standing in the lounge, we knew without a doubt that we loved the apartment even more upon a second look. It seemed to speak volumes to us and it distinctly *felt right.*

Vince immediately turned his focus on inspecting the bathroom, while I examined every aspect of the kitchen. The refrigerator was small, but there was adequate counter space and even though a dishwasher was lacking, a clothes washer was installed near the sink. As I opened cabinet doors, tried to ignite the gas stove and visualized myself cooking in this snug little kitchen, I was convinced that I could create amazing meals here.

I also surveyed the unusual "makeshift" bedroom. Climbing into the loft to enter the space, before crawling onto the mattress to get into bed, didn't discourage me from imagining how we could live here happily.

I methodically moved from room to room, taking pictures and documenting every nook-and-cranny, while Vince was examined the bathroom with a fine-toothed comb. The shower stall was in adequate condition, however, one of the interior walls appeared to be extremely moist. A slight pressure from Vince's hand against the surface caused water to seep onto the floor. He asked Massimo where the water source might be, however, Massimo was bewildered and unable to provide a logical answer. Needless to say, the wet wall was a prime concern, even though both agents assured us that the owner was required to make all repairs before accepting an offer.

We were equally concerned about the lack of access to the terrace. Would the community approve our plan to replace the window with a door? How long would the approval process take? Or, if the plan was denied, would we be content living in a home with a phenomenal view but without the outdoor space we coveted? Suddenly we realized how many questions remained unanswered and issues unresolved.

After spending hours assessing the apartment's condition, we finally concluded our meeting with Vanessa and Massimo, but agreed to consult further with Maria Laura and an engineer. We needed a concise understanding of the process to gain community approval for remodeling the window and obtaining concurrence from the owner to repair the leaking wall. We parted ways with the understanding that Vanessa would schedule the meeting for the following day.

"Wait a minute," Vince said, in deep thought. "I want to take a quick look at something." He walked around the outside perimeter of the apartment to locate the seeping wall's exterior. To our enormous surprise, Vince discovered that the apartment's bathroom was technically built in the space of an ancient cistern; a water collection point for the village during the Middle Ages. What a revelation! An epic renovation of the historic building's basic structure was required to stop the wall from its intended purpose of collecting water. Nevertheless, we were looking forward to discussing this issue in detail with Maria Laura and an engineer tomorrow.

Our afternoon exploration of Bolsena was very insightful. We visited the Church of St. Christina; where the Miracle of Bolsena occurred centuries ago. Seeking out the local amenities, we found several markets, coffee bars and casual restaurants. Also, conveniently located in the historic center was a bank, a gelatoria, a few bakeries and artisan shops. The village was clean and manifested a welcoming vibe, especially near the lakeshore where the view of the medieval village was quite majestic. We meandered to the harbor, past luxury three and four star rated hotels.

"Lake Bolsena is a marvelous lake for sailing," Vince noted as he pointed out two J-24 sailboats docked in their slips. "I wonder if there is a yacht club here?"

It was easy to fantasize living in this pristine area of unparalleled scenic beauty. A charming trattoria advertising lake fish on a handwritten menu posted by the entrance attracted us as a perfect place to have lunch. We chose a lovely table overlooking the lake. After the wine was served, we prepared for our meeting with Maria Laura, talking over different scenarios regarding our concerns. We agreed that it was important to get her advice and an engineer's expert opinion about how to resolve these matters before further pursuing ownership of the apartment.

Our precious vacation was sadly drawing to an end. Today was our last full day in town and we were dedicated to making effective use of our limited time. Since it would be many months before we returned to Italy, we wanted to soak up as much of our beloved Italian culture as possible.

It was market day, our last chance to grab a roasted porchetta sandwich for breakfast from the food truck to chase down with our last cup of coffee from Paolo at Cafe Barrique. Other last purchases included a tablecloth for Vince's mother, kitchen towels for me and the *cinghiale* sausages which we planned to smuggle home in our luggage for Vince. We also bought a potted geranium to leave on the table at Casa Flavia as a gesture of gratitude for Roberta and Mauro's hospitality. Vince petted the calico cat for the last time and we said goodbye to the shopkeepers we had befriended. It was a melancholy day.

As we took our last stroll window-shopping up the Corso Cavour from Piazza Cahn, we were suddenly stopped in our tracks by an advertisement posted in another real estate agency's window.

"Oh my gosh, Vince! Look at this." I almost shouted. "An apartment in our price range is for sale in Porano! It's one bedroom, fully furnished, with a balcony and a garage!"

Vince came over to read the sign. "I wonder why our agents didn't tell us about this property?"

"I don't know. Maybe it's a new listing. Let's find out if we can see it today." I snapped a picture of the listing on my mobile phone to show to Vanessa. Our appointment with Maria Laura and the engineer was not for another hour, but in our eagerness to view the apartment, we headed for her office immediately. The three ladies were in the office when we arrived.

Buongiorno Vanessa, Mandy and Maria Laura greeted us almost in unison. "You are early," Maria Laura added.

We showed them the picture of the listing which we found on our own, by sheer coincidence. As agents with up-to-date knowledge of the local market and an acute awareness how much we desired Porano as a location to secure a home, we were disappointed that no one mentioned the listing to us proactively. Caught off guard and a slightly embarrassed, Maria Laura looked at the listing, recognized the selling agent's name and scheduled a meeting for us later in the afternoon. We were cautiously ecstatic and hopeful that this was the home for us. It would be a remarkable stroke of fate if the apartment we capriciously found, turned out to be our dream home.

Meanwhile, Maria Laura enlightened us about the property buying process in Italy. We needed a *codice fiscale;* an Italian tax identification number, similar to an American Social Security number. Codice fiscale numbers are assigned to Italians at birth, to non-Italian nationals, upon request. The number is required to perform any significant transaction, such as opening a bank account, applying for utility services, buying property and even purchasing a phone. Contrary to what we had heard from others, according to Maria Laura, obtaining lawyer representation is not required. The immobiliare collaborates with a *notaio*; a public officer whose fee is paid by the buyer. The notaio represents both the buyer and the seller and is the highest-ranking official serving as a neutral party. He conducts formal document checks, confirms the parties' identities, calculates the taxes, collects them when the deed is signed at the close of escrow and pays them on behalf of both parties. Property transfer contracts must be signed in front of the notaio. Once the taxes have been paid and the title deed has been filed, the notaio keeps the original in his records and provides the parties with official copies. Authorizing Maria Laura to be our Power of Attorney would enable her to sign all documents on our behalf if we were not present at the deed signing. Our first formal step to becoming property owners, however, was to apply for the codice fiscale. Without it, we could not proceed with an offer if we should find the home of our dreams. Maria Laura offered to escort us to the tax office in Orvieto Scalo to file the appropriate paperwork. Strangely, we were not apprehensive about taking this first official step and filled out the applications without hesitating. Using the immobiliare as our current local address, Maria Laura offered to notify us when our codice fiscale cards arrived.

It was finally time to head out to Porano for the property tour. Vince and I had a good feeling about it. Although the apartment was located outside the medieval wall, Maria Laura told us that it was in a pretty part of the village, on a tree lined avenue, near a good restaurant, a coffee bar and a pharmacy. We drove the scenic route past Castel Rubello; my favorite way to Porano. Maria Laura recommended the castle as a wonderful place for guests to stay overnight. Soon we were at the apartment, where the seller's agent was already waiting for us. After the introductions were made, the seller's agent indicated that the apartment was only a short fifteen-minute walk from Porano's medieval center and located directly across from Paolina Park, the gateway entrance to Villa Paolina; a magnificent mansion of the eighteenth century, surrounded by splendid ancient gardens with Etruscan tombs from the fourth century B.C.

The apartment building was a newer construction with a detached garage in front. Maria Laura joked by saying that anything outside of the village walls was considered "new construction." Typical of many European style apartment buildings, this was a two-level structure with residential dwellings on the top level and retail spaces below. The seller's agent guided us around the building, past a music shop and a small cafe, before pointing to a unit above a charming flower shop with colorful potted blooms attractively displayed at the entrance, beneath a green striped awning.

"That's the apartment," she said, "let's go inside."

Vince and I looked at each other smiling, both of us instinctively knowing that we were optimistically pleased with our initial reaction.

As soon as we entered the living space, we liked what we saw. The tasteful furniture and an extensive list of accessories was included in the sale price. Even though it was a newer apartment, the thick, exposed wooden headers above the windows and doors provided rustic character. The open concept floorpan with plenty of natural light consisted of a kitchen, a cozy dining and lounge area with French doors that opened to a balcony large enough for a bistro table and two chairs. The terrace view overlooked Paolina Park. The seller's agent noted that as a landmark protected by the Italian Heritage Society, the park would never be commercially developed. Throughout the year, various food and wine festivals were held on the premises and village parades periodically marched down the street directly below the balcony. We were truly enamored with the possibility of living here to experience the Umbrian countryside lifestyle. As we gazed at the local traffic below, a kindly old farmer maneuvered his toy-sized, blue tractor stacked with hay through the narrow country road, gesturing exasperated followers to pass by while he continued on his way at a snail's pace.

"Oh my gosh, honey!" I exclaimed. "Look at that. Isn't that endearing?" Then turning to the agents, I added, "Is that a traffic jam in Porano? I love it!"

To conclude the property tour, we looked at the bedroom, comfortably proportioned for a queen-sized bed and a floor-to-ceiling closet with a large window facing Paolina Park. The attractive bathroom was functional and came equipped with all the essentials.

Lastly, we looked at the garage. Maria Laura informed us that Italians refer to a garage as a "car box." The car box was large enough to accommodate a mid-sized car, a workbench, and storage for tools and seasonal items. I was overjoyed to discover a clothes washer installed in a corner, while Vince raved about the sink with a faucet for hot and cold running water. This apartment was absolutely perfect for us. It had everything we were looking for and it was in close proximity to Orvieto. We couldn't ask for anything more. We were convinced that we had found our Italian dream home.

The seller's agent wrapped-up the tour by asking if we had further questions. When she left, I felt free to show my enthusiasm, although, since Vince and I had not discussed our thoughts in private, I was afraid to seem overanxious. I was completely smitten by the apartment and hoped that Vince could read my mind. Then, I heard him ask Maria Laura to cancel our appointment with the engineer and draw up the paperwork for an offer and I cried tears of joy!

Our First Offer!

Due to several years of a slowing economy and a serious recession throughout Italy, it is not unusual for properties to remain for sale for many months, or even, years. The apartment in Porano had been on the market for several months without generating any interest or offers. When Vince suggested making an initial offer of 15% below the seller's asking price, Maria Laura quickly agreed and guaranteed to prepare the paperwork before our arrival in California. She would send the preliminary offer via electronic mail (email) for our review and signature before submitting the official offer to the motivated seller who resided in Rome. With a strategic plan in place, we walked out to our cars, when Maria Laura unexpectedly asked if she could accompany us to what she described as "a very special place." A bit mystified, we followed her on the country road toward Orvieto, when suddenly she pulled over to the side, stepped out of her car and made a hand motion directing us to do the same.

"Before you leave, I want to show you my favorite view of Orvieto," she explained as she walked across a field of grass to the edge of a cliff. "Look," she continued with a sweeping motion of her arm. "Look at Orvieto."

It was indeed an amazing view seldom seen by the average tourist. This secret spot, known only to her, was Maria Laura's own discovery. We appreciated her sweet gesture to bring us to this unique panorama of Orvieto; Umbria's ultimate Gothic hilltop town. The sun-dappled glow on the cathedral and the slabs of tufa stone on which Orvieto appears to be hoisted, intensified the dramatic outlook of the city and made this an appropriate, lovely place to say goodbye to Maria Laura. We thanked her for all that she had done for us, reiterated how much we appreciated her encouragement and looked forward to working with her on achieving our dream of owning a home in Italy. We promised to review and sign the documents as soon as we arrived home. Confident that fate was guiding us through this endeavor, we assured her that we were extremely eager to proceed with the buying process.

In Orvieto, we were on a mission to complete our last-minute shopping. We dropped by Patrizia's shop to say goodbye. She was very nice and offered us a bottle of local Orvieto Classico wine as a parting gift. I took a picture of Vince standing next to her, which Patrizia proudly posted in a conspicuous place in her shop. We also stopped by our favorite delicatessen to buy a few local specialties for family and friends. Vince bought a fresh truffle for Bob, spices for neighbors and friends and while he was still engaged in making a few more selections, I discovered the tiniest bottle of balsamic vinegar I had ever seen.

"Look, honey," I interrupted. "Isn't this cute?"

I loved the way it was packaged in a miniature box and thought it would make a delightful Christmas Tree ornament; a reminder of our house hunting trip, however, when I looked at the price, I reluctantly returned it to its place on the shelf. Additionally, Vince bought some sausages and a few slices of *cinghiale* to munch on during our ride to the airport in the morning. When he was ready to pay for his selections, the proprietor totaled the items on his time-worn, brass cash register, then came out from behind the counter and took the little bottle of balsamic vinegar I had shown to Vince and placed it inside our bag.

"For you," he said as he looked at me, "for you, a present."

"Awhh!" I exclaimed. "Really? Thank you, signore. Grazie." I thanked him profusely as this was yet another affirmation of how inherently warm and friendly the Orvietani are. Vince shook his hand and asked him for a business card. The name of the shop was *Dai Fratelli* and the owner's name was Emilio. I asked Emilio for permission to take a picture of his shop. It was entirely charming, a typical Italian deli with sides of beautiful prosciutto hanging on meat hooks from the ceiling, some looked like the substantial sides of cured pork we were familiar with, while others were covered with bristly dark brown hair. Vince pointed to a hairy one and asked Emilio what it was.

"*Cinghiale!*" He retorted proudly with his chest slightly expanded. Then Vince pointed to one of the others and asked, "What about that one? What is that?"

Emilio's chest deflated as he made a dismissing gesture and answered, "Oh, that is just pig." We were amused by his reaction and response. Vince made an effort to explain that we were going home to California, but planned to return to Orvieto soon.

"*Arrivederci, Emilio. Ciao*! See you again soon." When we shut the door behind us and stepped out into the narrow street of the *via del Duomo*, we were startled by the unusual hustle and bustle outside. The street was more crowded than normal and huge spot lights mounted on roof tops brightened up the area below, but the strangest sight of all, was a laundry line that was being suspended across the street from the top floor windows of a prominent residential *palazzo*. We had never seen laundry hanging in the streets of Orvieto's historic center and we certainly had not noticed those big spot lights earlier in the day. A man with a bullhorn loudspeaker directed a throng of people to move aside to clear the way for a policeman who came running down the street, blowing a whistle and waving a fist in the air as if he was chasing someone. Curious about all that was occurring, we questioned fellow spectators, who informed us that the street had been transformed into a movie set for the filming of a night-scene in a major motion picture. Immediately, I wondered who the movie-stars were, what the name of the motion picture was and where I could stand so that I might end up in the film's background as a movie "extra."

Our early morning drive to Rome's Leonardo DaVinci International Airport; more commonly known as *Fiumicino*, was a bit challenging because we knew that once we reached the *Grande Raccordo Anulare* (the Great Ring Road) highway approach to the airport, the exit to the terminals was easy to miss, which would consequently require us to drive the entire circle around Rome again to get back on the right track. Nevertheless, we departed Casa Flavia in plenty of time to compensate for any unexpected delays, including potentially getting lost. Fortunately, rush hour traffic had not yet reached peak congestion and we were able to follow the highway signs to the correct exit, leaving returning the rental car as our only concern. Since Fiumicino is the second busiest airport in Europe, we expected to see plenty of car rental return signs, blatantly marked in English; the universal language, leading us to the drop-off location, however, not so. Frustrated and nerve-wracked, we drove around the airport multiple times looking for a clue or indication of where to return the car, until I finally referred to my Italian dictionary to translate car rental to *autonoleggio*. Once we knew what to look for, the autonoleggio signs easily directed us to the drop-off location. We were finally done with the more exasperating issues and on our way to the more familiar chores of international travel.

During the horrendously long flight to San Francisco, Vince and I found solace in perpetually discussing the apartment in Porano. We couldn't wait to get home to review the preliminary offer Maria Laura was preparing for us. We were actually on the verge of buying our Italian dream home! Who would believe it? We deemed it remarkably serendipitous to have found a property so ideally suited to us on the last day of our trip. We loved absolutely everything about it and in my imagination, I had every room redecorated to reflect our style. Despite only one bedroom, I already had a million ingenious ideas of how to furnish the intimate space with dual purpose furniture to accommodate overnight guests. Vince developed his own ideas about utilizing the garage to its fullest potential, as a workshop, a place for storage, a laundry area and, in due course, a safe place to leave our car when we are not in Italy. I cannot describe how much I adore talking with my husband about our dreams. I love to watch his face when he radiates with positive energy. It makes me feel as if we have the world on a string and my heart swells with emotion.

When we finally arrived home, I must admit that we did not immediately start up the computer as promised, to look for Maria Laura's email. After our sixteen-hour journey from Casa Flavia to our front door in San Carlos, we were completely exhausted. After Vince briefly reconnected with Henry; our cat, to let him know we had returned, we showered and crawled into bed. In fact, it was the morning of the second day when we finally gathered our wits to read Maria Laura's email and review the documents she attached. We were impressed that she provided an English translated copy along with the Italian version.

The offer was unquestionably straight forward, without intent to negotiate closing costs or other miscellaneous fees, it stated our offer price and request for a response within three days. Without further ado, we signed where required, scanned the documents and sent them back to Maria Laura, who almost instantly confirmed receipt. To our dismay, she also informed us that on the morning following our property tour, the listing agent showed the apartment, quite unexpectedly, to another potential buyer; a single young man who discovered the listing on the internet. We found it utterly unbelievable that no one had shown a lack of interest in that lovely apartment until we were prepared to make an offer.

As the saying goes "For those who wait, waiting is a lifetime" and although it was only forty-eight hours instead of three days, it seemed like we waited a lifetime for Maria Laura's phone call letting us know that the seller did not accept our offer. I was crestfallen when Vince told me the news.

"Is there anything we can do? Is it over? Are there no options?" I asked in despair.

"The seller rejected our offer because our price was too low," Vince explained. "If we want the apartment, we can present a new offer at a higher price." Oh, I was devastated. Could we afford that? Vince clarified further that since our offer was rejected without the slightest consideration, there was no counter-offer from the seller, therefore we would be starting anew. Regardless, Maria Laura sent a new offer, which we signed immediately, so it could be presented to the seller the next day. We were hopeful that our strong offer of only 5% less than the asking price would be readily accepted.

Again, it was wishful thinking. The next morning, we were informed that the seller's counteroffer was for no less than 1,000€ below his asking price. Vince and I were beginning to doubt that fate was still on our side. We debated not raising our offer price because we felt that we were dealing with an arrogant, unreasonable seller, but after considering every aspect long and hard, we decided that the apartment was worth fighting for and after three years of internet property searching, we were convinced that this was our Italian dream home. Therefore, we decided to follow our hearts and directed Maria Laura to accept the seller's counter offer without further negotiations! Understanding the compelling, difficult decision we just made, we were elated and extremely pleased with ourselves for reaching a collective resolution. We were nearly the proud owners of a home in Italy!

We promised each other not to reveal a word of our unbelievable news to anyone until Maria Laura confirmed, unequivocally, that we were under a signed contract. Since we accepted the seller's counter offer, surely, we would hear from her by the next morning.

In anticipation of Maria Laura's phone call, we hardly slept a wink all night. Predicting what our final cost would be, Vince contrived several financial scenarios as he perused through bank statements and check book registers. We discussed a return trip to Italy at the close of escrow. Unfortunately, Vince would have to represent us both at that paramount, *once in a lifetime* event, because as an employee, the remainder of my limited vacation time-off from work, was already allocated to our travel plans scheduled throughout the year. Nevertheless, I preferred to forgo the formalities of signing the deed, to attend our official move-in day sometime later. I was looking forward to taking a detailed inventory of the kitchen and household items supplied with the apartment. At first glance, it appeared that the space was tastefully furnished, but I anticipated adding my own creative touches, including replacing the colorful sheer window coverings in every room.

It was nearly 6:30 in the morning when the phone rang. I noticed that my hands shook slightly when I poured Vince a cup of coffee while he answered the call. Undoubtedly, Maria Laura had news for us, but I could not determine if it was positive news, since Vince's facial expression and voice inflection provided no indication. Immediately after he ended the conversation, however, I instinctively felt despair and without Vince saying a word, I knew that we were not successful in obtaining ownership. Notwithstanding our willingness to meet the seller's price, he changed his mind and decided not to sell the property. We could not fathom such a callous attitude! We found it rude and arrogant, even though, according to Maria Laura, in Italy it is the seller's prerogative to remove the property from the market at any time without warrant.

We felt as if we had been kicked in the teeth and it took several weeks to recover from the heartbreaking experience. Through Maria Laura's outstanding follow-up work, we learned later, that we were outbid by a local resident, the apartment had been sold to the young man who toured it after we did. Eventually we chalked it up to God's plan. Although we adored that apartment in Porano and fought a good fight to own it, God had a different plan in store for us and I couldn't wait to discover what it was.

Our Second House Hunting Trip

The remainder of the year was an atypical time for us as we adjusted to Vince's first year of retirement. It was not easy for Vince to acclimate to a new kind of work schedule, one that he set for himself when he realized how many projects had been waiting for him to retire. The ceiling needed painting, the stone floor resealing, the trees trimming, the garage organizing, the backyard fence needed replacing. The list was endless! He established a plan to tackle the projects one by one and the effects of his labor soon became apparent in our home and garden. Everything appeared "more loved," cared for and polished than before. I endured the feeling of envy every morning as Vince sent me off to work with a smile and a melodious, "Have a nice day, honey. See you when you get home." (Argh!) I could hardly wait for my turn to be free from the corporate rat-race!

No longer bound by Vince's mere two-week vacation schedule from work, we travelled extensively. In early summer, we flew to Alaska with our friends Larry and Marla, to cruise one hundred and thirty-five miles into Prince William Sound on an incredible twenty-six Glacier Voyage to get face-to-face with those towering masses of ice. The glaciers were so close that we could hear them moving as they calved above sea level. We had the time-of-our-lives fishing on the Talkeetna River where Larry and Marla each caught a monstrous salmon weighing more than twenty-five pounds!

Deeper into the summer, we vacationed in Costa Rica with Stan and Carole to explore the mist-shrouded Monteverde Cloud Forest by taking a thrilling two-mile, eighteen platform tour on zip-line cables suspended high above the treetop canopy. In Arenal, we heard the volcano rumble as it erupted explosive plumes of smoke and ash right before our eyes. We spotted sloths, iguanas, kudamundies and mingled with more monkeys than people!

Our most adventurous trip, nevertheless, was a combined land/sailing vacation in Turkey with Bob and Karen, Stan and Carole. At Europe's gateway to Asia, we explored the historic, populous city of Istanbul to tour all the important sites: The Blue Mosque, Hagia Sophia, the Topkapi Palace, the Grand Bazaar and the Egyptian Spice Market. At Pierre Lotti's Cafe overlooking the magnificent Golden Horn, we drank Turkish coffee, lunched at a restaurant with a splendid view of the world-famous Galata Bridge; the link between Europe and Asia and took a sunset cruise on the Bosphorus Strait; the dividing line between the same two continents. The sailing area of the Lycian Coast was a pristine and tranquil Mediterranean paradise. Our visit to Turkey was unlike anywhere we had been before and a truly memorable experience.

When we were home in San Carlos, we maintained a well-balanced social life, spending quality time with family and friends. Yet, Italy was always on our mind, somewhere in the background of our thoughts. During quiet times, Vince and I reminisced frequently about brilliant, beautiful Umbria in the spring, when every shade of green makes the perfect backdrop for the wild red poppies that cover the landscape. Moreover, in hindsight, we were amazed at how quickly we developed friendships with the locals during our stay in Orvieto and how much we thoroughly enjoyed attending the neighborhood market on Thursdays and Saturdays to savor the best porchetta sandwiches in the land. We missed Italy tremendously.

Tenaciously we dedicated several hours each week to our quest of finding a home in Umbria. Now, being somewhat familiar with the region, we recognized many of the village names mentioned in the listings. Vince became an *aficionado* at navigating web mapping programs to pinpoint and determine their proximity to Orvieto. He showed me satellite image street views of the properties and surrounding areas so that we could expertly determine if the listing interested us enough to forward the information to Maria Laura for her local knowledge and professional perspective. Periodically, we edited our collection to the finalists we would request to inspect when we returned to Italy after my sixtieth birthday.

Not long after we returned from our vacation in Turkey, I came home from work to an overly enthusiastic greeting from Vince, who met me at the door, avidly waiving some printed computer pages in his hand, pushing them in mine, announcing his great internet discovery.

"Treat, look what I found! Can I pick 'em, or can I pick 'em?"

He couldn't wait for me to join him at the computer to show me the full description and photos of the property he found on an Italian property internet portal called Gate-Away. It was a stunning two-bedroom, one bathroom apartment located in Morcella; a medieval borgo in the Comune di Marsciano; approximately a forty-minute drive from Orvieto. It appeared to have absolutely everything on our wish list. It was bright, spacious with plenty of storage and a wonderful terrazzo boasting an incredible view of verdant farmland, surrounded by mountains studded with enchanting hilltop villages. The apartment was in excellent, move-in condition and seemed perfect for us. It was unbelievable that this amazing property was priced within our budget.

The following is the original listing as advertised by Casambiente Immobiliare. I silently hoped that finding this listing would not be a "timing issue" for us, because realistically, we could not take another trip to Italy for at least six months!

Casambiente's Advertisement

CASAMBIENTE
A Passion for Real Estate

Umbria,
Nel Vecchio
Granaio- 2026

CASAMBIENTE s.r.l.

Strada San Felicissimo n. 8/ter
06134 Ponte Felcino - Perugia

Phone: +39 075 509 17 05
Fax: +39 075 509 17 05
Cell: +39 393 3322012

mailbox@casambiente.com
www.casambiente.com

Agency Commission: 3%

House Features

Building Type & Condition: *modern apartment in historical palazzo*

Position & Views: *hamlet near Marsciano - panoramic views*

Storeys / Rooms: *2 bedrooms - 1 bathroom*

Living Area: *70 m²*

Land Size: *panoramic terrace of approx. 10 m²*

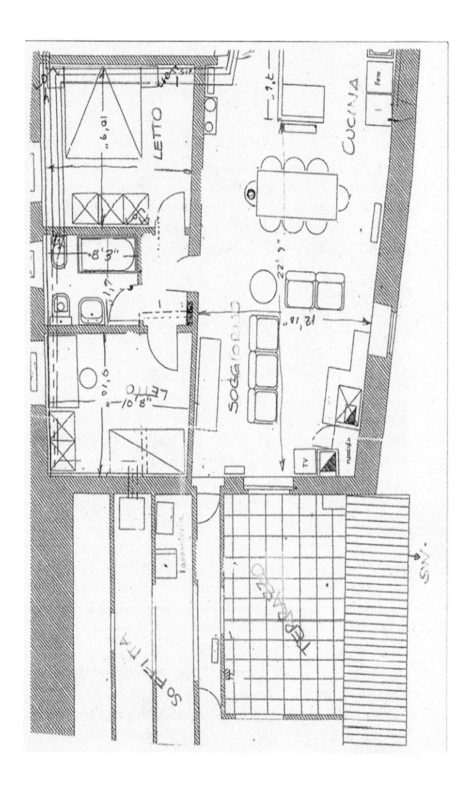

Orvieto; B&B Garibaldi
"We're Back!"

In January, my sister and her daughter came from Connecticut to help celebrate my sixtieth birthday. It was more than wonderful to have them in our home. Ellen had not been to visit since our mother died, almost four years ago and I was elated to have her and Meghan in our surroundings. Vince made dinner reservations at the Van's Restaurant; one of my favorite restaurants nearby. Larry and Marla, Stan and Carole and Vince's mother joined in the celebration. After dinner, Vince invited everyone to our home for coffee and a piece of the extra special birthday cake he baked for me. It was a perfect evening and I certainly felt loved and extremely blessed.

When Ellen and Meghan left the following day, I booked our flights to Italy. We were leaving right after Valentine's Day.

Although we planned another extended stay in Orvieto, curiosity persuaded us to rent a studio apartment more centrally located this time. *Bed and Breakfast (B&B) Garibaldi;* in the historic center of town, near the Piazza de' Ranieri seemed ideal and offered a winter discount rate of 47€ per night. Prior to securing a reservation, I communicated with the owner-manager, via email to request a more detailed description of the accommodations. David was forthright in describing the modest but adequate amenities, nevertheless, since we were visiting when the weather was predictably cold and gray, the lack of an outdoor area with an attractive vista did not concern us. Focused on house hunting, we didn't plan to spend much time in the apartment.

We arrived in the middle of February and met David at the entrance to the Porta Romana near Orvieto's historic center. From the photo posted on the B&B website, I recognized David instantly, although I must admit, that in person he looked huskier and surprisingly older. David was extremely polite, hospitable and made us feel like special guests when he explained that despite the B&B being closed during the winter months, he accepted our reservation as an exceptional case.

David currently lived with his grandmother in his childhood home, which he converted into the popular B&B Garibaldi several years ago. As the sole owner operator of the business, he is quite busy at the height of tourist season when all his apartments are booked throughout the summer. A separated area of the home, the modest accommodations were precisely as David advertised; no frills, spacious, comfortably furnished and equipped with everything we needed. It was more than adequate for our intended purpose. Following hours of thought-provoking house hunting, all we wanted a relaxing retreat where we could unwind and feel at home like local residents.

After a speedy unpacking and a bit of settling in, we took our first walk to get our bearings in town. Following our seventeen-hour journey, breathing recycled jet air, the cold, crisp evening breeze was rejuvenating and it felt great to stretch our legs. Orvieto enveloped us in a cozy sense of familiar territory and we were thrilled to be back.

This was our first-time visiting Italy in winter, because as future part-time residents, we felt that it was utmost important to experience Umbrian life in all seasons. Orvieto looked like a dreamy, fairy-tale village, uncrowded with tourists and only a few locals milling around. The Duomo was luminescent against a backdrop of a crescent shaped moon beginning to climb the evening sky. Even though Emilio's and Patrizia's shops looked inviting and Cafe Barrique beckoned us to come in, we weren't ready to interact with anyone yet and resisted the urge to stop in. Through the window of the real estate office, we saw Vanessa and Mandy engaged in a sublime discussion, however, feeling too weary to be social, we walked past without saying hello. Before returning to the B&B for some well needed rest, we ate a quick meal at a casual eating establishment nearby. Tomorrow morning we planned to "hit the ground running."

Morning I quickly for us and we were excited and rearing to go, beginning our day at Cafe Barrique, we ordered Italian coffees as if we were naturals at it. Paulo recognized us immediately and acknowledged our return with a smile and an exuberant *"Buongiorno! Sei tornato. Come stai?"* "Good morning! You have returned. How are you?"

"Va bene!" Vince said. "We are well." We drank our coffee slowly on a bench outside and wondered if the neighborhood calico cat that befriended Vince on our previous trip was still in the vicinity. It wasn't long before his four-legged pal appeared in the doorway across the street, unfortunately the cat was evidently not ready to reconnect with us. She stayed in the passageway watching Orvieto come alive as retailers began to open their shops.

Suddenly, Vince who had been in deep thought all morning, proposed several strategies to guarantee a more successful day of house hunting. A few weeks prior to our arrival, we provided Maria Laura a list of eight properties that seriously intrigued us and were intent on seeing, in addition to others that she might have proactively sought out for us. Although we did our due diligence; cyber researching each listing's neighborhood, local amenities and traditions, Vince suggested taking an exploratory trip to each village before scheduling an appointment to see the property with Maria Laura and the seller's agent. What a grand concept! No use monopolizing everyone's valuable time needlessly, if the village did not resonate with us. Furthermore, Vince insisted on seeing the apartment in Morcella with an agent from the listing agency; Casambiente Immobiliare. Morcella is located in the province of Perugia, in the province of Terni. He reasoned that an agent based in the territory where the property was located would be more expertise about the real estate market pertaining to that area. Besides, we had been working with Maria Laura for more than ten months and although she knew precisely what we were looking for, she failed to steer us to the well-suited apartment listing in Morcella. Consequently, we made our own arrangements to tour the apartment with Johannes from Casambiente. We were to meet at an agreed upon location near Morcella in a few days.

We finished our second cup of coffee and filled with optimistic enthusiasm, wandered over to the immobiliare. It was nice to receive a warm welcome embrace from Mandy and Vanessa. Vanessa had long been aware of the list of properties we were interested in seeing; however, we were rather disappointed that no tours had been scheduled yet. Nevertheless, both ladies would begin contacting the listing agents immediately to set up as many property viewings as possible within the first week of our time in Orvieto. Frustrated that our property search was temporarily suspended, we were left to our own devices and set out to explore unescorted.

One by one, we visited the towns on our list. Allerona; depicted in the advertisement as a quaint medieval village with splendid views, boasted good local services and amenities. We explored Fabro and Civitella del Lago; a village located so high up in the mountains it nearly touched the sky. We stumbled upon Acqualoreto; a tiny jewel box of a picturesque hamlet that appeared to invite us in to investigate closer.

"Let's explore Acqualoreto on foot," Vince suggested. "Maybe we can find a place to have some lunch."

As Vince parked the car in the small piazza, adjacent to an ancient wishing well, I noticed a sign indicating that there was a restaurant in the only non-residential building in sight. Curiosity lured me to enter the cozy hotel-style breakfast room. With no one in the vicinity, I was free to wander through the establishment to gaze at the fascinating black and white photographs on the walls. When Vince came through the front door, he asked, "What is this? Are they serving lunch? It looks like this place is closed. Is anyone here?"

"I pointed to a hand-forged iron sign hanging above the stove. *La Cruccola*. I think it is an inn, or a bed and breakfast and this is must be the dining room." Just then, an elegant, kindly looking woman wearing her hair fashioned into a tight bun at the nape of her neck, appeared behind the counter, carrying a tray loaded with two wine glasses and two plates layered with slices of luscious Umbrian meats. She greeted us.

"*Buongiorno. Prego.*"

We have learned that *prego* can mean "You're welcome," "May I help you?" or "What would you like?" depending on the context. Vince asked if it was possible to have lunch.

"*Pranzo?*"

"*Si,*" the woman replied and motioned for us to sit at one of the tables while she continued to prepare an appetizing lunch for the lucky recipients of that tray, which she proceeded to carry out to one of the guest rooms upstairs.

"*Uno momento,*" she said as she passed us. I remained seated at the table, while my inquisitive husband wandered around to look at the vintage photographs hanging haphazardly on the wall. He stopped to stare at a picture of a young girl standing between two men, holding their hands. When the woman returned, Vince asked, "Is this you?"

"*Si. E mia padre e zio,*" she answered. "Yes, this is me with my father and uncle."

While placing a few eating utensils and napkins in front of us on the table, she explained furthermore in Italian and hand gestures, that the Bed and Breakfast had been in existence for more than one hundred years. Awestruck, we sat at the table while she served us an ample portion of an array of sliced meats and cheeses, some bread and a bottle of olive oil. It all looked delicious and we greedily dug in immediately. As we were enjoying the savory delicacies, she brought over a bowl, a mandolin slicer and a vegetable I had never seen before. She sliced the slightly yellow, cabbage-like vegetable, filling the bowl with thin slivers that broke apart when she tossed them with extra virgin olive oil, a syrupy, rich balsamic vinegar, salt and pepper, topping the mound with generous shavings of Parmesan cheese. She placed a liberal heap on each of our plates and left the remainder in the bowl, which she pushed toward us.

"Buon apetito," she said.

We couldn't believe how out-of-this-world delicious the simple, rustic salad was and how well it complemented the rest of our bountiful meal. Today, Vince and I often recall this memorable experience fondly and in hindsight, we regret not asking the woman what she used to create that flavorful salad.

After we paid the bill, the woman walked us to the front door as if we were leaving her home. Before closing the door behind us, she invited us to explore the medieval hamlet through a stone arch entrance by pointing to the arch and citing on a yellow sticky-note that Aqualoreto was twelve hundred years old. The meticulously maintained tiny, fable-like borgo was the most picturesque we had ever seen and surprisingly, completely inhabited with flourishing container gardens adorning every doorway. I took an impromptu picture of several conspicuous pairs of denim jeans hanging on a clothes line to dry in the sun. There was something utterly charming about that scene and I couldn't resist capturing it in a photograph.

Although the multitude of villages we visited in consideration of buying a home there were enchanting, none stirred our emotions the way Porano did, consequently, our exploring effort narrowed down our list of desirable properties to only a few credible finalists. When we arrived at the immobiliare to inform Vanessa that we dismissed some properties from our list, she was on the telephone with a listing agent, confirming an appointment to view a detached home in Baschi the following day. Located only a few minutes from Orvieto, Baschi was the quaint medieval village on the other side of the A1 autostrade that we fell in love with on our previous visit to this region. Vanessa was also able to schedule a tour of a small vacant apartment in a village with the beautiful name of Castiglione in Treverna. Tomorrow looked promising and we hoped it would be a very successful day.

We met Vanessa and Massimo early right after breakfast. First on the agenda was the tour of the home in Baschi. It was a gorgeous day and as if Baschi stretched out open arms to greet us, the village appeared particularly charming with colorful, neatly trimmed, filled-to-the-brim terra cotta pots lining the cobblestone streets leading to the vacant home.

The unit for sale, was a substantial free-standing building with living quarters on three floors. The entrance to the second level led to a spacious kitchen and dining area. In Italy, it is quite common to discover that the kitchen cabinetry, counters and appliances have been completely removed because the home owners often take the entire kitchen to their new residence, leaving the space as a blank canvas for the new owners. The vintage style kitchen was appealing and appeared to be constructed of good quality materials. The floor upstairs housed two sizable bedrooms, a bathroom, and a laundry area with lots of extra space for storage. The floor beneath the kitchen, offered a formal dining room and a cozy lounge with a lovely fireplace that kindled visions of cuddling up on the sofa in front of a romantic fire, or entertaining friends in this attractive space. A door opened to the outside, but regrettably the property lacked a suitable area designated for outdoor dining and although the windows throughout the home were plentiful, they were small and without panoramic views. Nevertheless, Vince and I agreed that the place inspired us and we could imagine ourselves living in this home. Just as we were about to leave, Vince flicked his hand along one of the interior walls, over an apparent wet spot, as small bits of mortar fell to the floor.

"There's moisture accumulating inside this wall," he declared as Vanessa and Massimo came over promptly to assess the conspicuous mottled area for themselves. "Look at this. It smells like mold," Vince asserted.

After careful examination, Massimo determined that the evident water damage was easily repairable at the owner's expense. Furthermore, he suggested consulting a building inspector or an engineer for a professional opinion, greatly easing the obvious doubtful expression on Vince's face. We milled about the apartment while Massimo made several phone calls and before long, a meeting was scheduled for three o'clock in the afternoon.

While Massimo ventured off to another appointment, Vanessa escorted us to Castiglione in Teverna for a tour of the second apartment on the agenda. This property, in a pleasant community near Orvieto was adorable, boasted outstanding views and plenty of antique charm, nevertheless, it was infinitesimal and required more work than we were willing to undertake. This concluded our property tours for today.

While Vince and I lazied over a long casual lunch in B&B Garibaldi, before taking a drive to a rocky hilltop hamlet ideally located just outside Orvieto's ancient city walls. We spotted it a few days ago and were curious about the village that appeared to be hand-carved right out of the rock. Perhaps there would be an apartment or a house for sale that would be perfect for us. It took a while to navigate our way to Rocca Ripesena without a map, unfortunately, once we arrived, we knew immediately that the tiny locality would not be a suitable place for us to own a vacation home. The streets were too narrow even for two cars to pass, there were no local amenities or services and resident parking was only possible in a community parking lot situated at the entrance to the tiny village. The panoramic views, though, were undeniably breathtaking.

At three o'clock, Vince and I were the first to arrive at the unit in Baschi to discuss the moisture problem in the interior wall. As we walked around the attractive building for a comprehensive look at the exterior, Maria Laura and Massimo, accompanied by two men arrived. After quick introductions to the building inspector and engineer, Maria Laura informed us that the professionals had been briefed on the issue at hand. The building inspector scrutinized the problem area with a protimeter which measured the moisture in the wall. He quickly determined that water indeed caused the non-carcinogenic mold to develop in the voids of the stone. Everyone spoke in Italian among themselves, talking through each other in genuine Italian style, complete with the typical exaggerated hand gestures. Eventually, the engineer directed the conversation to us in English and recommended building a spurious wall in front of the damaged one, reasoning that the persistent mold was extremely difficult and dangerous to remove. We couldn't believe his suggestion! Needless to say, Vince adamantly disapproved of such an inadequate solution to such a serious problem. Hiding the culprit by covering it up was an absolutely unacceptable way of dealing with mold spores, which have a propensity to spread if not properly removed. Although we both knew that this wonderful detached house would not be our Italian dream home, Vince still asked if it was possible to install a panoramic window in one of the exterior walls. Maria Laura replied discouragingly that approvals from the community, the region and the Italian government were required for such a renovation, which could take many months to obtain. That confirmed our decision to repress the pursuit of this property. Instead, Vince suggested taking a scenic drive over the mountains to visit Morcella.

Morcella

Once again, we drove down the winding road that had become so familiar to us, along the shore of Lago di Corbara toward Todi, where we turned north onto the E45 highway. The terrain was often industrialized and as I gazed out of the window, I secretly wished that the scenery was more lush and verdant like the area around Porano. However, soon countless enchanting hilltop villages dotted the landscape and rich farmland created a stunning, informal, backdrop for what appeared to be authentic "every day" life in Umbria. Vince turned off at the Marsciano exit and headed toward the business center of town where a banner stretched across a train trestle, with the words "*BENVENUTI A MARSCIANO*" emblazoned in bold letters and displayed more discreetly below "Welcome to Marsciano," greeted oncoming travelers. How utterly charming! My doubtful attitude quickly subsided as I became open to the idea of considering buying property in this area. We wound our way to the top of the hill where the road became the SS317, when a road sign indicated that Morcella was at the next left turn. By now, the surrounding landscape was absolutely breathtaking, but the newly constructed homes we passed were not the lovely, stone colored, enchanting property jewels I wished for. Although we were clearly in the countryside, I was disappointed that no centuries-old charm was tugging at my heartstrings.

"No," I said to Vince. It was a long-drawn-out "noooohhh" followed by "This is not what we're looking for, is it?"

The country road made a slight turn to the right and then to the left and then without warning, we came upon a small borgo surrounded by a medieval stone wall. Now, 'this' was much more like it.

"Well, maybe," I said, glancing at Vince who was smiling adorably.

"That is the medieval part of Morcella," Vince declared enthusiastically.

"Let's drive down this road and see where it goes."

On a computer web mapping service, Vince intensely studied this area, practically knowing every twist and turn in the road, he recognized landmarks from his endless hours of research. We drove down to the bottom of the hill, to a small one-way stone bridge with a portable stoplight. We loved the allure of only one stoplight in the village. When the light turned green, we drove across the bridge, stopped at the first inlet and got out of the car for an unencumbered view of Morcella. The ancient village looked like a beautiful castle perched up on a hill. Vince was determined to find the sight-points he identified on zoomed-in satellite computer imagery, specifically two trees framed by the arch entrance into Morcella's historic center. As he looked around, he discovered them in the distance and exclaimed with joy, "There they are, my two trees!" With that, he pointed to the trees in the landscape and then to the printed photo he held in his hand. "Those are 'my' trees!"

Vince guided me across the street, on the road facing the village, he showed me exactly where the apartment was.

"That's the terrazzo, that's the living room window and the little one next to it, that is the kitchen window. What do you think?" he asked. "Can you imagine the views from that terrace?" It honestly looked like a fairytale village. Morcella was undeniably stunning.

"It's beautiful, honey. Anyway, since we have the appointment with Johannes tomorrow, let's just go and see the inside," I suggested. Almost breathing a sigh of relief, Vince felt as if he had won a battle by successfully persuading me to tour the apartment with an agent. We drove back to Orvieto, and after a casual dinner in town, returned to the B&B to anxiously await the following morning when we were scheduled to meet with a representative from Casambiente Immobiliare.

Monday, March 2, 2011, at 9:30 in the morning, we met Johannes in the parking lot at the Metano gas station located near the E45 highway exit toward Marsciano. As usual, we arrived early and wondered how we would know who Johannes was. Martine; Casambiente's Administrative Assistant, only instructed us to meet at the gas station. Vince waited in the car while I checked out Bar Tevere; the adjacent coffee shop, to see if anyone looked as if they were waiting to meet a stranger. An obvious local favorite, this country roadside gas station/coffee shop felt friendly, although the place was hectic with rush-hour customers paying for gas and demanding a morning jolt of espresso. One of the interior walls was brightly decorated with the words *Buona Fortuna*; Good Luck in Italian written boldly across the entire mural. I considered this a positive sign for us.

No one at the coffee shop looked like a real estate agent. When I returned to the car, a handsome man with wavy dark hair drove up next to us simultaneously, smiled, rolled down his window and asked, "*Di Lorenzo?*" Vince nodded his head, acknowledging agent and client had found each other.

Johannes approached with a warm, firm hand outstretched to greet us. He was tall, well built, seemingly in his mid to late forty's and appeared to be an energetic, professional who gave us the immediate impression that we would enjoy working with him. He was engaging and spoke perfect English with a wonderful German accent as he suggested that we could leave our car parked at the gas station and ride with him. Prior to viewing the apartment in Morcella, Johannes offered to show us a fair comparison unit in the historic center of Marsciano. We were duly dazzled and delighted with his wonderful demeanor and proactive approach, an immediate, clear difference from the customer service Maria Laura provided.

As we left the parking lot, Johannes became a tour guide, enlightening us with interesting historic facts about Marsciano. Marsciano was the most important township of the Mid-Tiber Valley, boasting a fortified castle entrusted to the Bulgarelli family of Montreale in 975 AD. Due to Marsciano's central position in relation to Perugia, Todi and Orvieto, the territory inhabited during the Bronze Age and Etruscan times, has been flourishing in its existence since the Middle Ages.

Monday was the weekly market day in Marsciano; therefore, parking would be easier at one of the public lots below the historic center. A unique outdoor elevator took us to the top of the village where an American woman named Marcia was selling her apartment located on the most prominent street in the central part of town.

"Here we are," Johannes said as he guided us to a corner building with a narrow front door. "We are in the historic center and this is the apartment I want to show you."

Johannes knocked on the front door before opening it with a master key. We walked up a narrow staircase to the living room where the seller was engaged in a phone call, but motioned for us to enter the living room. While she finished her conversation, Johannes highlighted the features of the living space. Marcia's obvious artistic flair was evident by the way she decorated her home in the rich jewel-tone colors that have always appealed to me. The fireplace was adorned with hand stencils and the walls were faux painted to mimic age-old charm. Since the apartment was officially a one-bedroom dwelling, a strategically placed partition created a cozy private sleeping nook for an occasional overnight guest.

After Marcia concluded her phone conversation, she introduced herself and invited us to feel at home as we looked around. An expat from Portland, Oregon, Marcia bought the apartment four years ago to utilize as a part-time home during her multiple visits to Umbria annually. However, as life often dictates, an unexpected change presented an opportunity to reside in Italy full time which demanded more living space. Therefore, Marcia reluctantly placed her ideally located apartment on the real estate market. We were the first potential buyers to tour the property since the listing was published.

The second floor encompassed an adequate storage area and sizable eat-in kitchen with great big French doors that opened to a balcony overlooking the street. It was lovely to see the local market in full swing. Marsciano looked like an interesting, thriving town.

Johannes led the way to the third floor as we continued touring the master bedroom, bathroom and a cozy laundry area with a clothes washing machine. Marcia's apartment was indeed an attractive, comfortable space, but we disliked a multi-level house and the balcony was only large enough for a bistro table and two chairs. This was not a suitable home for us.

As this was our first meeting with Johannes, he was only slightly aware of our property Wish List based on our request to see the apartment in Morcella. However, after hearing our assessment of Marcia's home, he quickly realized our mission, assuring us that we made a genuine connection with an agent who clearly understood our dream.

On our way back to the car, Johannes pointed out the Palazzo Pietromarchi, informing us that the ancient, completely restored palace was the current location of the Living Museum of Brickwork and Terracotta; the most vital industry to the area. All the little bits of local information Johannes provided, helped us to form a bond with the vicinity.

From Marsciano, we headed to Morcella via the same road that Vince and I travelled the day before on our exploratory visit. Johannes drove through Morcella's newer construction neighborhood and past the archaic bell tower which marked the entrance to the picturesque medieval hamlet through a massive stone arch, where he stopped precisely at an imposing door that epitomized age-old charm. It was truly a magnificent arched door, made of heavy wood, adorned with period appropriate iron embellishments. We were overly enthusiastic to finally tour the apartment that Vince discovered on the internet more than six months ago; the apartment of our dreams, the apartment that seemed ideal for us!

"This is the front door," Johannes said, "it opens to a common entry way to the four apartments housed in this building. The apartment we are going to see, is on the top floor and it is the only one with an outdoor terrace."

When our agent opened the magnificent door, Vince and I gasped with excitement at the sight of the foyer, with a vaulted ceiling, imposing brick arches and a terra-cotta stained, porcelain tiled staircase leading to the higher floors. A *cantina*; a cellar located in the corner of the ground-floor foyer belonged to the apartment we were going to inspect. We were pleasantly surprised to see that the cantina had ample space for storing at least two bicycles, or a vespa motor-scooter, firewood, wine and more. Vince's eyes lit up and became the size of saucers when Johannes pointed out a sink with hot and cold running water mounted to the back wall. Vince was thrilled!

As we walked up the stairs, we heard children's laughter and friendly voices coming from the two apartments on the second floor. It was a pleasant sound I liked very much.

"This is the door to the apartment," Johannes said, as he aimed for the door on the right. "That one," pointing to the door on the left, "belongs to a family who lives in Rome. They use this as their residence when they come for occasional week-ends."

Johannes pushed the door open and moved aside to let us enter. Vince entered first and I instantly recognized by the look on my husband's face that *this* was our Italian dream home. It was the same look I saw on his face when we entered our home in San Carlos for the first time. We never looked at another house after that. When you know…you just know! We had found our apartment! Beyond a shadow of a doubt, we had found our home! I was almost too excited to breathe.

"Very nice" were the first words Vince uttered as he looked around while Johannes opened the windows and shutters to let in the natural light. In spite of the gray morning, the apartment appeared bright and spacious.

"Excellent" was Vince's second comment. I was reluctant to reveal my feelings in case we could not afford this amazing apartment. The high vaulted, sloped ceiling with an attractive brick fireplace was the focal point of the great room with which could easily accommodate a dining and lounge area. Johannes pointed out the recessed lighting and the stone-accented architectural detail in the pony-wall that separated the entry way from the kitchen. The handsome kitchen cabinetry and granite counters appeared to be in excellent condition and the gas stovetop and oven were just what I had hoped for. Then Johannes opened the large glass door to the terrazzo and nearly "sealed the deal" for Vince. We both gasped in awe as the most amazing view imaginable revealed itself.

"The terrazzo overlooks the Tiber Valley," Johannes explained, "and the river in front of that ancient estate is the Nestore. Over there in the distance, is Todi and to the left is Marsciano. You're just minutes from town."

We couldn't believe the expansive breathtaking panorama before us. It overlooked verdant farmland, rolling hills, medieval castles, a small church, the Nestore River and hilltop villages in every direction. We were astounded that this gorgeous apartment was priced just slightly above our budget.

Back inside, a large empty area, which we both immediately referred to as the "Man Cave," featuring a cabinet sink and a clothes washer was a perfectly convenient space to stockpile a barbecue and idle outdoor furniture. Vince commented that the apartment provided more storage space than our home in California. The cozy bathroom was in excellent condition with a shower, bidet, toilet and a large porcelain sink mounted in an attractive quartz counter vanity. Oddly, there was even an extra lockable space accessible by a ladder in the bathroom. The same vaulted ceilings were featured in the two bedrooms, each large enough to accommodate a queen-size bed in addition to spars furnishings. The largest bedroom featured a charming stone niche, which gave the space period-style character by paying homage to the past. All the windows were set in 16-inch-thick stone walls, topped with the typical sturdy, dark wooden headers. The apartment was fantastic! Everything about it was perfect for us, we felt it deep in our souls!

To see the entire borgo, Johannes suggested taking a stroll through Morcella. There are not enough words to adequately describe how much the tiny medieval village resonated with us. It was lovely enchanting, charming and down-right adorable. The apartment was located on Via Del Priorato, an attractive street that branched out from Piazza San Silvestri; Morcella's main square, where the Chiesa di San Silvestri was built in 1027AD. Only a few streets comprised the ancient village, one even prettier than the next. There was a house with an old water well by the front door, a street with an arched cross-over that housed a room with a window, and there was a turret hidden away deep in one of the village corners, hinting to Morcella's primordial past as a medieval castle. Indicative of homeowner's pride, many of the front doors and balconies were beautified with potted plants and flowers. Through the church breezeway, Johannes escorted us to the predominant community parking lot adjacent to a sports court and a children's playground, complete with swings and hobble-horses where mothers and grandmothers sat in white plastic chairs as they watched their children chase playfully after each other. Morcella emanated a wonderful, friendly feeling and Vince and I loved it!

Our Second Offer
THIS Is It!

Unfortunately, due to a previously scheduled appointment with another client, Johannes reluctantly turned us over to an associate from a collaborating agency for the rest of the afternoon. Graham Lane was the co-founder of La Porte Verde; a property sales and management service located in the heart of Umbria. Expats from England, Graham and his wife Lin moved to Italy thirteen years ago to pursue their dream of buying a historic country manor to restore and transform into a lodging establishment and permanent residence. In the quaint village of Castello della Forme near Morcella, they eventually created Villa Rosa; which today operates as a thriving Bed and Breakfast.

Graham was concisely briefed about the apartment we inspected in Morcella, but nevertheless, he insisted on showing us another ownership option in neighboring Compignano, where a developer who acquired a derelict estate, surrounded by typical rolling hills and wooded landscape, was spearheading a project to restore the former landholding to an old-world style, condominium complex built to the highest standards. The Commune di Marsciano and the capital city of Perugia already approved an elaborate proposal, which included several residential units with picturesque views, access to a community swimming pool, a coffee bar and an alimentari. Graham bloviated that the project was a wise investment, as substantiated by a young American couple from Illinois who already purchased one of the condos to use as an occasional vacation home and rental income property. Although it was indeed a fascinating concept, the project was of no interest to us.

Since Vince and I were impatiently searching for an opportunity to discuss our ideas about the sensational apartment in Morcella, we asked Graham to take us to a local restaurant so that we could organize our plan of action over a leisurely lunch.

Graham brought us to Trattoria Rosatelli; a popular neighborhood restaurant located on a busy intersection in the center of Marsciano. I must admit that at first glance, Rosatelli did not appear to be the charming, congenial eating establishment that we had hoped for. Nevertheless, from the moment we walked through the front door, we recognized that undeniable feeling of welcome which we loved so much in these small-town Italian restaurants. The dining room crowded with guests, was a bit noisy, but in a good way. A waiter rushing to deliver plates heaped with scrumptious mounds of pasta smothered in sauce, acknowledged our presence immediately and nodded toward a vacant table, as if to say, "Ciao! Benvenuti! Just sit anywhere." Graham wandered through the restaurant as if it was his home, greeting several of the diners while he searched for a suitable table for us. Suddenly, he spotted his wife and a friend sitting in one of the dining rooms. While Graham walked over to say hello, a perfectly cozy table for two near a corner fireplace became vacant. Vince expeditiously guided me to it and pulled out a chair for me, inviting me to sit. The warmth of the fire on my back felt toasty and warm and as I became absorbed in our surroundings, I suddenly felt completely comfortable being a part of this local crowd. Overwhelmed with excitement, I was looking forward to beginning our conversation. Vince and I had so much to talk about.

Before leaving the restaurant, Graham stopped by our table to say that he would return in a few hours to drive us back to our car. He seemed to understand that we needed to talk privately.

Rosatelli was an amazingly popular restaurant, with a three-course menu offering a choice of several entrees at a paltry pre-fixed price of only 13€ per person. The first course *(Primi)* was a pasta dish, followed by the second course *(Secondi)*, including a course of vegetables *(Contori)*. Each serving was a generous portion of tasty, made-from-scratch, Italian home cooking. The food was an unbelievable value for the money.

"This is our kind of place," Vince said, "if we lived here, this would be our local hang-out!" A tall, lanky, waiter came over with his notepad.

"Prego," he said, anxiously taking our order. Vince ordered our menu selections in the best Italian he knew, including a liter of the house red wine and a bottle of sparkling water. When the wine was served, my husband held his glass upright and moved in closer to me as he made a toast and we began our heart-to-heart discussion.

"So, what do you think of the apartment?" Vince asked.

"I think it is gorgeous and it has everything on our wish list; plenty of storage, a nice kitchen, two bedrooms, it's located in a beautiful medieval village and. (that was a long drawn out "and" to emphasize the importance of the next statement) most importantly, it has that fantastic terrace with an amazing view!"

"I know. Honey, I love it too!" I replied. "I love the apartment, but nevertheless, it is so far from Orvieto. Isn't that deviating from our original plan? Furthermore, I don't like the atypical industrial area we have to drive through to get here and there are no services in Morcella, no coffee bar or bakery, therefore we would have to drive to Marsciano for everything. Didn't we want to live in a village within walking distance of local amenities?"

"I agree, but, my dear, Marsciano is only a five-minute drive away and it has all the stores and services we need, including a weekly market. Wouldn't it be fun to go to the market every Monday? And Orvieto is only a forty-minute drive away. I drive forty minutes to Bob's house every week and we drive that distance to visit Stan and Carole all the time. In fact, we drive forty minutes to go almost anywhere, all the time, without thinking about it," Vince pleaded. "Just compare going to Orvieto to going to San Francisco; it could be our day trip to 'the city.' Besides, it is much less touristy on this side of the E45." Vince stressed every positive point of buying the apartment and, honestly, I agreed with everything he said.

"Yes, all that is absolutely true and I love that Morcella is obviously a multi-generational village," I added to Vince's enthusiasm. "Children of all ages were playing on the sports court and I believe that as long as there are children growing up in the village, Morcella will continue to thrive. Do you love the apartment enough to make an offer? Can we afford it?" In a brainstorming manner, I blurted out all my questions at once.

The seller was an American named Ann Geneva; a graduate from the University of California in Berkley. Ann lived in England for a brief period of time before relocating to Morcella, where she resided for five years. She was currently living in Morocco, intending to buy a beach-house. Eighteen months ago, Ann listed the Morcella apartment for sale at a substantially higher price, subsequently, no offers were generated. Armed with this information, Vince recognized an opportunity and proposed making a strategic initial offer slightly below the current asking price.

"What do you think?" he asked with his eyes twinkling and a small amount of perspiration glistening on his forehead. "I think we should make an offer, although, I don't want to carry a mortgage," he added almost thinking out loud, "I wonder when we will have to come up with the money?"

"At this point, I suppose there is no harm in asking Johannes to review the buying process with us to make sure that we understand what to expect," I suggested, hoping to initiate a phone call to indicate that we were seriously *contemplating* buying the apartment, without uttering words of commitment which, at the moment, still seemed too bold and nerve-wracking to me.

"OK then, hand me the phone and let me ask Johannes what happens next if we make an offer today. I'll ask him specific questions, just for informational purposes," Vince said. "I suppose it will be necessary for us to open a local bank account for transferring funds," he continued, as I handed him the phone. I was smiling from ear-to-ear and as kindred spirits, I knew that in spite of the serious expression on Vince's face, his heart was smiling too.

I heard the phone ringing on the other side.

"*Pronto! Ciao, Vince?*" Johannes obviously had the Caller ID feature enabled on his mobile phone. It felt surreal listening to Vince's side of the conversation as I concluded that once an offer was accepted, we would have to leave an "earnest" deposit, which would eventually be applied toward the purchase price of the property. A few months following acceptance, a deed signing would be scheduled in Perugia, at which time the remaining balance of the purchase price was payable in cash or by check from a local bank. If we were unable to attend the deed signing in person, we could relinquish Power of Attorney to Casambiente to sign on our behalf. A notaio would oversee our best interest in contractual closure.

Vince took a deep breath as he concluded the conversation with a promise to call back after discussing his newly acquired knowledge with me. Together, we needed a moment to establish a plausible timeline and absorb the reality of the big step we were about to take toward homeownership in Italy. Johannes's unsolicited comment described Ann as "a dogmatic piece of work" meaning that she was a difficult seller to work with.

When Vince hung up the phone, we looked at each other with smiles that felt as if they were frozen on our faces and for a moment, neither of us said a word waiting for the other person to speak. Then, after more brainstorming, discussing, and carefully weighing the odds, Vince declared that he was ready to make a verbal offer! Oh, my goodness! I felt sure that everything would work out in our favor this time. 'This' apartment was the reason why we lost the apartment in Porano. God was watching over us when that offer fell through because He had a better plan in store for us and from the bottom of my heart, I felt that THIS was it. This apartment was meant for us. This one had God's blessing.

I trembled like a baby-bird as Vince placed the call and spoke pragmatically when he made an offer of 20% below the list price. Johannes felt that it was a good, strong offer and vowed to contact Ann immediately.

We were on a nervous adrenaline rush, when our lunch was brought to the table. Famished, we dug right in and just as we predicted, the food was healthful and delicious! We shared our pasta choices unable to decide which tasted better. The sausages and veal were cooked to perfection. Vince poured more wine just when the phone rang. I heard Johannes's voice on the other side. Surprisingly, Ann's counteroffer was only a few thousand dollars higher. Vince accepted without remission, unequivocally, sealing the deal and *just-like-that we bought our Italian dream home!* I couldn't believe it. This was momentous and monumental!

"Oh, my God!" I exclaimed, clapping my hands in victory and unable to breathe. "Did we do it? Did we just buy a home in Italy?"

Like me, Vince was outwardly emotional. Simultaneously, we stepped away from the table with our arms outstretched as we reached for each other in a congratulatory hug.

"Yes, Treat, I believe we did. All we have to do is pay for it." Vince replied. "Now," he continued as he let out a long pause, "when are we going to tell my mom?"

"What do you mean? We'll tell her when we get home and we'll tell Ellen too. I can't wait to share our happy news with our family!"

"No," Vince said adamantly, "I want to wait until we sign the papers and it is official. Johannes wants to meet us tomorrow morning for coffee at Bar Rosetti in Marsciano. We have to fill out and sign some documents, because all we have at this moment, is an accepted verbal offer."

It wasn't long before Graham appeared at our table ready to take us back to our parked car at the gas station. It was difficult not to mention a word of what had just happened. We were on cloud nine!

After some idle conversation, a cordial thank you and goodbye, we watched Graham drive away before Vince and I exploded with ideas. Mine were about furnishing and decorating our sensational new home while Vince was consumed with ideas of how we were going to pull funds together.

"I would like to ask Johannes if we can see the apartment once more before we fly home so I can to take room and window measurements."

"Honey, that's a great idea, I can't wait to decorate," I replied. "I won't be able to sleep tonight. I just love the kitchen. I can't believe it has granite counters and beautiful wooden cabinetry. It's obvious that an American had a hand in designing the apartment."

"We must open a bank account in Marsciano," Vince replied, without reacting to my comment. "I am sure that Johannes will help us with that. More than likely, we will have to give him the earnest deposit immediately."

"The first thing I am going to do," I continued with comments about what was important to me, "is get rid of all those dingy, old-lady curtains hanging in every window. I don't want any curtains anywhere; I want to flaunt the apartment's natural light and airy ambiance. Nevertheless, we will need some kind of window covering to shield us from the sun on the terrazzo door. I bet it gets very hot in that living room on a sunny day."

Before turning onto the E45 highway to Orvieto, we took a slow drive through Marsciano to familiarize ourselves with the city. Although there were no large shopping malls (thank God), there was a good Home Improvement store called the Brico, Euronics sold home electronics and appliances and the Conad; an American-style supermarket rivaled the supermarkets I patronized at home. There were several *mom-and-pop* butcher shops, clothing stores, banks, bakeries and a few small establishments that sold specialty items from the area. It seemed that anything we required to setup our home or our hearts desired was available in Marsciano. In an industrial neighborhood closer to approaching the highway, I noticed a warehouse that appeared to be a second-hand shop. I was so excited and asked Vince to stop the car so I could investigate. The huge warehouse was filled to the rafters with used furniture, house hold items, mirrors, doors, wrought iron and decorative objects. I was looking forward to hunting for treasures when it was time to move in!

We were exhausted when we arrived at B&B Garibaldi. It had been an incredible day, an important day, a successful day! Our search for our Italian dream home was over!

4. We Found Our Home in Italy

Bright and early the next morning, we returned to Marsciano for our important meeting with Johannes. Vince drove to the Rosetti Coffee Bar as if he was already familiar with the area. Although the coffee bar was located next to a tire shop in the industrial neighborhood, it was also across the street from a winery and the freshly brewed coffee smelled divine, the warm *cornetti* (croissants) and pastries looked temptingly delicious. Johannes arrived just as we were getting out of the car. He greeted us eagerly and ordered cappuccinos while I settled at a suitable table for us to conduct business and review the necessary paperwork.

As Johannes pulled a stack of documents from his briefcase, he concisely explained that our signature reconciled our verbal offer into a legally binding formal agreement. Vince asked pertinent questions while visions of decorating danced through my head as I allegedly tried to follow their conversation. We readily signed the paperwork where instructed and agreed to follow Johannes to his office in Perugia to draw up the official documents for the actual sale of the property. Everything was going so smoothly, almost dreamlike, as if manipulated by fate.

When we walked out to our cars, Vince asked Johannes if we could stop by the apartment again to measure the rooms. I knew that when we got back to California, I would be planning and imaging how each room would look. Oh, how I couldn't wait to begin glancing through magazines and scouring thrift shops for just the right accessories to enhance the medieval charm of the apartment and the building. It was wonderful to establish our Italian home completely from inception!

"Wait a minute," Johannes suddenly said when we arrived in Morcella's community parking lot as he reached for one of the documents in his briefcase. It was a rough outlined drawing of Morcella.

"Before we go inside, let's take a look at something here." With the map in his hand, he walked through the village arch entrance to the rear of the apartment building and said, "Yes, here it is," as he pushed open a chain-link fence gate and guided us through it.

"That small garden belongs to the apartment," Johannes said, pointing to a tiny piece of land overgrown with weeds directly underneath the apartment's living room window.

"Really?" Vince replied.

"OK, that's nice. If we are ever here long enough, I can plant a lemon tree and grow a few tomatoes."

We accessed the apartment building through the magnificent, imposing front door and walked up the stairs. This time, when Johannes stepped aside to let us in, even though a bit pre-mature, ownership pride filled our hearts soon as we entered the apartment. Soon, this beautiful apartment would be *our* home!

Vince and Johannes measured each room while I examined the kitchen cabinets for actual storage space. I also took a closer look at the state of the appliances and captured a snapshot of the clothes washer display panel so that I could translate the control selections from Italian to English when I got home. There was an unattractive, free standing, white cabinet in the guest bedroom that I hoped to repurpose as a nightstand. The apartment was in excellent condition with no cracks or chipping paint anywhere, nevertheless, there was a plethora of tiny picture nails that would have to be extracted from the walls, leaving holes to be patched. Consequently, the walls would need an entire fresh coat of paint. We operated all the windows and shutters and were pleased to discover that all were in good working order. With our comprehensive inspection completed, we followed Johannes to Perugia.

Casambiente

During the thirty-minute drive to the Casambiente Agency office, Vince and I talked non-stop about the apartment. Seeing it through the eyes of soon-to-be owners, we looked at things differently. Ann left three beautiful terra-cotta planters and a large market umbrella on the terrazzo. I was eager to incorporate the planters into my decorating design and Vince was looking forward to utilizing the "man cave" as a space to store a barbecue and outdoor furniture, tools and other *manly* things.

When we arrived at the office, Johannes proudly invited us to view the expansive panorama of Perugia before us, surrounded by snow-capped mountains, it was breathtaking. He explained that the day-to-day's business operation was managed in his private residence; a low-energy, sustainable home which he built from the ground up with his father and a small crew of laborers. The contemporary style, wooden house was quite impressive, with temperature-controlled floor-to-ceiling living room windows that adjusted automatically to the sun's light. The energy efficient building, designed to eliminate negative environmental impact through sensible planning, was created by Johannes's father who lived in Germany. Together, father and son established a lucrative business. Selling these structures in Germany and in Italy was Casambiente's primary focus, while selling Italian real estate was a secondary trade.

After a brief tour of the residence, Johannes led us to the business office where he introduced us to Luisa; his wife and Martine; Casambiente's Administrative Assistant. As coincidence would have it, Martine was an ex-pat from Belgium and spoke fluent Dutch; another sign that the apartment in Morcella was meant for us! Both ladies were extremely warm and cordial and we became instant friends.

Vince and I were motivated to fill out the necessary paperwork and sign on the dotted line; solidifying our commitment to purchase the extraordinary property in Morcella. Luisa and Martine worked diligently as they turned our verbal offer into a formal agreement and the preliminary bill of sale into a contract. Lacking patience was my foible, I became restless and stepped outside for a breath of fresh air, leaving Vince to answer methodical questions about our financial stability and other equally boring subjects. As I lingered outside admiring the scenic beauty, I noticed a small pile of seemingly discarded, terra cotta tiles on the ground. I stooped down to admire more closely the workmanship of each of the exquisitely hand-painted, star-shaped pieces unlike any I had ever seen. Each one was a little *fresco*. I asked Luisa about their origin, how old they were and why they were tossed aside. She explained that they were salvaged tiles from a remodeled home recently sold to a client. Acutely aware how much I liked them; Luisa offered one of the tiles to me.

"You can choose one," she said sweetly.

"Really?" I responded, looking at Vince for his reaction, overwhelmed by Luisa's generosity.

"Look at her," Vince said as he chuckled at my excitement, well aware of my compulsion for handmade Italian tiles. "Now she won't know which one to choose." Of course he was right. I inspected each one carefully before identifying my favorite; depicting a woman combing her long yellow hair. The tile appeared to have some history and I couldn't wait to find a place of honor for it in our California home. I loved this very special souvenir from this very special trip to Italy.

At long last, the forms were completed and signed. Martine consolidated the paperwork and handed us a folder thick with documents representing our copies of the offer, formal agreement and the bill of sale. Luisa gave us a letter from Ann Geneva which was simply addressed to: *Dear Clients.* We couldn't wait to read it. In a week or two, Martine would notify us via email when the Deed Signing was scheduled so that we could arrange to arrive in Italy a few days prior. To complete the final necessary step, Luisa offered to meet us at the UniCredit Banca di Roma in Marsciano to assist with opening an account so that we could transfer the initial deposit to the seller immediately after our return to California. Following several handshakes and many all-around hugs, Vince and I drove back to Orvieto. We were thrilled beyond belief!

In the car, I reached for Ann's letter. Her amazing, heartfelt composition will be a treasure for as long as we own the apartment:

Information for clients about the wonderful apartment in Morcella

Dear Clients,

From before I moved into the apartment five years ago, I was sure I'd made a happy choice. All the Italians I mentioned it to said, "Oh, Morcella, that's a NICE village!" When pressed as to why, they didn't seem to know how to respond. Indeed it turned out to be a place, with people who welcomed strangers, always had a good atmosphere and was well-maintained, quiet yet thriving.

Each August the village gets together and runs its annual festa for a week or so of festivities and people come from all around to eat and enjoy. Everyone pitches in to do the cooking, serving, cleaning up, etc. The revenue for this pays the costs of maintenance for the village for the whole next year.

The pride of Morcella is its beautiful painted eighteenth century church, right across from the apartment entrance. It seems as if every other person I met went misty eyed and said they'd been married in that church! I have never seen another of its kind. It originally dates from the eleventh century!

One thing about Morcella you should be especially pleased about is that three or four years ago, the Marsciano Commune voted to spend the entire grant for village improvement from the European Union (600,000 Euros) exclusively on Morcella, rather than any of the many surrounding villages. This was because Morcella was judged as the most beautiful village in the Commune!

In practical terms this meant that for an entire year, all the streets were dug up! It was a real nuisance, all the beautiful pots of plants had to be moved inside, we walked over planks, but at the end of the year the entire village had new tasteful period lighting, totally new water pipes, new electric wiring, new gas pipes, all the substructure was replaced and the cobblestones relaid. At the end we were all proud and the only cost to us at each house was a connection fee of 60 Euros. This work should not need to be touched for 100 more years at least! This is a rare thing for a medieval village such as Morcella.

Now for the best part, the neighbors! This building could easily have been converted into six or even eight apartments. So we are lucky we are only four. Each of the people converted their apartment (including the Perugian family who did mine), to the highest standards. The fact that they did it for themselves rather than for resale says it all (the Perugian family lived in this apartment for seven years before they sold it due to the grandfather's ill health).

All the neighbors are the nicest people in the world, as only Italians can be. The first two apartments belong to two families. One has Irma the widowed grandmother, her lovely son Silvano and his wife Sara, with their young son Michelangelo (only in Italy). They are the kindest people with a good sense of humor! Silvano is a builder and Sara a hairdresser who works in Perugia. Silvano supervised the waterproof lining and re-tiling of my terrace.

Next door to them are Mirko and Mirella, again the loveliest people imaginable, with their two young sons Vittorio; quiet and studious and Giacamo; young sweet and energetic. Mirella stays at home with them and is admirable in every way, as is Mirko who is a geometer whose offices are in the castle viewed from the sitting room window. Mirko providentially organizes our collective annual building and contents insurance, which costs much less this way. It amounts to a mere 100 Euros annually; cheaper than we could have gotten it individually and it also helps that we have had no claims. We also pay about the same amount per year for the electricity and upkeep of the common areas. In addition, each apartment sweeps and washes the stairs and the common entrance. You can do this yourself, or do as I do and hire a village girl to do it (for eight Euros per month for one hour per week). This way the "house" is always immaculate, and the relationships among the neighbors have always been harmonious.

The people on your floor are again a lovely small family of three who live in Rome. Claudio is a senior electrician, Allessandra works for the phone company, and their young daughter is a very girly girl, a delight and very friendly. Alex speaks English, and my only complaint is that they are able to make it to Morcella so rarely.

I often had problematic neighbors where I lived in the US and England, so this has been a pure joy! I always loved coming back to this beautiful medieval village; it always looked magical to me, especially after a long absence.

One more thing, the two antique stone troughs in front of the building were mine (originally from my English garden), but I am leaving them as a tribute to my lovely neighbors and the beautiful medieval granary they decorate.

Enjoy!

Ann Geneva.

Although we were not scheduled to meet Luisa at the bank in Marsciano until eleven o'clock, we arrived early the next morning to wander around town. As soon-to-be home-owners and part time residents, we looked at everything from a new perspective. When we were in Italy, Marsciano was going to be our home town, where we would attend community events, go to the weekly market, shop, dine in restaurants and make new friends.

As we did with Johannes, we parked the car near the community elevator and took the lift up to the historic center. We acknowledged passerby when our eyes met and bid them *Bouna giornata;* Good day. We window-shopped at the boutiques on the Corso Umberto, somewhat surprised at the high-quality merchandise for sale in such a humble village.

Soon, we saw Luisa searching for a parking space, we walked over to meet her, feeling enthusiastic about opening our own account. Signor Luigi Vincenti welcomed our business. He didn't speak a word of English, nevertheless, with Luisa acting as our translator, we had no problem completing the necessary paperwork and before long, Signor Vincenti presented us with a checkbook and an Automatic Teller Machine card for cash withdrawals at local ATM machines. We were elated to be an official part of the community!

We offered to take Luisa out for lunch to celebrate our new status, although she was unfortunately unable to join us. Familiar with only one restaurant in town, we returned to Rosatelli and ordered the lunch *menu di giorno;* the lunch menu of the day. I felt as if we were in a charming Italian movie. *How could this possibly be real?* Our lunch was more delicious than the first time we dined at this restaurant, or even the second time, and our conversation was more spirited. We vowed to take Italian lessons as soon as we returned to California. Instead of relinquishing Power of Attorney to Casambiente, Vince was bound and determined to attend the Deed Signing ceremony in Perugia, which meant that he would sign on my behalf so that I could accumulate my vacation time at work until autumn, when we planned to furnish the apartment and officially move in.

It was gently raining and already dark when we arrived at the front door of B&B Garibaldi in the early evening. Vince inserted the key into the front door lock, when much to his surprise, he felt the key snap in two as he turned it to unlock the door, leaving the stem in the keyhole. "Oh great! Now what do we do?" Vince said as he pulled the remaining part of the key out of the lock and looked bewildered at it in his hand.

"I don't know," I answered. "David emphatically asked us not to ring the doorbell because his grandmother was always asleep. Let's try knocking on the door or calling his name. I believe that's his balcony."

"I'm not going to yell out his name in the street," Vince retorted.

I reminded him that the only people we knew in Orvieto were the real estate agents.

"Let's see if anyone is in the office. Maybe they can call David for us on his mobile phone," I suggested. Since it seemed like it was our only option, we headed to the Corso Cavour, when as luck would have it, we ran into David who was on his way home. Without hesitation, Vince showed him the piece of the key and explained what had occurred. David laughed and said that it was not the first time this had happened, he should have changed the lock long ago. He asked us to follow him to a locksmith in town, where we were fixed up with a new key in minutes. At the B&B, David produced a pair of needle-nose pliers from his pocket which were attached to his keychain and dug out the key fragment from the lock as if he had done this task before. Once inside, we all laughed about the comical mishap, then Vince and I scurried up to our room, eager to unwind from our busy day.

We spent the remaining days of our time in Umbria enjoying long drives in the countryside and exploring local stores. We made the rounds to say goodbye to Carlo from Trattoria da Carlo, Patrizia from the Sapore dell'Umbria store, Paolo from Cafe Barrique and Emilio from the Dai Fratelli specialty meat delicatessen. We told them that we would see them again when we returned in September.

Signing on the Dotted Line; May 20, 2011

During the long flight home, we spoke about the best way to break the news of our Italian home ownership status to Vince's mother. Vince was concerned that she might feel abandoned, that we would move to Italy permanently, or that we spent our money foolishly. After brainstorming a few scenarios, Vince appropriately decided that he would announce our fantastic news in his own delicate way and in his own time. On the other hand, I couldn't wait to tell my sister. I knew that Ellen would be more than thrilled and share our joy. After telling Ellen and Vince's mother of our happy news, we were eager to tell Stan and Carole too. Carole had been seriously ill since early January and we hoped that the news of our Italian home with an extra bedroom to accommodate her and Stan as often as possible, would cheer her up.

I don't know how we made it through the next few months. We continuously felt as if we were on cloud nine! Everyone shared in our excitement and while Vince took care of mundane details such as money transfers and other financial matters, I could think and talk about nothing but furnishing and decorating our new home. *We bought a home in Italy, somebody pinch me!* Buying the apartment was a cash transaction, therefore, to determine the best time to transfer funds to our Italian bank account, Vince kept a constant watch on the ever-changing cost of euros.

Fluctuation of even a percentage point made a significant difference in how many dollars we converted to euros to pay the balance of the purchase price of the apartment. I definitely had the more enjoyable task of transposing our new apartment into a "home."

I corresponded with Martine frequently, asking her for website recommendations to research for furniture models and price comparisons. I acquired countless decorating magazines featuring French and Italian style furnishings and searched online auction websites willing to deliver the larger pieces of furniture to Morcella. All my senses were wholly fulfilled and I was completely in my glory. There was so much to organize, contemplate and envision. It was a new and exciting time in our lives and I realized every day how much I loved that Vince and I were energized by our new dream, our new goal.

Selectively, I collected items to incorporate into my decorating scheme, personal things indicative of our laid-back personality and my own original photo art to reflect my creative talent. A pair of wrought iron candlesticks, a hand-painted serving tray, quilts and a duvet cover, watercolor prints of sunflowers and photos of family and friends would all add a glimpse of "us" to our new home's interior decor. Shades of red were my color choice for each bedroom, as I focused my knack for decorating on keeping the apartment feeling spacious and light-filled. Photos of Ann's decorating flair with heavy, dark furniture and doily covered windows made me think that the apartment was just crying out for my sense of bright and airy styling. I imagined hanging mirrors to bounce light around and suspending crystals in windows to generate prisms that danced on the walls when kissed by the sun's gleaming rays. I had a myriad of ideas for our apartment, taking cues from the down-to-earth Italians, my goal was for us to live in comfortable elegance with a graceful blend of unmistakable timeless charm.

By reading internet blogs written by expats living in Italy, I gained from their experience, perspective and helpful tips. I learned that many Italian newcomers turned to IKEA; an affordable store offering a large selection of ready-to-assemble furniture and home accessories. An IKEA store was located near me in the Bay Area and also in the vicinity of the airport in Rome. Martine's suggestion of renting a truck in Perugia to drive to Rome for an IKEA pick-up, seemed like a feasible idea!

IKEA is well known for Swedish, contemporary style furnishings and since my taste leaned toward the Traditional style, I must admit that I had never been to an IKEA store before. However, deciding to investigate with an open mind, I was pleasantly surprised at the excellent quality of their products and the large selection of "soup-to-nuts" accessories to furnish a house from scratch. Within minutes of entering the showroom floor, I found myself fumbling through my purse for a notepad and pen to jot down style numbers to show Vince. Surprisingly, I quickly discovered that IKEA offered some bed designs that I could easily incorporate into a traditional decor. When Vince and I returned for a joint visit, I had a scrupulous list of items to show Vince for his concurrence. I selected everything from beds, bedding, chests of drawers, floor coverings, bath towels, kitchen utensils, dishes and cookware. I eliminated the guess work. In Italy, all Vince was required to do was rent a suitable vehicle, purchase the items on my list at the IKEA store in Rome and transport them to the apartment in Morcella.

When Martine notified us that the Deed Signing date in Perugia was scheduled on May 20, our enthusiasm went through the roof. Crestfallen and absolutely envious that I could not attend the milestone event, I became an avid planner and scheduler. Having used all my allotted vacation time, I had no alternative but to go to work until I accumulated time off for September, when we planned to officially move in and set up home in our new apartment.

On April 30, our happiness was greatly overshadowed when we received the very, very sad news that our dear friend Carole had passed away. We were devastated and knew quite well that without her, our lives would never be the same. Carole was an exceptional person. After 65 years of marriage, Stan's world was shattered. To help ease his pain and provide a change of surroundings, Vince invited Stan to accompany him on his Deed Singing Trip to Italy. It was just what Stan needed.

While Martine arranged to have the water and electricity services turned on for Vince's arrival, I booked flights and accommodations at the Relais Villa Valentini Hotel in the village of San Venanzo, near Morcella. I reserved two rooms for only a few nights, just until we became the apartment's official owners and the "baton was past" to Vince in the form of house keys. Once he had access to the apartment, the men could stay there for the remainder of their trip. I planned a regimented, arduous task list for Vince, which included painting all the rooms, purchasing two ready-to-assemble beds and everything else on my extensive list of items from the IKEA store in Rome. Once the beds were assembled, Vince and Stan could sleep in the apartment. As fate would have it, the Deed Signing trip encompassed a national holiday, which meant a long work free week-end for me and an opportunity to spend a few days with Ellen at her home in Connecticut. I would meet Vince's return flight from Rome in New York so that we could fly to San Francisco together. I was convinced that my foolproof plan would execute like clockwork.

When it was time to drive Vince and Stan to the airport, I was bewildered knowing that a part of me was going with them. It had been many years since Vince and I were separated by international waters and I found it difficult to cope with my apprehensions. Twenty-two hours later, Vince finally phoned to announce their safe arrival at the hotel in San Venanzo.

The Relais Villa Valentini was a simplistic, hospitable and charming place. Vince and Stan arrived late in the evening, completely ravenous and although the kitchen was already closed, the hotel staff was happy to prepare a beautiful plate of sliced cheeses and Italian cured meats. The rooms were small, nevertheless, adequate, comfortable and attractively furnished. The men had only one day to acclimate to the local time, the Umbrian surroundings and to locate Bar Rosetti where Vince was scheduled to meet Luisa on the day that the formalities were taking place. Vince and I spoke on the phone every night. He told me that the seasonal red poppies were in bloom, covering the hillsides. We missed each other immensely!

On May 20, 2011, Vince's nervousness waiting for Luisa's arrival at Bar Rosetti turned into delight when she showed up earlier than scheduled. After a brief introduction to Stan, Vince followed Luisa to the bank where the first order of business was to withdraw funds for the balance of the purchase price of the apartment. He found it interesting, quite comical and small-town-charming that the bank's limit for issuing a cashier's check was only 20,000€, therefore, multiple banknotes were issued. With the bank transaction completed, Luisa led the way to the notaio's office in Perugia, where the formalities would take place in a conference room. Vince was surprised by the number of people already present in the room. The *members of the cast* were: Ann with her companion who was also named Anne, the notaio, an English translator and her witness, Johannes, Luisa and Martine. Everyone was extremely cordial and appeared to be in a jovial mood.

The notaio was the evident dominant dignitary in the room, commenced the meeting by presenting Vince with an English version of the purchase contract. He read the document aloud, while Vince followed along with the translator and the Witness corroborated that the translation was accurate and correct. The buyer and seller conceded to the contractual agreement, followed by Ann's affirmation that the earnest money had been deposited into her escrow account. At that time, the focus turned to Vince, who was eager to complete the buying process by bestowing Ann with the final payment in return for the most important component in the entire transaction; *the keys!* Vince produced the series of cashier's checks and pushed them across the table in Ann's direction while Martine brought forth several sets of spare keys. It was the exciting "grand finale" moment Vince had been waiting for. He asked if someone in the room would take a photo of Ann handing him the keys.

"I want to document this moment for my wife who couldn't be here," Vince said. Everyone in the room was touched by his thoughtfulness and several people readily took out their cameras to photograph Ann's exaggerated gesture of holding the keys up high, ready to drop them in Vince's hands.

"This is for Joyce," Vince said as he heard the cameras click to capture the momentous event. The apartment was now officially ours and Vince had the keys to prove it!

Before the meeting was adjourned, Vince wrote checks to the notaio, the translator and the witness. Ann's companion and Stan came over to congratulate the buyer and seller, the Notaio also shook their hands. Then Johannes and Luisa walked over and did the same, followed by Martine, who presented Vince with the numerous sets of extra keys. Chuckling, Vince commented on how I was going to love the large skeleton key that opened the door to the apartment. Pleased with the truly congenial experience, Vince thanked the Casambiente team for their professionalism and guidance through the entire home buying process. Then he looked at Stan, put a hand on his shoulder and said, "Come on, Stan. Let me show you our new home!"

Vince drove like the wind. Now quite familiar with the area, he knew the way from Perugia to Morcella without a map, parked in the community parking lot, walked through the church breezeway to the impressive wooden door and opened it for the first time with his own set of keys. Stan was speechless at the first sight of Morcella.

"Wait until you see the apartment," Vince boasted as he guided Stan into the foyer with the brick arches. He opened the door to our cantina to show off our storage space. As they continued up the stairs, Stan commented about the amazing condition of the ancient, completely restored building. Then, with the adorable skeleton key, Vince opened the front door to our apartment and said, "Welcome to our Italian home, my man. What do you think?" He immediately led Stan out to the terrazzo to take in the glorious view of the Tiber Valley's freshly plowed, vivid green farmland, strewn with profusely red poppies blooming in the distance.

"This is amazing!" Stan replied. "This is magnificent. Congratulations, Buddy! Let me take a picture of you as the official owner, there on your terrace, looking over your domain." Vince posed at the railing, gazing over the landscape, feeling somewhat emotional as he realized that we had accomplished our dream. We finally owned a home in Italy and what spectacular one at that! If my mom and Orry could see us now, they would have been immensely proud of us. In our heart of hearts, however, we knew that they were "up there" watching over us. In fact, they probably orchestrated the entire attainment.

With the Deed Signing behind him, feeling carefree and bursting with pride, Vince toured Stan through the apartment, reminiscing how the allure of Orvieto and careful, diligent shopping was the key to finding the perfect property in Morcella. Stan was duly impressed.

Before spending their last night at Relais Villa Valentini, Vince treated Stan to a well-deserved meal at Rosatelli. They shared a bottle of local red wine and after a long lunch, Vince declared that enough business was conducted today. "Let's drive over the mountain," Vince said. "I'll take you the scenic way to Orvieto. I'll introduce you to my 'ugly girlfriend.'"

5. We Bought a Home in Italy

It was a small consolation for me to speak to Vince on the phone every day. His enthusiasm was evident in his voice, as he was animated and excited when he described the Deed Signing experience as fun-filled and lighthearted, unlike the tedious process we went through when we purchased our home in California.

Immediately after breakfast the following morning, Vince and Stan checked out of the Relais Villa Valentini. Vince was looking forward to renting a moving truck today, going to Rome to buy the beds and furnishings so that tonight he would spend his first night in our apartment. Unfortunately, in my absence, to observe the centuries old ritual of carrying the bride over the threshold, Vince would have to carry Stan.

On the way to the apartment, Vince and Stan stopped at the Brico Home Improvement Center to purchase an ice chest and two inexpensive chairs. At the Conad Supermarket they stocked up on some basic food items, water and beer. Luisa was already waiting for them at the apartment by the time they arrived.

Today was a big day with much to accomplish. For an insignificant hourly fee, Luisa accompanied the men as their functionary personal assistant, translator and guide. Martine located a truck rental agency at the convenient Edigio Airport in Perugia and before long, Vince and "his crew" were rolling down the highway in a moving van to purchase and transport all the items on the shopping list which I painstakingly prepared ahead of time. Luisa was impressed with the thoughtful effort I put forth in creating such an elaborate, well sorted list.

It was an approximate two-hour drive from the Perugia Airport to the IKEA store in Rome, however, the time passed quickly as Luisa pointed out many sights of interest and travel shortcuts along the way. Vince was ecstatic to learn that there was a quicker route from Morcella to the airport in Rome.

Much to Vince's delight, the IKEA store layout in Rome was exactly like the store in the Bay Area, style and item numbers were also the same, therefore, he was quite familiar with the various departments. Vince divided the long shopping list by tearing it into three sections. Keeping a section with the furniture for himself, he handed one to Luisa, one to Stan and asked them to gather the items on their part of the list. As if it was a contest, each person readily accepted their responsibility, grabbed a cart and began their shopping spree. Stan focused on finding cookware, kitchen utensils, and dishes, while Luisa searched for bedding, glassware, bath and kitchen towels. Vince took charge of locating a queen-sized bed frame, a full-sized bed frame, two mattresses, two chests of drawers, a leather sofa, two side chairs and an area rug, notwithstanding that everything may not have fit in the van. The sofa was the only item not in stock and had to be ordered for a future delivery.

When everything on my list had been collected, Vince guided his shopping mates toward a queue at the cash register. One by one, they pushed three flatbed hand trucks and several shopping carts through the line. With all my heart, I wish that someone had taken a photo of the spectacle. What a sight they must have been! After all the items were rung up and paid for, the clerk handed Vince a receipt that was longer than Santa's "Naughty and Nice" list, the end of it almost reached the floor. Vince laughed out loud, as did Luisa and Stan.

Loading everything into the van for transport to Morcella was an arduous task. Stan and Luisa's help transferring the smaller items into the van was appreciated, however, Vince needed some serious muscle power to assist with the heavier pieces. Since Stan was not able to help lift the heavier bed frames, bulky mattresses and chairs, Vince relied on his own strength to partially load and strategically balance each piece on the truck bed, until he was able to pull or push the entire piece into the van. When the last piece was methodically loaded and secured, he closed and latched the van and jumped into the driver's seat.

"*Andiamo!* Let's go!" he ordered. The goal was to leave Rome before rush hour traffic jammed the highways.

Rather than parking in Morcella's community parking lot, Vince intended to park near the apartment building's front door where it would be much easier to unload the van. With the side rear view mirrors pulled in, he held his breath as he crept the moving van, unscathed, with mere inches to spare, through the medieval arched entrance into the Piazza San Silvestri.

Stan and Luisa cheered when Vince brought the van to a stop.

Now, came the strenuous chore of carrying the contents up four flights of stairs and into the apartment. Vince and Stan worked non-stop to unload the van. The most difficult challenge was getting the cumbersome mattresses into the apartment. Those darn things buckled in the middle and had no place to grab a good hold of them to carry them up the stairs. Stan wore a brace on one leg to support a painful knee, he also lacked the strength to do heavy lifting, leaving Vince to walk and scoot the weightiest items up each step, one at a time until he could drag them inside the apartment. Hours later, the van was finally empty and ready to be returned to the rental agency. The beds still had to be built so that Vince and Stan could sleep in them tonight.

It was nearly two o'clock in the morning, Italian time, when Vince finally phoned. He called me as soon as the beds were assembled and Stan was sound asleep. Our conversation was exciting and happy, we must have spoken for more than an hour as Vince shared the events of his day with me in detail. The most comical part of his shopping spree story was having lunch at the IKEA Store Restaurant, famous for their gourmet meatballs with gravy and other Swedish-style delicacies. During the long drive to Rome, Stan's eyes sparkled with anticipation as he mentioned several times how much he looked forward to ordering a big plate full of Swedish meatballs and gravy for lunch. When it came time to eat in the cafeteria style restaurant, Luisa and Vince chose panini and soft drinks while Stan ordered a three-course meal, which he ate at leisure. Eventually, Vince reminded him, somewhat harshly, that Luisa was getting paid by the hour and Stan's lingering lunch was costing him a fortune. Failing to see the humor, poor Stan was woefully disappointed that he didn't get to enjoy his tantalizing meatballs in the manner he wished for.

I hated for our conversation to end, nevertheless, I empathized that my husband labored all day and was dog-tired. Tomorrow promised to be another exerting day, Luisa agreed to escort the men to a home improvement center to buy paint and the plethora of supplies needed to coat the apartment's interior walls in a fresh new color.

At nine o'clock the next morning, Luisa met a very tired Vince and Stan in Morcella's community parking lot. The home improvement center was located in Perugia near Casambiente, therefore, Luisa suggested that the men follow her to the Leroy Merlin store, paying attention to the routing for future visits to the mega store for the Do-it-yourselfer.

The Leroy Merlin store was much larger and offered a wider variety of products than the Brico store in Marsciano. Vince brought a paint color sample that matched the walls of our home in California. We loved the sentiment that our American and Italian homes, although separated by an ocean, were connected by ownership and paint color. Kinda silly, isn't it? While the paint was being mixed, Vince and Stan gathered drop cloths, buckets, brushes, rollers, a ladder and an array of other necessities. When everything was purchased, packed in the car and Vince had no further need for a translator, Luisa headed back to Casambiente, leaving the men to find their way back to Morcella.

Painting walls has always been one of my least favorite chores in the entire world and as much as I yearned to be with Vince in our new apartment, I did not envy the job that he and Stan were faced with. Properly preparing the surfaces before applying paint was tedious, but a necessary step to achieve a professional result. The men repaired cracks and filled nail holes with spackling paste, scraped away peeling paint and sanded rough areas smooth, removed dirt, grease and mildew with trisodium phosphate (TSP) and while the walls dried, they gobbled down a quick lunch on the terrazzo. Improvising the ice chest for a table, Vince laid out a feast of the usual sliced bread, cheese, salami and prosciutto, along with luscious grapes, a garlicky mixture of olives and several bottles of Italian beer. While they ate, the men discussed paint techniques that would minimize brush strokes and roller marks. They agreed that Vince would do the cutting-in (paint along the trim, ceilings and corners), while Stan would fill in the open spaces with a roller.

As Vince filled the roller tray with paint, he noticed that the emulsion seemed thin and watery, although, being circumspect and unfamiliar with the Italian paint mixture, he continued what he was doing, shrugged his shoulders and said, "If I wanted everything to be the same, I wouldn't have bought a house in Italy." He handed Stan the loaded tray and a roller. "Here you go, my man. Let's start there," he said, as he pointed to an area in the room. "Give me a head start, then come in after me."

Since the weather was forecasted to be unseasonably hot by mid-afternoon, the men focused on painting the *soggiorno* (living/dining room) early in the day, before the sun's heat pierced through the doors and windows and made it unbearable to work in that area. Stan took the paint tray to a corner of the room, leaving ample space for Vince to position the ladder. As Vince began cutting in along the ceiling, Stan assumed a position almost directly underneath the ladder, where he could easily fill in with a roller. Despite the fact that the men's technique was flawless, the thin paint did not adhere to the roller, providing a very uneven coverage. The watery mixture dripped down Stan's arms as he rolled it on the wall, coating him in paint up to his elbows! Frustrated by what he saw, Vince stepped down from the ladder to examine the paint mixture. Puzzled as to how to resolve the problem, Vince again determined that Italian paint must just be different and asked Stan to do his best under the circumstances. The men worked steadily for hours, making slow progress as Vince moved the ladder along the walls, Stan followed below, maintaining the same pace. Suddenly, Stan felt moisture dripping on his head.

"Hey, is it raining in here?" he asked, befuddled looking up at his buddy. Yet, as soon as Stan uttered the question, he recognized that what dripped on him like rain was Vince's perspiration! Without realizing it, the apartment had become uncomfortably warm and muggy. Ughhh, it was difficult to continue painting. Stan looked at Vince with a wistful expression, hoping for a temporary reprieve from the messy project. Vince was also ready to abandon his paint brush for a while.

"Let's grab some dinner," Vince suggested, adding, "it's my treat." Stan jumped at the invitation and although there was not hot running water in the apartment, the men cleaned up with wash rags and before long, they were refreshed and on their way to Oasi Villaggio; the restaurant that Johannes recommended when he showed us the apartment last March.

Oasi, located about two and a half miles from Morcella on the country road to Marsciano, is well known among the locals for serving fresh Umbrian cuisine, specialty truffle dishes and mouthwatering pizza. Once an old farmhouse with stables, cellars and outbuildings, the eating establishment's interior is marked by brick arches, typical beamed ceilings and terra cotta floors. A cordial waitress seated Vince and Stan at a pleasant outdoor table, perfect for eating under the stars on a balmy evening. She promptly placed a brown paper lunch bag filled with Italian breadsticks and freshly baked sliced bread on the table. With the bag's top folded down like a cuff, it was an adorable presentation.

The men had worked up quite an appetite and were looking forward to a hearty home cooked meal. The varied menu had just enough choices to create a dilemma. Everything looked delicious! Ultimately, Vince ordered the gnocchi with gorgonzola sauce and Stan ordered a pizza. For their first course, they shared a house *tagliere*; an appetizer plate of sliced cheeses and cured meats traditionally served on a cutting board. A liter of house red wine was also ordered to balance out the meal.

The food was amazing. The appetizer plate was generously loaded with sliced Capocollo; characterized by the reddish veined-with-fat "marbling" of the tasty meat, Coppa; a product with deep Umbrian roots, made from the remaining parts of the pig and head skin that has been boiled and seasoned with orange zest, Guanciale; pork jowls salted with the pigskin attached, seasoned with garlic, salt and pepper and Lardo; a compact layer of white pig fat, sliced thinly and seasoned with fresh ground black pepper, served on top of a slice of toasted bread. The cheese selection was interestingly diverse and accompanied by a tiny cup of chestnut honey to drizzle on top. Stan's gourmet pizza was beautifully cooked on a crispy crust that didn't sag in the middle when it was picked up. The most memorable dish was Vince's gnocchi; a plate full of light-as-air, tiny pillows of fresh potato goodness, smothered in a mouthwatering, rich and creamy gorgonzola sauce. Vince had never tasted anything so divine. It was delicious! The men savored their well-deserved, exquisite dinner, engaged in happy conversation about the day's events. Stan was relieved to be away from the sadness which encompassed his home in California and Vince was grateful to have Stan's companionship and moral support.

When they returned to the apartment, Vince was too energized to sleep. Intending to paint only a small area, he opened a can to dip his brush, when he suddenly noticed that the consistency of the color mixture was much thicker.

"Hey, Stan, look at this!" Vince exclaimed. "You won't believe this, but the paint is thicker now. Maybe it just needed time to develop." Strange, but true, the consistency was much more like standard latex paint. Although mystified, the defeatist men suddenly gained renewed hope that the slightly thicker mixture would provide better coverage without creating a drippy mess and that it might truly be possible to finish painting the entire apartment before their departure to California in less than two days.

While Vince wrapped up his projects in Morcella, I thoroughly enjoyed spending some serious sister-time with Ellen in Connecticut. Every evening, after my phone conversation with Vince, I couldn't wait to tell her of the progress he had made in preparing the apartment for our return in autumn when we were scheduled to move in. My sister was genuinely happy for us, I could see it in her eyes and it gave me great pleasure to know that she shared in our exuberance, consequently, I persuaded her to join us in Italy to help me organize the kitchen, arrange the furniture and decorate while Vince assembled storage units, built shelving, hung pictures and set-up the utility room. When Ellen agreed, I was thrilled to my core. I couldn't wait for the day that we would meet each other at the Rome airport and drive to Morcella together. I couldn't wait to see her reaction at the first glimpse of our village as we drove in on the country road from Marsciano and I was dying to show her our apartment and terrazzo with the mesmerizing view of the Tiber Valley.

Italy's time zone is six hours ahead of the local time in Connecticut. The beautiful morning, enticed Vince and Stan to take a last stroll through the village before departing to the airport. I was busy packing before I went to bed that night when my phone rang. I felt my heart throb in my chest when I heard my hubby's voice. He sounded very excited that something special appeared to be happening in Morcella as several blue pennants depicting white flowers, a medieval arch, or the name MORCELLA decoratively illustrated, were suspended from windows and balconies. Large arrangements of Sweet Broom adorned the church breezeway and lined the piazza in front of the church. Sweet Broom is a shrub of glorious yellow flowers, with a spicy-sweet fragrance that delights the senses. His voice became even more high-spirited as he described his enchanting surroundings. I learned later, that throughout Italy, the religious feast of honoring Saint Theresa; the patron saint of Morcella was celebrated that day. The feast is marked by decorating the village with Sweet Broom floral arrangements, suspending pennants and laying extravagant flower pedal carpets (Infiorata) over the cobblestone pathways infant of the church for the special late-day service when the Host is carried through the streets in procession.

I could barely sleep after our phone conversation, I watched the clock, counting the hours until morning light and then.it was finally here! Sunday, May 29, 2011, it felt as if I had been waiting for this day since forever! Vince was coming home today and I was very anxious, to meet his flight from Rome at the Newark Liberty International Airport. I bought a new outfit to wear for this special occasion. I hoped to look my best for my hubby, we hadn't seen each other in twelve days and I wanted so show him what he's been missing. I was dying to give him a giant hug and kiss to welcome him home. I couldn't wait to see and touch our Italian house keys and hear Vince's stories all over again when I could watch his facial expressions as he spoke in person. Since we were flying to San Francisco together, we had at least five hours to make up for lost time.

Ellen dropped me off at the airport in plenty of time to meet Vince's flight. Since he would have to go through customs, we arranged to meet at the departing gate for the flight to San Francisco. This was one of those circumstances when one appreciates the convenience of having a mobile phone. As I was walking toward the International Terminal, Vince called to tell me that he and Stan were already on their way to the Domestic Terminal. We were still speaking to each other when suddenly I heard Stan say, "Hey, there's a familiar face, here she is!" And at that moment I laid eyes on my husband for the first time in almost two weeks. We were crazy happy to see each other. Oh my Gosh, we hugged and kissed and then I asked him the all-important question.

"Well, honey. How do you feel? Do you have buyer's remorse?"

"Are you kidding!" Vince exclaimed. "I have the direct opposite. I can't wait to go back with you in September. I love it there; I love our apartment."

"Oh! Thank God," I replied. "Where are the keys? Let me see the skeleton key." Vince produced a bunch of keys on a keyring from his pocket and dangled them within my reach, Stan took a picture of Vince holding one key and me holding the skeleton key! It was a very momentous photo.

Finally Moving In

"For those who wait, waiting is a life time." Isn't that how the saying goes? It was going to be a brutal, long summer waiting for September when we would return to Morcella together to furnish the apartment. I spent a big part of everyday focused on what I planned to bring from California to add those personal touches to our new home. I created a list of priorities to follow after we arrived and I was constantly imagining how I wanted to decorate each room. As I poured my energy into our Italian dream home, my heart was full.

I wondered if the clothes washer was the kind that dried clothes after the washing cycle. I read about such machines and decided to send an e-mail to Ann to ask some questions. I was thrilled when I read her reply:

From: ann@libero.it
Sent: Monday, June 13, 2011 1:20 PM To: Di Lorenzo, Joyce
Subject: Morcella apartment

Dear, Joyce,

I was delighted to hear from you. We had such a good time at the deed signing and you were sorely missed!

About the washer I am leaving in the apartment; it is a German made Bosch, the same as is sold in the U.S. and the best manufacturer for a washer in the world. It is a basic model (I am not much of a Martha Stewart type) and does a great job. I found that there are very few times during the year when it was not possible to dry clothes outside on the terrace. They will be bone dry and sunny smelling in no time. Alternately, I have dried clothes on racks and the lines which pull out from the wall in the utility room where the washer is or topped them up on the radiators (knickers on the long ones). I washed everything on cold and only once a week or so.

Life is too short for worrying, especially in Italy. Spend your time dreaming about wine-filled dinners on the terrazzo in the sunshine. Enjoy the beauty of the region. I have some bits of local you may find useful:

First, if you drive one mile past the left turn-off for Morcella on the SS317 you will reach Cerqueto, which has a bank with an ATM, a post office, a cafe with good cappuccino, a small grocery store and a bakery where you can get fresh bread every morning. More importantly the first Perugino ever painted hangs in a church in this village. You have to adjust to Italian priorities and art is number one! You should open a back account here. The man at the counter is very nice (tell him you bought my apartment)! Banco Populare di Spoleto is a good bank and it is never busy. The entrance is hidden behind two big trees. You can park in the little public parking lot opposite the entrance. Ditto for the post office, it's very convenient.

Every Monday in Piazzo Carlo Marx in the center of Marsciano is a famous market where everyone goes. I am not a good shopper, but friends who are, tell me they get fabulous clothes and everything else there for pennies. Great produce, local meat and cheese specialties, plants, household items, etc. You should really go even though parking is a nightmare in town on Mondays.

Do you know that Ryanair flies directly from London Stansted to Perugia? You are only 22 km from Perugia and it is much easier to get to Morcella from there instead of from Rome. Don't know how you get to Stansted though, but there might be some San Francisco/London flights then maybe to Stansted by train?

If you drive downhill from the parking lot in Morcella and cross the little stone bridge you will come to Oasi, an excellent trattoria. They serve all the local dishes and the service is friendly. Oasi makes a good "local favorite." Another few miles away is a very good LIDL German discount store, good for bulk supplies. Near the LIDL is a very good large Super Conad grocery store where you can get everything imaginable!

Now going back to the apartment, don't know if you'll ever want satellite TV, but the white cable on the floor in the living room is connected to the satellite dish on the terrace. The dish actually belongs to Silvano, but as each dish can take two connections, he kindly let me connect to his.

The two beautiful antique stone troughs in the front of the building were mine. They are English antiques and fairly valuable. I left them there in honor of the lovely medieval building, but I noticed that Irma has just put her plastic plant pots on top of them. If you ever wanted to plant them up, I'm sure no one would mind.

The last thing is that you really must learn some Italian. It will make all the difference for your life there—besides the fact that in Italy NO ONE speaks any language other than their own. After several years of getting nowhere with lessons in London, I finally "bit the bullet" and went to a wonderful little school in beautiful Arezzo. I'd suggest you take a week off and do the same. I am the worst at languages, but it is a wonderful school and even I came out babbling Italian.

It means so much to me that you both really love the apartment and understand what makes it so special. I hope and trust you will have many happy years there.

All my best wishes to Vince. Ann.

I read Ann's letter several times, each time I found myself lingering on different words that sparked daydreams of us shopping at the farmer's market in Piazza Carlo Marx, buying fresh bread at the bakery in Cerqueto and dining at Oasi.

Finally, after what seemed like the longest summer in history, it was time for our departure to Italy. Friends and colleagues were thrilled for us, their names quickly became a growing list of guests eager to visit, once we were settled in our new home.

I warned our car service about the excess baggage we were taking to the airport this time, consequently, our car service came to pick us up a bit earlier than scheduled. In addition to our roll-aboard luggage and flight bags, we were also transporting four cardboard boxes, each packed to the maximum weight of 70 pounds, with all the household items and personal treasures that I had diligently collected to make our Italian house a home. I must admit that it was quite stressful getting everything to the airline ticket counter, however, once we were checked in for our flight and rid of all that baggage, I was convinced that it was well worth the assiduous effort.

When the security process was behind us, Vince and I settled in at an airport wine bar, where we had plenty of time to relax with a lovely glass of Vino Rosso before boarding. I phoned Ellen to synchronize our arrival times and meeting place at the Rome Airport. Her direct flight was scheduled to land an hour before our connecting flight from Frankfurt. After every detail was thoroughly discussed, we wished each other a safe trip and a Buon Viaggio. I was very excited and already looking forward to the end of our eighteen-hour journey to Italy.

Since our European port-of-entry was Frankfurt, no further passport checks were required in Rome and we were free to leave the airport once our baggage was claimed. We arrived on our twenty-third wedding anniversary. My eyes searched for Ellen, who was waiting for us somewhere in the Arrival Terminal by now. Then, simultaneously, we spotted each other in the Baggage Claim area. In a touching sweet gesture, she held up a handmade colorful sign to greet us. It said, "Happy Anniversary, Vince and Joyce. Welcome To Your New Home!" in big red letters on a bright yellow background, decorated with drawings of the Golden Gate Bridge and the Coliseum. It was a beautiful sign! Apparently, our timing was flawless, we flew into each other's arms, relieved to be together safe and sound.

Soon our belongings were collected and loaded precariously on two carts which we pushed into the elevator for the cumbersome shlep to the car rental agency. Vince did a masterful job of loading everything into the car, although nearly burying my sister in the back seat under flight bags, purses and one of the large cardboard boxes. In hindsight, I wish that I would have taken a picture of that comical situation. It was an uncomfortably tight fit for the two-hour drive to Morcella, nevertheless packed in the car like sardines, off we went. Despite being weary from the long flight, we were in good spirits and no one complained.

As we left Rome further behind, Ellen surprised me when she asked, "What is Firenze?" Since I considered her as a world traveler, it never quite occurred to me, that as a former Pan American flight attendant, she had only flown to Rome, therefore she knew that in Italy, Rome is called *Roma*, but she was not aware that Florence is called *Firenze*.

After an hour on the road, we stopped at an Autogrill to buy a few provisions for breakfast at home the next morning. Ellen had never been to an Autogrill before and as a shopper-at-heart, her eyes lit up when she saw the abundant array of food and snacks. She couldn't resist buying decadent Italian white chocolate bonbons for the road. It was already so much fun to have my sister with us. Vince thoughtfully informed me that we had wine and coffee at home, but not much of anything else. (It was the first time Vince referred to our new apartment as "home.") Some fresh oranges, milk and pane (bread) and a freshly baked golden focaccia sprinkled with rosemary and garlic would make a wonderful breakfast in the morning.

When we turned off the A1 autostrade onto the more rural E45 highway toward Perugia, the terrain became more green and picturesque. Vince ceased every opportunity to point out the impeccable hilltop villages and enchanting castles along the way. As any first-time visitor to the area, Ellen was mesmerized by the rustic beauty of the Umbrian countryside. By the time we took the exit leading to Marsciano, the magnificent dome of the church in the historic center was softly aglow under the remaining streaks from a glorious, fuchsia colored sunset. Then finally, Vince turned onto the country road to Morcella.

"Well, do you see your village yet?" he teasingly asked me. My eyes searched the darkening distance for the first sight of our magical hamlet when it suddenly came into view.

"There it is!" I almost shouted, my heart bursting with pride as I pointed to Morcella, the most beautiful, romantically charming medieval village in the whole wide world! "There it is, Ellen. What do you think?"

"Wow! It is beautiful, it looks surreal," she answered, almost holding her breath.

It was also my first view of Morcella at night and it was truly breathtaking to see the stone buildings and clock tower illuminated by the amber lights of the village against the evening sky, embellished with a far-flung full moon and the brightest stars imaginable. As we crossed the stone bridge by the single traffic light and wound our way up through the narrow street to the arched portal, my eyes welled up with tears of joy until Vince stopped the car at our front door and turned the engine off.

"We're home," he declared.

"Oh my God, Ellen," I said overcome with emotion. "Isn't it beautiful?" As I got out of the car, the heavenly sound of a congregation singing a melodic, sweet hymn drifted through the open church door and I realized that a worship service was in progress.

"Shhh!" I whispered to Ellen pointing at the church and then to our apartment building. "That's where we live."

I removed the large box and a flight bag from Ellen's lap so that she could (literally) peel herself out of the car. When she heard the singing, she remarked, "Wow! Perfect timing. Did you plan this or do they always sing when you arrive?"

"Yes, they are singing to welcome us," I answered jokingly. Vince was already opening the massive door to the common foyer. "Our apartment is up there," I said, directing Ellen's gaze upward to our bedroom windows as I guided her inside the building. She was immediately dazzled by the brick arches and terra cotta staircase.

"Oh 'Wow,'" she reiterated again. ('Wow' is my sister's favorite word for anything that impressed her.) I indicated where our storage room was on the ground floor and as we moved up the stairs, explained that our neighbors lived on the second floor and we lived on the third.

I entered first and was pleased to immediately notice the hard work Vince had done. The walls were freshly painted, the leather sofa and linen covered chairs were just perfect and the partially opened IKEA boxes that were strewn about were simply waiting to be unpacked. I showed Ellen to the guest bedroom, pulling her roll-aboard behind her, she commented, "How nice. I didn't know that I was going to have my own bedroom."

The unmade beds looked so inviting, clearly, we were all exhausted, however, there was still a lot more baggage to bring upstairs. After several trips back and forth to the car, everything was finally in the apartment, we loosened our clothes, removed our shoes and just as I thought that we were going to bed, Vince produced a bottle of wine and three glasses from the kitchen cabinet.

"I saved this bottle for our first toast," he announced. "Let's go outside on the terrazzo!" That's my Husband, what a wonderful idea! It was a beautiful, balmy evening, but the twinkling lights of the surrounding villages in the distance were an inadequate preview of the jaw dropping view that would reveal itself in the morning. Vince poured the wine and handed us each a glass. "Welcome home, Treat," he said, followed by, "glad you could join us, sister-in-law," as he tipped his glass to Ellen.

"Cheers!" Ellen said, deliberately dragging out the word for emphasis before we took our first sip "Congratulations, you two." The happiness I felt at that moment left me speechless.

We slowly drank our wine as we felt our bodies relax. Suddenly, Vince pointed toward the sky and shouted, "Look at that!"

Almost at the same time, Ellen exclaimed, "Oh! Wow! What was that?" By the time I looked in the direction that Vince had indicated, I saw the tail end of shooting star. "That was unbelievable," Vince commented as Ellen added, "That went all the way across the sky!" I was disappointed that I missed seeing it, but thrilled that Vince and Ellen did.

When our bottle of wine was empty, we were certainly more than ready to get a good night's rest. I asked Vince where "we" kept the linens and bath towels, he was adorable and showed me where he stored them neatly stacked in the utility room. I handed Ellen one of the brand-new sets of linens and a bath towel and invited her to sleep as late as she needed to, although I couldn't wait to show her the apartment and the incredible panorama in the morning. Needless to say, the three of us fell asleep the moment our heads hit the pillows.

I felt a bit disoriented in the morning, when I woke up to the wonderful aroma of fresh brewed coffee. I heard the astounding lovely sound of birds chirping and my sense of smell caught a faint whiff of an intoxicating, flowery-sweet fragrance in the air. For a moment, I didn't know where I was and then I remembered that I was in Italy, in Morcella, in our new home and my sister was with us! Exhilarated, I jumped out of bed to find Vince in the kitchen preparing a platter of fruit and focaccia bread for our breakfast on the terrazzo. When I approached him for a "*Buongiorno*" kiss, he shooed me away and told me not to look at what he was doing. He obviously wanted to surprise Ellen and I with breakfast. I stepped out on the terrazzo to find two plastic chairs and an ice-chest covered with a tea towel posing as a table set up for our breakfast. What an endearing man I married.

It was an unbelievably beautiful morning. The variegated colors of the scenic hills and freshly plowed farmland below looked to me like an exquisite agricultural painting and I was awestruck. I went to Ellen's room and caught her stirring, sensing that I was near, she said with a scrunched-up face, "Buongiorno. I thought you said that we could sleep as long as we wanted. What time is it?" I actually hadn't even looked at the clock, but when she asked, I saw by my watch that it was nearly nine thirty. Just as I was about to answer, the most magnificent thing happened, I was stunned to silence when the church bells tolled! Oh my God, it was amazing to hear them for the first time, their rich, deep, lingering tone reverberated throughout the village. The bells rang nine lingering times to announce the nine o'clock hour, followed by two shorter chimes for each fifteen minutes past the hour. I couldn't believe it! I grabbed Ellen's arm and practically yanked her out of bed.

"Listen to those bells, El it is time to get up. Come look at the panoramic view," I clamored. "You are going to die!"

Not soon enough for me, my sister entered the living room, shouted out a cheerful Bongiorno to Vince and then literally dropped her jaw when she saw the abundant sunlight pouring into the apartment from the wide-open terrazzo door and the living room window. "Wow," she said again, dragging out the word for emphasis as she continued to the terrazzo, "this is gorgeous!" Last night we arrived in the dark, therefore, Ellen was completely surprised by the landscape in the morning light and readily confessed that she had never seen such an alluring view anywhere. I was extremely pleased that my sister was genuinely impressed.

Vince stepped out to join us, carrying a beautifully arranged platter of sliced oranges and the rosemary Focaccia bread and a pot of hot coffee, which he placed on our ice chest table.

"Buongiorno, mangia," he said, inviting us to eat. I found three mugs in a kitchen cupboard and grabbed some paper towels to use as napkins. Vince offered the plastic chairs to Ellen and me, while he sat on an inverted bucket. Each time the church bells tolled, we stopped our conversation and listened in awe, while the three of us enjoyed a lovingly prepared breakfast as we soaked in the beautiful scenery.

"Can you believe you own this place?" Ellen asked as she snapped pictures from every angle. "I can't get over how stunning the scenery is here. No wonder you two fell in love with this region."

While we ate and drank unhurried, we devised a plan to tackle the myriad of projects on our "To Do" list: unpack and organize the kitchen, arrange the furniture, organize the bathroom, buy a dining room set, mop the floors, figure out how to use the clothes washer, stove and vacuum cleaner. There was so much to do, it was difficult to decide where to start.

Taking my first shower, I was thrilled to discover that we had hot running water and excellent water pressure. Although the shower stall was small, it was an adequate size. My mind was racing with creative ideas about disguising the bidet which I had no intention of using for its intended purpose. It could possibly make a nice planter for red geraniums or function as a convenient foot bath. If Vince could build a box around the darn thing, it could be a place to set my towel within easy reach of taking a shower.

Dressed and ready to go into town, we walked downstairs to head toward the community parking lot. This gave Ellen her first look at our street, the church and Piazza San Silvestri in the light of day. She shook her head in disbelief, because just as it appeared to me the first time I saw it, our narrow street of Via del Priorato looked like a movie set and it seemed surreal that her sister owned a home in this enchanting village. Before we entered the church breezeway to the car, Ellen looked at the stone arched entrance and said, "I love that!" I walked her through the arch to see the war memorial and the stately eagle statues that were mounted there. In all her worldly travels, Ellen had never been in a medieval village like Morcella.

Vince drove us to the Brico Home Improvement Center in Marsciano to buy buckets, mops and cleaning supplies. Ellen was proactive and jumped right in to help me find what we needed, translating labels on bottles of floor polish, dish soap, glass cleaner and laundry detergent to ensure that we were buying the right products. In another section of the store, Vince was looking for a set of screwdrivers, a drill, drill bits, electric cords, a hammer, saw, tape measure and various other basic tools that a man needs to fill his utility room.

After we bought out the Brico store, Vince took us to the adjacent Conad supermarket to buy groceries. Seeing Ellen walk down every aisle with such avidity and interest was a joy for us. She was overwhelmed by the enormous whole hind-legs of gorgeous prosciutto hanging in the deli department. She *oohed-and-aahed* over the variety of salumi, olives of every type and size, creamy gorgonzola, huge hunks of nutty Parmesan and pepper studded Pecorino cheeses and the most mouthwatering fresh baked goods imaginable. Unable to decide what to buy, we bought a little bit of everything.

Returning to the apartment, we put the groceries away and went to work immediately. We listened to Italian music on the radio while we washed kitchen cabinets and unpacked the boxes full of dishes and cookware. Being in Italy with Ellen, listening to European music, brought back vague memories of my early childhood. Growing up in Holland, where music was broadcast in every European language, our mother always listened to the radio. Although the songs sung in Dutch were most popular, my mom's favorite music was German. As I grew older, I also learned to love French, Greek and Italian music, notwithstanding that I didn't understand a word. I climbed up a ladder to line the top shelves inside the cabinets, while Ellen washed and dried our new glasses and dishes. I placed each item according to size; big pots and pans in the back, smaller ones in front. We arranged drawers of silverware, serving pieces, knives and kitchen utensils and sewed a curtain for the under-the-counter waste-bin storage space. Vince busily constructed shelving units and organized all his "man cave" things in the utility room. We were blissfully happy, I felt it with every ounce of my being.

After hours of diligent laboring, Vince entered the kitchen and complimented us on our progress. He took a picture of my sis and me in the midst of our hard work, unflattering as we looked at that moment, it served as a cheerful reminder of our first day at home in Italy. To make them easier to carry to the trash bins outside, Vince broke down the empty boxes we had tossed in a corner near the front door. By midafternoon, the kitchen was efficiently organized and immaculate. There was plenty of space for everything, with cupboard room to spare for food and wine storage.

At one o'clock when the restaurants opened for lunch, we were famished and ready to take a break. We sat at an outside table in the attractive courtyard at Oasi, Ellen was looking forward to her first meal at a local restaurant. We recommended the gnocchi but also suggested that the Daily Special was always a wonderful choice, as well as the pasta with truffles, or maybe the lemon risotto. The waiter, who was beginning to recognize us as frequent customers, brought the Vino Rosso della Casa which Vince had already ordered and placed it on the table with the usual paper bag filled with fresh bread. Ellen reached for the carafe of wine when Vince stopped her and offered to pour it for her. Caught by surprise, she was delighted by his chivalry, Vince laughed and said, "Oh, I didn't know that my sister-in-law was going to be a fun 'drinking buddy.'" It was an amusing, lighthearted moment.

Eventually Ellen selected the gnocchi with truffle sauce for lunch, I ordered the angel hair pasta with fresh tomatoes and basil, Vince ordered sliced steak with rosemary and red pepper berries. We started off our meals with a shared appetizer plate of meats, cheeses and bruschetta with tomatoes and garlic. As usual, the food at Oasi tasted heavenly and I was enraptured watching Ellen experience and enjoy every moment of her first authentic Italian meal. *This* was the picture Vince painted for me when he suggested buying a second home in Italy; a place to welcome visiting family and friends;

a place in the rural, Italian countryside where we could make extraordinary memories together.

After a gratifying and most relaxing lunch, we stopped at an outdoor furniture store to search for a dining set which Vince's mother graciously offered to buy as a housewarming gift for us. Located on a country road in Marciano, the EMU Outlet Store displayed stylish outdoor furniture on their front lawn and in their window. I was eager to see what else they had on hand. Upon entering the store, we were immediately greeted by Paolo who introduced himself and asked if we needed assistance. We readily confessed that we spoke very little Italian, while Paolo confessed that he did not speak English at all, nevertheless, not knowing the language was an irrelevant problem. We always seemed to be able to communicate with the Italians.

It was wonderful to shop with someone else's money. My mother-in-law gave us "carte blanche" to buy whatever we desired. Not the indecisive types, Vince and I quickly chose a sturdy, dark metal, rectangular table with four matching chairs, however, just as we were about to pay for our selection, a round table with a glass top and a white wire base shaped like an hourglass caught my attention. The table's attractive contemporary flair, was a beautiful contrast to the apartment's old-world style and as an indoor dining table, it was perfect for the open and airy ambiance I strived for throughout the living space. At first, Vince and Ellen could not see my vision, but after I selected just the right white woven chairs to accommodate the table, they agreed that the set was a diverse, ingenious choice for our apartment. Paolo seemed extremely happy with our business and scheduled a delivery for the following afternoon.

At home, we had every intention of going back to work, arranging the living room furniture and unpacking more boxes, but the effects of jet-lag dictated that we turn in early. Tomorrow was Market Day in Marsciano and with happy anticipation, we looked forward to shopping with the locals, bright and early. We would tackle the living room at another time.

Ellen and I were raring to go in the morning, poor Vince, as he searched for a suitable parking space in the busy town, he now had to contend with two women telling him where to park. The market was buzzing with local color and flavor. With our love of cooking and even eating, for that matter, it was impossible not to get inspired as we walked through the market together. Almost immediately, I spotted a porchetta truck; a plain and simple porchetta panino was Ellen's perfect introduction to one of Italy's best loved street foods.

She was excited to see the severed pig head on the side of the golden roasted body and took pictures of the seller building our sandwiches with just the right balance of lean and fatty meat.

"Oh my God!" Ellen exclaimed after taking her first bite. "This is to-die-for!" We ate our sandwiches out of hand while we walked past the multitude of produce stands, then without warning, Ellen stopped dead in her tracks in front of a vendor selling fresh Mozzarella di Bufala out of a small white truck.

"Wow, Joyce, look at that guy! He is gorgeous!" Ellen said.

"Well," Vince replied quickly with finesse, "then I think we should buy some cheese."

Ellen was adorable when the handsome salesman asked her in Italian what she wanted to buy, she was slightly giddy, almost blushing as he handed her a plastic bag of his freshly made mozzarella cheese submerged in water. I will forever appreciate Vince's foresight to take a picture of Ellen and that sexy vendor, who we referred to as "her cheese guy" for the remainder of her visit with us. It was an unforgettable, comical moment.

We loved being a part of the bustling energy, moving from stall to stall with the locals was intoxicating. A table full of tiny *carciofini* (baby artichokes) caught Ellen's eye, (she had never seen the small purple ones), we stopped to smell a bunch of perfectly red, ripe *pachino* tomatoes, and we found an overflowing table of intensely fragrant oranges sleeked by the Umbrian sun. We were flabbergasted at how reasonably priced the best quality fruits and vegetables were; less than 1€ per kilo. One kilo is equal to two and a half pounds! Our visit to the market with my sister was a very memorable way to spend the morning.

The weather was outstanding and ideal for eating lunch on the terrazzo. We prepared an amazing salad with the wonderful produce we bought at the market, which Vince pared with a lovely bottle of wine. The mozzarella cheese was outstanding and the tomatoes were bright red, juicy and actually *tasted* like a fresh, vine-ripened tomato, instead of the ludicrous watery, tasteless versions from the supermarkets in the Bay Area. During lunch, we giggled about Ellen's cheese guy, talked about the amazing porchetta sandwiches and how much Vince and I enjoyed mingling with the locals at the weekly market. We felt completely at home among the crowd.

After lunch, Ellen and I took a stab at arranging the living room furniture. Design projects often start with magazine clippings, but mine always starts with something completely intangible; a feeling. I would just know when the room *felt* right, when it *felt* like "us." Generally, I let a home speak to me. From there, I base the decor on what the bones of the house have to offer, however, evidently there was not a square corner in the apartment and it distorted our eye's perception when we positioned the furniture. To begin, we placed the sisal rug in front of the fireplace, then tried several different configurations with the rustic red sofa and slipcovered chairs to explore the room's potential. The focal point was the fireplace, however, the sweeping view from the terrazzo was foremost and we also needed to consider a sensible place for a television near the cable outlet in the wall. Eventually we settled on a pattern conducive to entertaining guests, moving around comfortably within the space and with easy access to the door leading to the utility room. We still lacked essentials such as coffee and side tables, a T.V., a shelving unit for books and personal items and art for the walls. I was looking forward to collecting these crucial items over time.

As expected, Paolo arrived to deliver the quintessential dining sets. I was delighted to see them in our home and determined immediately that our choices were a good juxtaposition to the medieval ambience of the space. With a certain propensity, Vince settled on a suitable placement of the outdoor set while Ellen and I positioned the indoor set to create a clear division between the lounge and dining areas in the room. Balance and proportion were important and when I stood back to observe the entire space, I was extremely pleased with the impeccable result. When you bring together white-painted walls, warm terra cotta-colored floors, windows capped with rustic beam trimmed headers and marry them with classic furniture lines, rooms come alive with timeless character. To express our gratitude for the dining room set, Vince phoned his mother. I smiled deep inside when I overheard him say with pride "Joyce and Ellen are making this place look fantastic." As the finishing touch, I couldn't wait to adorn the new dining room table with a vase full of sunflowers.

"Ellen, grab those scissors and let's cut some sunflowers!" I called to her. We walked to the banks of the Nestore River below our apartment and in a field across the little stone bridge, we cut armloads full of sunflowers. We carried them home, trimmed their woody stems and made several free-form arrangements in pitchers, bottles and jars to place on the dining table and in every room of the apartment. Our home looked like a page in an *Italian Living* decorating magazine.

Vince's "man cave" looked equally impressive. I framed the Welcome Sign Ellen made for us, along with a few artful photos of laundry; a charming collection of well-worn blue jeans hanging on a clothes line and a collection of adorable baby clothes strung on a clothes line against an ancient stone wall. The metal shelving unit that Vince built provided storage for his tool chest, jars filled with screws and nails, electrical cords and a surplus of items large and small. There were specific areas to keep mops, brooms and a garden hose. Our apartment was beginning to feel like home.

Unbeknownst to Vince, I planned a surprise dinner party in honor of his birthday the following day. Only my sister was aware that we were meeting our friends from the Casambiente Agency; Johannes, Luisa, Martine and their families, at Rosatelli for dinner at eight o'clock. At the appropriate time, I suggested taking Ellen to the first restaurant we ever patronized in Marsciano. Fortunately, Vince agreed without being suspicious. When we arrived, on cue, we were shown to a table where our guests were already seated. Vince was completely caught off guard. It was a wonderful evening; the surprise party was a complete success. That night, we certainly had everything we ever wanted; family, friends and a home in Italy.

The next morning, we decided to take the day off from working in the apartment to commemorate Vince's birthday. During a celebratory breakfast at home, we toasted to his honor with mimosas and sang a slightly off-key rendition of Happy Birthday, while Vince opened cards and gifts from us and his mom. Later, we drove the scenic route to Civita di Bagnoregio to take Ellen sightseeing. Vince wanted to show her the fairy-tale like village unlike any other. Ellen gasped at her first glance of the intimidating footpath approach to the ancient village, but it equally also added to the allure and ambience and she was eager to reach the entrance at the top of the hill where the spectacular views of the surrounding, desolate landscape left her breathless. Inside the village, every pot brimming with flourishing pansies and barren stone walls transformed into masses of creeping pink and red geraniums were photographic opportunities for her. Like most visitors, she took countless pictures of every nook and cranny.

From Civita di Bagnoregio we drove to Orvieto to have lunch at Trattoria da Carlo. Carlo was indeed happy to see us, when I told him that it was Vince's birthday, he made a big wonderful fuss over him. As I introduced him to my sister, Teresa came out to greet us, muttering something in Italian, she gave us a hug and hugged Ellen too. My sister was astonished at the warm welcome we received. Teresa seated us in the lovely courtyard, handed us menus and asked what kind of wine we preferred. Without a word of English on the menu, it was fun to help Ellen translate her selections. Carlo recommended the *Stinco di Maiale*; a pork shank, seared until dark, golden brown on all sides, then cooked low and slow with onion, garlic, rosemary, juniper, and clove until softened, and finished in the oven until crispy. It sounded inconceivably delicious and Ellen and I couldn't resist ordering it!

Sipping the bold red house wine Vince ordered, we were still in the midst of studying the menu, when a strolling accordionist stopped by to serenade us. As if we were in an Italian movie, it was all too perfect. Ellen thought that I might have ordered the musician for Vince's birthday, instead it was just a superb example of a typical Italian afternoon, sitting at an intimate outdoor table in one of our favorite Trattorias in Umbria. Before taking our order, Carlo came to our table with a jovial Cheshire Cat grin on his face, carrying a beautiful carpaccio salad covered with peppery, fresh arugula. Upon closer inspection, we saw that Carlo had written "Happy Birthday" with a syrupy, dark balsamic vinegar right on top of the arugula.

"I deserve an Oscar for this! No, two Oscars! Happy birthday, Vincenzo, *Buon Compleano!*" he said, as he presented the extra special salad to Vince with wild applause. Vince was deeply honored by Carlo's wonderful and extremely friendly gesture.

As an appetizer, Ellen and I selected a tomato aspic pudding. However, when Vince placed his order, Carlo replied, "No, my friend, you are not having that. I will make you something special today." He smiled and disappeared into his kitchen, returning promptly with the tomato aspic pudding. It was lightly refreshing, bursting with tomato, garlic and basil flavor, a profoundly delectable fare. I shared a taste with Vince in exchange for one of his carpaccio salad, both dishes were an excellent complement to our main entree. Carlo's special course for Vince was a *Grigliata Mista*; a mixed variety of grilled-to-perfection meats, served with a drizzle of olive oil and a squeeze of lemon. Our Stinco was enormous. The meat was tender and fell off the bone. To this day, whenever we bring anyone to Da Carlo's Trattoria, it is the dish I recommend and it never fails to impress.

Carlo capped off our meal with the usual offerings of Limoncello, grappa and coffee. We complimented and congratulated him on his outstanding cuisine. He is an incredibly talented chef. As the last guests to leave the restaurant, Carlo and Teresa walked us out and with a round of hugs and kisses for all. Our next stop was at Gelatoria Pasqualetti.

The last two days of Ellen's visit with us were filled with laughter as we combined work with pleasure. We shared so many amusing moments arranging bedroom furniture, creating wall art from photos, and hemming a linen panel for the terrazzo door to shield the living room from the harsh afternoon sun. Vince constructed a curtain rod from bits and pieces of wrought iron for the door and assembled a chest of drawers for the guest room. When we needed a break, we toured the neighboring villages. In Civitella del Lago; high above Lago Corbara as a stunning backdrop, Vince took a picture of Ellen and I sitting on a stone wall with our backs against each other, we looked like a pair of book-ends. In Aqualoreto, Ellen photographed every charming doorway, shutter and narrow cobblestone street, just as we did when we were first-time visitors to this lovely little hamlet.

In search of a local eatery, we arrived in Montecchio when most trattorias already stopped serving lunch, fortunately, we stumbled into a hotel with an adjacent restaurant that appeared to be in full swing. Nonchalantly, we seated ourselves and before we were settled, a waiter came to our table with a huge platter of grilled zucchini, drizzled with olive oil.

"Prego," he said, as he dished out a heaping forkful of the bright green vegetable and placed it on each of our plates. We were excited, hungry and loved places where you just sit down and without ordering from a menu, delicious food magically appears. Another server placed ceramic pitchers of red and white wine and small carafes of *frizzante* (carbonated) and *naturale* (natural) water on our table. Then, the first waiter returned with a ladened tray of lean prosciutto, cappicola and mortadella, followed by a second tray of my favorite bruschetta; pomodoro, garlic and basil.

Each time, smiling, without saying a word, he served our plates with generous portions of the delicacies on the trays. This was so amazing, the restaurant staff had their home-style serving down to a flawless routine. After our appetizer dishes were cleared, bowls of pasta with a flavorful, slightly spicy, tomato-based sauce were brought to our table, succeeded by the main entree of grilled *Salsicci Mista* (mixed sausages). When it was all over, the three of us looked at each other, assumed a reclined position in our chairs and let out a lethargic sigh of relief. At a cost of only 12€ per person, we were satiated, dumbfounded and completely fascinated by the entire lunch experience.

There was certainly no need for dinner that evening or breakfast the following morning, we just had coffee and a banana and reminisced about the plentiful lunch we had in Montecchio. This was Ellen's last day with us and for her "grand finale" we decided to take her to Deruta to see the local crafts up close and personal. Ellen had always heard of Deruta, but never dreamed that she would ever visit the town world renowned for its exquisite hand-painted ceramics. Knowing my sister, I anticipated her going crazy over the wide selection of pottery for sale direct from the artists in the family-owned studios. Deruta was also well worth a visit just to see the beautiful antique ceramic decor throughout the historic village.

When we took the highway exit, I pointed to the enormous blue and white ceramic star, marking the entrance to the famous city, Ellen felt an adrenaline rush of enthusiasm build in her soul. Our maiden name is *de Ruyter* (pronounced by most Americans like Deruta with an extra "r" at the end), therefore, my sister thought it would be quite important to take a "selfie" photo of us standing under a storefront Deruta sign, which she spotted immediately as we drove past the many showrooms in the lower part of town. What a marvelous idea! The sign was mounted high above a window, requiring us to jump up simultaneously while we clicked the camera. Vince, who watched the whole hilarious fiasco, readily offered to take our picture, since it was obvious that our many attempts were unsuccessful. Nevertheless, we laughed until we cried and finally settled on a pose that included unbecoming partials of both our faces and a mere hint of the sign in the background.

Vince parked the car in the lot on top of the hill, where Ellen caught a glimpse of the first ceramic studio before we even opened the car doors. Located at the arched entrance, the magnificent hand-painted, ceramic table top, brightly colored serving platters and oversized urns on permanent display, were my sister's impactful introduction to Deruta's quaint historic center. "Wow, look at that!" Ellen exclaimed, as she headed toward the store before I could tell her that all the pieces in the studios are truly hand-painted, meaning that each brush stroke was actually applied by a master artist who took hours of labor to complete each original piece and that each one was an exceptional, unique work of art, different from its predecessor. Instead, I followed her to the entrance to the village. As if trying not to disturb, Ellen gingerly tip-toed into the shop to watch an artist choose just the right color to apply to an intricate design-in-progress on a delicate bowl. My sister was mesmerized and gained an immediate respect for the handcrafted ceramics that have been made in the traditional way for centuries.

We browsed through every store, with Vince following patiently as Ellen and I indecisively discussed patterns and designs; which pieces to buy and how to use or display them once she got them home. To break the ice and begin the buying streak, I introduced Ellen to Luca at Majoliche Artistiche Fanny; one of my preferred shops, where I bought a wonderful rectangular serving platter that looked like an antiquity, decorated with life-like bunches of yellow grapes on a white background. Ellen was on a tight budget and couldn't afford to be a compulsive shopper, leaving her with difficult decisions to make. There was the pepper grinder decorated with lemons, cherries and sunflowers that she loved at first sight, but there was also a beautiful salad bowl with an ancient white lace pattern accented with blues, greens and yellows and with the matching olive oil dispenser, the pair would make a stunning statement on a dinner table. There were also numerous small accessories and mementos Ellen wanted to buy for friends at home.

Always the wise one, Vince suggested a *reboot*, "Let's fortify our brains and bodies and have lunch somewhere. It is seriously time to take a break from shopping," he commanded. Trattoria Taverna del Gusto, a local favorite, with outdoor ceramic tables under a shady canopy and an excellent menu looked like the perfect place to eat lunch, recuperate and narrow down Ellen's options. Ahhhh, it felt great to sit down. As if he read our minds, a waiter promptly placed a blue and white ceramic pitcher filled with red wine on our table. A few minutes later, we were presented with menus, a *tagliere* (cutting board) of sliced Umbrian meats and cheeses along with a basket of bread. We were grateful for the speedy service, we didn't realize how hungry we were, until the food arrived.

Spending the day in Deruta with the two people I loved most in the world was everything I ever wished for. I heard the muffled sound of metal bistro chairs scraping against the cobblestone street as locals and tourists sparred for seats and the restaurant became more crowded. I found myself beaming with happiness as I listened to Vince share his opinion with Ellen about the ceramic pieces he liked most. It was another one of those *"aha"* moments for me; a moment of realization that I was blessed beyond my wildest wishes.

Our slow and relaxing lunch made us sprightly, with renewed energy, Ellen asked us to confirm her three final selections at one of the studios. The pieces were truly works of art, but when she realized that the total cost of all three pieces exceeded her budget, she was faced with a profound dilemma. Which piece should she eliminate? She must have changed her mind a dozen times, until finally, seeing how torn she was, Vince came to the rescue.

"Here," he urged, while he slipped her a 50€ note, "buy them all, already. Take this, then you won't have to choose." At first, Ellen shyly tried to hand the money back to him, but when he insisted, she was grateful and with a twinkle in her eyes, asked the artist to wrap up all the items. She was thrilled. Before we left the store, we captured Ellen's precious moment on camera, taking a picture of her and the artist standing in the studio.

When we returned to the apartment, we unwrapped the salad bowl and the olive oil dispenser, placed them on the window sill to clearly see the pieces in the light. Then we unwrapped the pepper mill and examined the masterful craftsmanship. Ellen gave Vince an extra special big hug to thank him for his contribution. She would forever cherish her ceramics and the experience of buying them in Deruta direct from the artist.

It was a gray and rainy morning, the weather matched my mood, I certainly hated taking Ellen to the airport, however, I understood very well how anxious she was to get home to be with her family. On the other hand, I knew that in her heart-of-hearts, she also wanted to stay with us a little while longer. Vince got to know his sister-in-law much more during our time together and the three of us honestly enjoyed each other's company.

The two-hour drive to Rome seemed particularly long, I wished that she didn't have to go. The closer we got to Rome, the worse the weather became and upon our approach to the airport we saw several waterspouts in the sky. I hoped that Ellen's flight would not be delayed and that her journey back to New York would go smoothly. Fortunately, we arrived at the terminal in plenty of time for Ellen to go through the security process and head to the departure gate without rushing. She has always been a bit nervous about flying alone. We hugged and kissed, thanked each other for the wonderful time we spent together and said goodbye as if we were never going to see each other again. Ellen said that her days with us were the best vacation she ever had. Inside the terminal, my sister disappeared into the crowd and Vince and I were on our own. Although feeling a bit sad, we were looking forward to going home. We only had one more week before our flight to California and there was still much more to do.

Home Alone

The four-hour roundtrip drive to Rome was a bit draining and by the time we returned to the apartment, Vince and I were quite weary, however, we felt strangely happy to be home alone for the first time!

We changed into more comfortable clothing and retreated into our perspective areas of the apartment to tackle more projects. I framed the picture I had taken of the clothes washer display panel with the English translations typed in red to hang in the utility room. With Ellen's framed Welcome Sign and the two laundry pictures I already had, the four made an attractive display. Vince was poring over a creative idea for a container garden and an arbor to provide overhead shade on the terrazzo. It would be lovely to grow seasonal herbs and flowers in the future, the space was definitely large enough.

To resemble a weathered, cast stone finish that provoked imagining its past, I suggested applying a sponge-paint technique to the walls above the hearth. At first, Vince was reluctant to try my idea, but in the end, he agreed to let me attempt my hand at it and helped me tape off the corners and prepare the surface for my handiwork. I must admit, that I only had limited experience doing this, but with the first few strokes of the sponge, I knew that I would love the end result. I asked Vince to refrain from commenting until I completed the project. The warm and earthy colored stain in contrast to the stark white walls added an attractive dimension to the room and when I stood back to admire the overall effect, I was pleased with how it made the fireplace stand out in the room with enhanced refinement.

Vince and I were just about ready to clean up, take showers and decide where to go for dinner when our doorbell rang. It was our downstairs neighbor; Mirko with his two sons; Vittorio and Giacomo.

"*Buona sera*," Mirko said, with a big adorable smile on his face, offering his hand in a handshake. Vittorio and Giacomo followed with a warm but somewhat shy "*Ciao*." I gave Vince a puzzled look and wondered how we were going to communicate with our guests. However, Mirko made it easy when he pointed to Vittorio and said "English" indicating that Vittorio knew how to speak a few words of English, which he learned at school.

I gestured for them to enter and sit down, then I pointed to a bottle of wine and held up a glass. "Grazie, no" was the response as everyone took a seat around the dining table. Mirko pulled a piece of paper from a notebook and presented it to Vince; it was a bill for 16€. Vince looked at Mirko and shrugged his shoulders, signaling that he wondered what the charge was for. Mirko understood the inquiry, opened the door, pointed to the stairs and pretended to push an invisible broom. We instantly grasped that the bill was our charge for keeping the common stairs clean. No problem, we gladly paid it and laughed at how easily we were able to communicate with each other in spite of the language barrier. By speaking a little Italian, a bit of English, using sign language, gestures and the translator application on our mobile phones, we were able to convey that we were going back to California in two days and returning in the spring. Officially meeting our neighbors for the first time was a very pleasant experience.

Instead of dining out, we assembled a few finger-food appetizers, sat at our new outdoor dining table and ate dinner on the terrazzo. We will never outgrow the ever-changing-with-the-seasons, staggering view across the Tiber Valley. We watched a spectacular sunset unfold while we slowly drank our wine and munched on delectable chunks of fragrant melon, plump ripe peaches, mozzarella cheese and Umbrian salami. When the sun was completely beneath the horizon, the moon appeared in a silvery sliver just above the first star.

Shining in our direction from a village across the valley, a light came into view that became brighter and brighter, until it was nearly a spotlight. Inquisitively, I mentioned it to Vince.

"That's *Poggio Aquilone*," he said, "another medieval borgo on top of the hill. I noticed the light a few nights ago and a lot of traffic seems to be going in that direction. Maybe there is something special going on over there. It might be a soccer game."

Ohhh, this was our last free day in Italy, I thought with a heavy sigh when I woke up the next morning. Tomorrow was dedicated to finishing last minute chores, tying up loose ends and confirming our travel arrangements before flying to San Francisco the following day, therefore, I hoped that we could do something fun today. I was very happy with how much we had accomplished to transform our empty apartment into a beautiful home; however, we still needed a few small pieces of furniture and Italian decor to add those uniquely special finishing touches that one can only find at flea markets or antique stores. In preparation for this trip, I conducted in-depth internet searches for local thrift shops, used furniture stores and flea markets when I came across *Arte e Giano Antichita,* located in the village of Canale. Arte e Giano Antichita appeared to be the kind of place that was chockfull of hidden treasures just waiting for me to discover them. When I asked Vince if we could investigate, he didn't hesitate.

Canale is a sleepy little village, on the outskirts of Orvieto. As we made our way to Orvieto, it was tempting not to stop at Trattoria da Carlo for lunch, but we were on a mission to locate the antique store in Canale. We drove past impressive old homes on a tree-lined street, when suddenly, right smack in the middle of a residential area, we came upon it. Arte e Giano Antichita; a yard full of old iron gates, well-loved garden furniture, baskets oozing with history, charming wooden doors, interesting window frames and gorgeous fifteen gallon, two and a half feet tall, wine bottles that resembled magnificent green glass bubbles.

"Vince, Look! I love, *love* these bottles," I cried out, overcome with desire to buy one. "Wouldn't they would look wonderful in our apartment? What is more Italian than these wine bottles? I wonder how much they cost." To my great disappointment, I discovered that the antique store was closed and I was left standing outside the locked gate clamoring to get in. I literally pouted until Vince said that we could come back later in the afternoon when they might be open.

"I am so excited!" I exclaimed, "if that green bottle is less than a hundred dollars, I am buying it. It's so Italian and in California, an antique wine bottle like that would cost more than two-hundred and fifty dollars. I'll show it to you in the Napa Style catalogue. I just saw it there the other day."

"OK, OK," Vince said, trying to calm me down, "if it costs less than one hundred dollars, I will buy the bottle for you. We can collect wine corks in it. It will take twenty years to fill it but meanwhile, it will look great in our apartment."

To pass the time, we took a drive through the verdant countryside, a long walk along Orvieto's defense walls and cobblestone streets until it was slightly after four o'clock when most shops open again for the evening. To my great joy, the gate was open and a man, whom I hoped was the proprietor, was standing in the yard. I nearly leaped out of the car before Vince brought us to a stop. When he approached me, all I could say in Italian was *"Buona sera."* I am sure that his reply was a friendly offer of assistance. Wishing that I could speak the language, I smiled and walked over to the fantastic bottle, which was prominently displayed on an old wooden spool; the kind that is often repurposed as a rustic table.

"Quanto costa?" I asked timidly, hoping that I was correctly asking, "How much does this cost?"

"Dieci euro," the man answered.

Vince looked at me and asked, "OK, so how much is it?"

"I think he said one hundred euro. He said *dieci*. Does that mean one hundred?"

I shrugged my shoulders and asked the man in English, "One hundred?" He took out a ten-euro bill from his pocket and showed it to me. I thought I was going to die from excitement.

"Vince, he said it was ten euro, not one hundred dollars, ten euro! Can you believe it?"

The shop owner lifted the bottle from the table and placed it next to me on the ground. It was heavy and even more beautiful when the sun shined through the glass. At that minimal price, I wanted to buy all his bottles, but Vince said that we only had space enough for two of them. When the proprietor realized my joy, he motioned for me to follow him to another part of the yard where he stored more of these amazing bottles. He handed me one that was a bit smaller in size and more blue in color, then he handed me another one, smaller yet, set in a woven basket.

"Per te, gratuito," "For you, gratis," he said.

Oh my Gosh! Really? I was thrilled and spontaneously gave him a hug. He seemed delighted that he had obviously made me very happy. I knew exactly where in our apartment I was going to display these gorgeous bottles. During the entire drive home, I couldn't stop talking about our fortunate purchase, in fact, I silently pondered how we could create a business exporting these wonderful, unbelievably inexpensive treasures to California to sell them for a cool and easy profit. They sold for a much higher price at the prestigious Napa Style store.

We used the community water fountain located just outside our front door in Morcella, to wash the bottles before bringing them inside the apartment. I ran upstairs to get a roll of paper towels, a scrub brush and a bottle of liquid detergent. Vince stuffed a wad of the paper towels, a couple of drops of detergent and a gallon of water in each bottle. He lifted them, one at a time, waist high, to gently swish the soapy water around until it loosened the dirt at the bottom. Then he poured out the suds and pulled out the paper towels, scrubbed the outside with the brush and rinsed them until they were sparkling clean. It was quite picturesque to watch Vince wash those antique bottles at our village fountain, on our cobblestone street lined with potted plants as his backdrop. I ran upstairs again to get my camera. When Vince carried the gleaming bottles upstairs, stepping sideways to avoid bumping into the railings and walls, I thought to myself: *this is another one of those moments that will stay with me forever.* I've had so many *moments* since we started coming to Italy.

Just before sunset, I was standing on the terrazzo, anticipating a glorious sunset. When I entered the living room again to ask Vince to join me, the realization of how lovely the apartment looked suddenly hit me. Maybe it was the way the light came through the windows at that very instant, or the sudden awareness that we were leaving the following day, but I knew that there was one final step I had to complete before our departure. I went downstairs to where the building's common mailbox was mounted on the stone wall, removed Ann's name from the mail slot and inserted ours: *Vince and Joyce DiLorenzo.* Perfect! I loved seeing our names on the mailbox.

Since it was our last evening in Morcella, we made a simple dinner from the left-over perishable foods in the refrigerator and dined at home. Vince opened our last bottle of wine, while I grabbed a quilt from one of the beds to wrap around us as we cuddled up at our dining table on the terrazzo. We were completely relaxed and absorbed in what we had accomplishment on our first official trip as owners of our new home in Italy. We talked about how happy, fortunate and blessed we were and began making plans for our return in the spring when I would have more vacation time from work accrued. All at once, Vince noticed the bright light in the village across the valley again.

"Curiosity is killing me. Let's go see what that light is all about. We'll follow the traffic flow up there."

I agreed immediately. As we neared Poggio Aquilone, we saw the posted signs along the way: *Sagra di Umbricelli a Poggio Aquilone.*

"Oh, it's an Umbricelli Festival," I declared. Umbricelli, we learned, is an Umbrian specialty pasta made without eggs; small rounds of pasta, about the size of a coin, are tediously formed by hand, then rolled and given a twist before they are cooked in water and smothered in sauce.

After we parked the car, like sheep, we followed the herd of people to the village entrance. Poggio Aquilone; a bit larger than Morcella, boasted a post office, tobacco shop, a thriving B&B and a small coffee bar. The main piazza in the center of the village was appropriately adorned with pennants strung from balconies to roof tops. There was a bandstand set up near the post office and long picnic tables with benches lined the main street all around the village. At a central station, the locals seemed to order food from paper menus on which they marked their selections, then proceeded to another station to buy their beverages before taking a seat at one of the long tables. Children carried trays loaded with generous portions of Umbricelli doused in a rich sauce made from sausage, garlic and olive oil, to the tables to serve hungry guests. We walked around the entire village, amazed at how well organized everything seemed to be. The *Sagra* (feast) was a festive family affair, everyone seemed jovial, engaged in delightful conversation and there was not a loud, obnoxious, wine intoxicated guest in the crowd.

We stood near the band stand, watching the crowd, waiting for the music to begin, when suddenly someone called out our names. Who could possibly know us here? It was Silvano; the man who lived with his family, in the apartment directly below ours. It took us a moment to identify him, but when he gestured for us to join him at his table, we recognized his wife Sara, son Michael-Angelo and mother Irma immediately. In that instance, we felt as if we transitioned from tourists to being a part of the community. We felt as if we *belonged* here. It was wonderful to be acknowledged and invited to sit and eat with Silvano's family. Unfortunately, we were too inhibited to join the family who only spoke Italian, so we communicated in sign language and gesticulation that we had already eaten dinner and were going home. *Awhhh, what a shame, next time*, I thought. We will be speaking Italian next time.

Before going to bed, we walked out on our terrazzo one last time. It was such a bright and balmy evening that we couldn't resist snuggling together in our original positions under the quilt, which I left draped over the chairs, before we drove to Poggio Aquilone. Flickering fireflies danced near the banks of the Nestore River now and every once in a while, a gentle breeze drifted the intoxicating honey-lemon scented fragrance from the Linden trees our way.

"Tomorrow we'll be on our way back to our American lives," Vince said.

"I know and I'll have to go back to work Monday. Please don't remind me, I am not ready. I wish we could stay here longer," I replied.

Vince poured the last of the red wine from the bottle, equally into the two glasses still left on the table and gave one to me. As he held up his glass, he made a final toast, "Here is to us. Thank you for letting me buy you a home in Italy."

"Here's to you, Bunny, thank you for my life. You made our dream come true," I replied, as we gave each other a kiss. "I can't believe we did it. We pulled it off. We bought a home in Italy!"

We settled back into our chairs, into each other's arms and snuggled up under the quilt. I love when Vince identifies the constellations for me. I adore him especially when he points out the Milky Way, Orion's Belt and the Big Dipper. Gazing up at the brilliant star-lit sky with my husband, on our last evening at home in Morcella, I was reminded of an inspirational quote I once read somewhere: "Aim for the moon, because even if you miss, you'll land among the stars."

Thank you, God, with your blessings, we most certainly landed among the stars…

Epilogue

As I am writing this book, Vince and I are about to celebrate our five-year anniversary as the proud owners of our beautiful home in Italy; the home that has enriched our life in countless ways.

We discovered that everything (in life) is about timing… 'the right timing.' After working at the same company for nearly thirty-six years, on January 19, 2012, without warning, I suddenly found myself without a job. As part of a reduction in the work force, my department was eliminated and I was forced into early retirement, leaving me free to travel to Italy whenever our hearts desired and our budget allowed. While my colleagues mourned the loss of their jobs and phoned their families to notify them of the devastating news, I phoned the airlines to book a ticket to Rome in February on Vince's flight, before announcing to my husband that I was no longer employed. If the offer we made on the apartment in Porano had been successful, we would not have found our perfect dream home in Morcella. If we had found Morcella before I became unemployed, Vince's conservative, faint-heart would have deterred us from following our unimaginable dream of buying a second home in Italy. *Timing* seemed to be on our side throughout the entire experience, as if we were being guided from above, everything appeared "meant to be."

When we returned to Morcella in February 2012, we met Achille Caporicci in the parking lot, while we were putting snow chains on our tires. Yes, it actually snowed in Morcella that year and the landscape was breathtaking. Achille approached us and said something in Italian, which we interpreted as, "Be careful. Leaving the parking lot can be slippery."

"*Grazie*," we replied, to his friendly warning.

"I am Achille," he said, "I was born in this village."

"I studied English over thirty years ago in Perugia, but now, I don't speak good English." Achille appeared to be approximately Vince's age. We were thrilled to meet someone who was born in Morcella, with whom we could converse, nevertheless only a little. Throughout the years, we have formed a wonderful friendship with Achille and his wife Giovanna. He told us many interesting stories of growing up in Morcella, attending the grade school now abandoned and playing with friends in the Nestore River by the historic mill as a young boy. He told us that Morcella was once a castle, with a heavy barricading door at the arched entrance to the village and that once a Count lived in the building that is now our apartment. Achille remembers the American soldier who gave him a piece of candy after the war, when the troops came across the stone bridge by the single stop light. He was three years old when World War II ended. Achille's mother lived in their ancient stone home until 2016, when she died at the age of ninety-seven.

Since buying our Italian piece of heaven, we have become friends with our downstairs neighbors and Guido and Rosanna; the couple who have been living next door to Achille since 2002, endlessly, lovingly restoring their house into a three-story home brimming with original character. Three years ago, they also acquired one of the adjacent apartments that partially forms one of Morcella's turrets. Guido's heritage is German, he is a wonderful story teller, Rosanna is originally from Perugia, she is an amazing cook. When they are at home, they speak a mixture of Italian and German to each other, however, they also speak English, which makes getting together with them especially interesting and fun because they commonly speak three languages in a single conversation. We are extremely compatible friends and enjoy spending time with Guido and Rosanna.

One evening while having dinner at Rosatelli, we met Gillian and Bruce. We heard the familiar lilt of an American conversation coming from their table; a comforting, welcoming sound after several weeks of struggling with the Italian language. Once our meal was ordered, I walked over to introduce myself. Bruce; an American from Boston, bought a vacation home eight years ago in Cerqueto; one of Morcella's neighboring villages. Gill; a "transplant" from Great Britain, lived in Cerqueto permanently and worked as a *Gill-of-all-traits* helping expats settle in Umbria. Both Bruce and Gill were very nice, therefore, I didn't hesitate to invite Vince to the table so I could extend the introductions. During the years we have watched Gill's endearing children; Stan and Holly, grow into teenagers. I'll never forget when Gill told us that Italians generally don't pronounce the H, therefore, when she introduces her children, she often accentuates the sound of the first letter in Holly's name to avoid comments, such as: "Oh, how charming, you named your children *Stan and Olly!*" Gill has supported us through minor difficulties and helped us "learn the ropes" of settling in Umbria. We have become very good friends. On a subsequent visit, we had the pleasure of meeting Bruce's wife Pam; who makes me laugh more than most any other woman I have ever met.

In no time at all, we became friends with Giovanni, his wife Paula, son Francesco and daughter Veronica. The first words Giovanni ever spoke to me were "I don't speak English" but he said them so perfectly that I thought he was joking. As the only Americans in Morcella, Giovanni made us feel welcome immediately by inviting us to join his family for pizza at Oasi. He came to our apartment with his cousin ILaria to coordinate going to the restaurant in multiple cars. ILaria's father and Giovanni's father were brothers. She lives in Rome with her husband Pasquale and daughter Alina. They own the family home in Morcella, where Giovanni lived until he was two years old.

"There will be three families," he said. "You," as he pointed to Vince and I, "are one family. She," as he pointed to ILaria, "two families and me," as he pointed to himself, "are three families. OK? We follow at eight o'clock. OK?"

It was absolutely, more-than OK. We were excited to be invited to dinner as part of a big Italian family. We rode in the car with ILaria, Pasquale and Alina. Giovanni's family, including his ninety-two-year-old mother, were already waiting for us when we arrived at the restaurant. Pasquale and ILaria spoke enough English to keep the conversations going and offered basic translations so that we could converse with the other people at the table. That first dinner has become a tradition for us, a trip to Morcella would not be complete without having pizza with Giovanni and his family. When we are not in California, Giovanni keeps in touch via e-mail, informing us of Morcella's church and social activities. He shares an interest in car and motorcycle racing with Vince. Pasquale, Ilaria and Alina were guests in our home while on vacation in California and when Francesco graduates from college, he will also be our house guest for a few weeks. We wholeheartedly enjoy being a part of Giovanni's big Italian family.

While shopping at the local EMI Supermercato one day, we met two ladies who worked there; Charolaine and Maria Pia. Unless I read her signs wrong, each time we shopped in the market, Charolaine flirted with Vince openly. She made eye contact and conversation only with him, until one day, my suspicions were confirmed when she twisted the hair behind her ear with one finger, looked up at him from her cash register with big adoring eyes and said, "Do you live in Italy?"

"Si, we have a *casa vacanza* in Morcella," Vince answered, "we are from California."

"Ahh," Charolaine replied, "do you like Italy?"

"We love Italy." That was our first conversation with Charolaine. Since then, we have met Francesco; Maria Pia's husband and the five of us have become best friends. We have dined at each other's home, attended Sagras together and through them, have met other locals. At least once each time we return to Italy, we get together as a group. Spending time with our Italian friends has improved our use of the language tremendously. We sincerely value their friendship.

Lastly, while having dinner at Johannes and Luisa's home one lovely evening, Johannes mentioned that Sue and Steve; a British couple, recently bought the beautiful yellow farmhouse located just outside Morcella's medieval wall and suggested that we pay them a visit. The following day, we came bearing a bottle of wine, potted plant and a card to welcome them to the neighborhood. A stone plaque mounted on the outside wall of their farmhouse named the estate *Villa Cipressa*; a lovely park-like property with an adjacent summer home, boasting a swimming pool, cypress, cherry and olive trees, rosemary, sage, lavender, a multitude of flowering plants and a stunning view of historic Morcella.

At first, there was no response to our knock on the door and Vince thought that we should leave our gifts on the steps near the entrance, however just as we turned to go to the car, a disheveled looking man dressed in his robe opened the door.

"Yes," he said, questioningly.

"Ciao, welcome to the neighborhood, my name is Vince, this is my wife, Joyce. Casambiente; our real estate agents told us that you just bought this house and that you are English. We are Americans and bought an apartment in the village two years ago," Vince said, pointing to Morcella, "so we are neighbors. Welcome to the neighborhood!"

"Oh, OK, well then, it's a pleasure to meet you. My name is Steve, my wife Sue is in the shower. Would you like to come in for a drink?"

At first, we hesitated to accept Steve's invitation, he was dressed in a robe and his wife was in the shower. We were afraid that we had disturbed an intimate moment, or woke them from a sound sleep, nevertheless, Steve insisted and offered to make a cup of coffee. We followed him upstairs to a living room full of scattered furniture, Steve straightened a sofa and cleared a space for us to sit. When he asked where in America we were from, we told him that we were from the San Francisco Bay Area. "Oh," Steve said, "we spent our honeymoon there. It was great. It was beautiful." Vince asked Steve where in England he was from. "A town in the south of London that you have probably never heard of," Steve replied. "It's called Croydon."

"Croydon?" Vince repeated for clarification. "I've been to Croydon. I was there with a friend in the mid-seventies."

This coincidence was an icebreaker and the beginning of a lovely first encounter with Steve. As the three of us talked in the living room, Sue appeared in a pair of adorable red flannel pajamas with white snowflakes and "Let it Snow" written on her shirt. We seemed to be close in age and I liked her immediately. She made a pot of tea, invited us to sit at the kitchen table, overlooking the pool, we chatted for hours, Steve dressed in his robe and Sue in her pajamas. Nowadays, we refer to that first visit as 'our pajama party.' We are great friends and have travelled to Sicily and sailed in the British Virgin Islands together and we hope that one day Steve and Sue will visit us in California.

When we are in Italy, our friends are our family. Presently, Vince and I are fortunate to spend fifteen weeks throughout the year at our home in Morcella, where we have created a second life in a culture where people embrace a slower paced, less combative existence without power lunches and a dinner sandwich in front of the computer while working late into the evening.

We love Morcella in the winter, when the surrounding countryside is particularly beautiful, the fields are dormant and the landscape is peaceful. Medieval villages throughout the region exhibit intricate and elaborate *presepes;* nativity scenes that seem to come alive at dusk. Holiday music literally fills the air, chestnuts are roasted on street corners and locals dress in period clothing. It is magical to wander past the enchanting displays in a different village every evening.

In spring, the red poppies are in bloom and the colorful extravaganza is at its peak during Cantine Aperte; when Umbria's most important wine tourism event takes place. Wine cellars open their doors and invite the public to taste the region's new wines with roast pork panini and bruschetta drenched in locally produced olive oil, topped with savory meats and cheeses.

In summer, sunflowers the size of dinner plates cover the hillsides; a sight more beautiful than I ever imagined. Gazing at fields of six feet tall, glorious sunflowers is one of summer's highlights. In August, we become immersed in the Mezz'Agosto; Morcella's annual festival, when residents transform our tranquil village into a nine-day neighborhood-party with an outdoor dining hall and dance floor. The resident women spend hours preparing mouthwatering meals by hand, the men grill savory meats over an open fire and the children serve more than 500 guests every evening. It is a festive community event which we sincerely love being a part of.

Autumn may just be the most colorful time of year when the rolling hills have been plowed into rich, dark clay fields waiting to be planted again in early spring and the vineyards are crimson red, orange and gold, ladened with jewel-toned grapes ready to be harvested. In November, when olive trees give up their fruits to be pressed into the peppery oil that lubricates the Italian lifestyle, the pungent fragrance of freshly pressed olives permeates the region.

Whether we are in San Carlos or Morcella, we never take a moment of our extraordinary lives for granted. We realize how fortunate we are to live in two cultures and experience the best of each. We are blessed beyond belief!